Lecture Notes in Computer Science 2263

Edited by G. Goos, J. Hartmanis, and J. van Leeuwen

Springer

Berlin
Heidelberg
New York
Barcelona
Hong Kong
London
Milan
Paris
Tokyo

Tony Clark   Jos Warmer (Eds.)

Object Modeling with the OCL

The Rationale behind the Object Constraint Language

 Springer

Series Editors

Gerhard Goos, Karlsruhe University, Germany
Juris Hartmanis, Cornell University, NY, USA
Jan van Leeuwen, Utrecht University, The Netherlands

Volume Editors

Tony Clark
King's College London, Department of Computer Science
Strand, London, WC2R 2LS, United Kingdom
E-mail: anclark@dcs.kcl.ac.uk

Jos Warmer
Klasse Objecten
Postbus 3082, 3760 DB Soest, The Netherlands
E-mail: J.Warmer@klasse.nl

Cataloging-in-Publication Data applied for

Die Deutsche Bibliothek - CIP-Einheitsaufnahme

Object modeling with the OCL : the rationale behind the object constraint
language / Tony Clark ; Jos Warmer (ed.). - Berlin ; Heidelberg ; New York ;
Barcelona ; Hong Kong ; London ; Milan ; Paris ; Tokyo : Springer, 2002
   (Lecture notes in computer science ; 2263)
   ISBN 3-540-43169-1

CR Subject Classification (1998): D.2.1, D.2.2, D.2.10, K.6.3

ISSN 0302-9743
ISBN 3-540-43169-1 Springer-Verlag Berlin Heidelberg New York

This work is subject to copyright. All rights are reserved, whether the whole or part of the material is
concerned, specifically the rights of translation, reprinting, re-use of illustrations, recitation, broadcasting,
reproduction on microfilms or in any other way, and storage in data banks. Duplication of this publication
or parts thereof is permitted only under the provisions of the German Copyright Law of September 9, 1965,
in its current version, and permission for use must always be obtained from Springer-Verlag. Violations are
liable for prosecution under the German Copyright Law.

Springer-Verlag Berlin Heidelberg New York
a member of BertelsmannSpringer Science+Business Media GmbH

http://www.springer.de

© Springer-Verlag Berlin Heidelberg 2002
Printed in Germany

Typesetting: Camera-ready by author, data conversion by PTP Berlin, Stefan Sossna
Printed on acid-free paper   SPIN 10846123   06/3142   5 4 3 2 1 0

Preface

Since its inception in 1997 the UML has become the de-facto standard for modeling object-oriented systems. As part of the standard the OCL provides the modeler with an expressive notation for capturing essential system properties such as state invariants and guards on state transitions. OCL has been adopted by practitioners in Industry and by academic researchers and is one of the most widely used languages for expressing object-oriented system properties; as such it makes a significant contribution to the quality of systems developed using the UML notation.

As the use of OCL has spread, there has been increasing interest in providing precise definitions for the notation, for example to support tool development. Extensions to the language have been proposed in order to support a wide variety of application domains from real-time systems to modeling business processes. As experience with OCL has grown, a number of researchers have proposed system development methodologies based on OCL.

Work on OCL has been reported and discussed in a number of different forums. The first workshop in Amsterdam (included in this volume as 'The Amsterdam Manifesto') produced the first paper about OCL, which has also been submitted to the OMG as an answer to the request for information for UML 2.0. OCL developments have been presented at the annual international UML conferences and in a series of OCL workshops held at the University of Kent, UK in 2000 and subsequently at UML 2000 at York, UK and UML 2001 in Toronto, Canada. At the time of writing the Object Management Group is currently reviewing the OCL standard and has issued a request for proposals for OCL 2.0. Many of the authors in this volume are contributing to this review process.

This volume contains a collection of papers representing key contributions to the development of OCL. In most cases the papers are developments of work reported at the conferences and workshops described above. Together they address many of the important issues faced by advanced practitioners and researchers in object modeling.

October 2001   Tony Clark
                                                                             Jos Warmer

Table of Contents

Introduction

"The conclusion is that Logic, conceived as an adequate
analysis of the advance of thought is a fake. It is a superb
instrument, but it requires a background of common
sense."

-- A. N. Whitehead (1861-1947)

"Whatever aptitude a man may have to exercise the
power of abstraction, and to furnish himself with general
ideas, he can make no considerable progress without the
aid of language, spoken or written."

-- L. Euler (1707-1783)

There is a widespread misunderstanding among both software practitioners and experts in the area of formal methods that the purpose of such methods is to prove, *conclusively*, whether some piece of software is "correct". This confusion is rather unfortunate, since it often leads to disillusionment and rejection of formality as impractical (e.g., it does not scale) and, therefore, irrelevant to software development. In fact, as the quote from Alfred North Whitehead indicates, the notion of conclusive and objective proof derived by formal methods has been all but abandoned even in mathematics itself, where it is now understood that "proofs" really represent social consensus among mathematicians rather than statements of objective reality. This should be even more apparent in the case of mathematical models of real-world systems, which are almost always approximations of some kind.

Despite this, we have not abandoned either mathematics or its application to solving real-world problems. Significantly, Whitehead still refers to (mathematical) logic as a "superb instrument". But, if it does not bring us certainty and irrefutable proof, what is it that makes it superb?

Many years of experience with the application of formal methods to software development indicate that the most beneficial effect, by far, is that formality introduces a heightened degree of *precision* into our thinking and our specifications. By "precision" I mean a clear and unambiguous statement of intent. While still imperfect, any conclusions drawn from precise specifications are more likely to be much closer to the ideal of certainty than those drawn from imprecise ones. (Like most things in our complex world, proofs are hardly ever conclusive but are, instead, matters of degree.)

Precision should not be confused with detail, although this often happens. In the case of specifications, precision implies a clear delineation between elements that are covered (included) by a specification from those that are not. Thus, a precise

A. Clark and J. Warmer (Eds.): Object Modeling with the OCL, LNCS 2263, pp. 1-3, 2002.
© Springer-Verlag Berlin Heidelberg 2002

definition of the class of motor vehicles will allow us to clearly conclude whether a particular object is a vehicle or not, while still leaving room for further detailing such as whether a vehicle is a truck, an automobile, or a moped. This means that there is no inherent conflict between precision and abstraction and that these two fundamental techniques used in design can complement and reinforce each other.

Clearly, precise specifications are necessary when those specifications are meant to be realized by a computer, since most computers do not tolerate ambiguity. However, they are equally necessary to accurately communicate our intent to others and, perhaps most importantly, to ourselves. It never ceases to amaze me how much complexity is exposed whenever we reflect in depth upon even the simplest of things. As David Parnas and his colleagues point out in a well-known example [Par87], a seemingly simple statement such as "the level of the water in the tank shall never drop below X", is fraught with ambiguity. (What do we mean by "water level"? Is it the instantaneous water level – which may be highly inaccurate due to the sloshing of water in the tank – or some average water level? If we mean the latter, how do we define "average"? And so on.) The problem is that the real world is a complex place and our rational thinking process is notoriously fallible. It is typically based on unstated assumptions, personal biases, and overextended mental shortcuts. Being precise forces us to tease out such fuzzy elements, expose them to closer scrutiny, and define the corresponding delineation boundaries.

The purpose of OCL is to support precision; that is, it is a tool to help us express our thoughts precisely. As such, it is nothing new since it merely packages standard basic concepts from mathematical logic in a specific form. However, what makes it unique and gives it tremendous leverage is that it is adapted to a UML context and is part of the UML standard. This creates an opportunity to introduce the benefits of precise specifications to a much broader community of software developers than most other formal notations. In the past, one of the major impediments of many such notations has been that they were not an integral part of a common development language or tool. From that perspective it is instructive to note the effect obtained when a syntactically and semantically integrated assertion construct was introduced into the C language. The net result was that a large number of software developers who had never heard of a Hoare triple (and may not have been interested had they heard of it), used the mechanism to improve the reliability of their software.

OCL provides a "programmer friendly" version of prepositional logic, bereft of upside-down "As" and backward "Es" that, unfortunately, seems to repel many software practitioners. Thus, the existential and universal quantifiers (truly scary and highfalutin names if ever there were any) are cleverly disguised as operation names ("exists" and "forall" respectively), to hide from users that they are actually applying mathematical logic. Rather than bemoan the need for such subterfuge – if that is what it is – we must do whatever is necessary to facilitate precise thinking in the development of software. It is clearly in the interest of us all.

Given this potentially enormous impact that OCL can have on the future of software development, this book is exceptionally timely and useful. I can think of no better group of authors to discuss the topic of OCL then the ones represented here. It not only covers the ideas and explanations of individuals who were the originators of OCL, such as Steve Cook and Jos Warmer, but also the views of most of today's prime experts in the theory and practice of OCL. It is no exaggeration to call this a seminal volume, since it describes the fundamental rationale behind OCL, and, we know that a grasp of rationale is key to all understanding. There will, undoubtedly, be more books on OCL as it evolves and its use becomes more widespread. It is, therefore, crucial that its origins are properly documented in a reference book. This is that book.

Bran Selic
Stockholm, October 2001

References

[Par87]   Parnas, D.L., van Schouwen, J., Kwan, P., Fougere, S., "Evaluation of the Shutdown Software for Darlington (SDS-1)", Interim Report for the Atomic Energy Control Board, 16 November 1987

A Meta-model Facility for a Family of UML Constraint Languages

Tony Clark[1], Andy Evans[2], and Stuart Kent[3]

[1] Department of Computing, Kings College, London, UK
anclark@dcs.kcl.ac.uk

[2] Department of Computer Science, University of York, York, UK
andye@cs.york.ac.uk

[3] Computing Laboratory, University of Kent, Canterbury, UK
s.j.h.kent@ukc.ac.uk

Abstract. With the move towards UML becoming a family of modelling languages, there is a need to view the Object Constraint Language in the same light. The aim of this paper is to identify a meta-modelling facility that encompasses the specification of the semantics of a family of object constraint languages. This facility defines a common set of model concepts, semantic domain concepts and semantic mappings that can be conveniently reused when constructing new family members.

1 Introduction

The Object Constraint Language (OCL) [Warmer98] is a language for expressing constraints on UML models. Recently, significant efforts have been made to provide a more precise description of the OCL. For example, a meta-model for the abstract syntax of OCL [Richters98] has been proposed. An outline meta-model of its semantics is presented in [Kent99], whilst a variety of other work has developed formal descriptions of the OCL semantics (see [Clark00a] for an overview).

At the time these approaches were developed, UML was viewed as a single, albeit large, modelling language. However, with the advent of UML 2.0 it is likely that UML will become a family of languages [Cook00]. In UML 2.0, it is intended that the semantics of each family member will be encapsulated by a single UML profile. Each profile will tailor UML to a specific application domain. For instance, one might have a UML for real-time modelling, e-business modelling or business process modelling. The impact of these changes will not just affect the diagrammatical components of UML. Specific extensions of OCL are also likely to be required. Indeed, there is early evidence of the need for such extensions in industry [Kleppe00, Knapman00a, Knapman00b]. The OMG's recent proposal for MDA (model driven architecture) [OMG01] also mandates the use of profiles, each with a potentially different constraint language.

A. Clark and J. Warmer (Eds.): Object Modeling with the OCL, LNCS 2263, pp. 4-20, 2002.
© Springer-Verlag Berlin Heidelberg 2002

A problem faced by the developers of profiles is to avoid the task of re-inventing meta-models for families of related languages. The aim of this paper is to show how the semantics of a family of OCL languages might be precisely captured within a meta-model. In doing so, it aims to highlight two key mechanisms which can aid in the large grained reuse of constraint language meta-models: language definition patterns and package extension and import.

The work presented in this paper is based on the Meta-Modelling Facility (MMF), which comprises a meta-modelling language (MML) a meta-modelling tool (MMT) and a method (MMM). This work has arisen out of an IBM funded project [Clark00] to investigate the feasibility of re-architecting UML as a family of languages. The work is currently being prepared as input to the UML 2.0 revision process under the auspices of the precise UML (pUML) group (http://www.puml.org).

This paper is structured as follows: Section 2 gives an overview of the MMF and the basic patterns and architecture used to describe meta-models. Section 3 presents the core meta-model of MML (a typical UML like core meta-model). Section 4 then extends the core model with the features of a static constraint language. Finally, section 5 discusses some general approaches to constructing profiles.

2 The MMF

The Meta-Modelling Facility (MMF) [Clark00a] aims to provide a modular and extensible method for defining and using modelling languages. MMF comprises a language (MML), used to write language definitions, a tool (MMT) used to interpret those definitions, and a method (MMM) that provides guidelines and patterns for good practice in language definition. This section introduces the language and the tool.

2.1 The Language

MML is a language for meta-modelling, which incorporates a subset of the UML. The language is defined in itself using a precise meta-modelling approach, in which mappings are defined between its modelling concepts and the concepts in its semantic domain. The development of the language is ongoing and has been supported by IBM.

The main modelling features of MML are packages, classes, attributes and a constraint language. These are introduced briefly below, being careful to identify differences with the standard UML interpretation. Examples of their use can be found in subsequent sections.

A package is a container of classes and/or other packages. This is familiar UML. Perhaps more unfamiliar is the ability to specialize and import packages, which has been borrowed from Catalysis [D'Souza98] and enhanced. Packages and package import and specialisation are the key constructs in MML that support modular, extensible definitions of languages based on a set of fundamental patterns. Our contribution is to provide a precise, tool-supported definition of this concept, and to show it can facilitate the development of precise meta-modelling definitions.

Package import is shown by placing a UML dependency arrow between the packages. The child package copies all (and therefore contains all) of the contents of the parent package. In addition, it may specialise the copied contents, in which case the copies are hidden and only the specialised contents are shown. A class, package, attribute or method within the scope of the package may be renamed through specialisation. This is indicated by a specialisation annotation on the corresponding import arrow. So if a package B imports A, copying class C and specialising it to D and copying attribute a in C and specialising it to b, one would annotate the arrow with [D<C[b<a]]. This is a nested syntax, reflecting the notion that there is a containment hierarchy of modelling elements.

An example of package import is shown in Fig. 1. The elements in red (lighter colour) represent those elements that appear in the child package by virtue of import from the parent(s). The blue elements (darker colour) have been added separately. They have been included to help clarify the meaning of package import. They could be generated automatically from the import relationship and renaming annotations, and, indeed, are by MMT. When an attribute is imported, its multiplicity may change, for example from "*" (zero or many) to "1" (exactly one). This can be included in the renaming annotation, so if, in the preceding example, the multiplicity of the attribute a was also specialised to 1, the renaming annotation would have been [D<C[b<a[1<*]]].

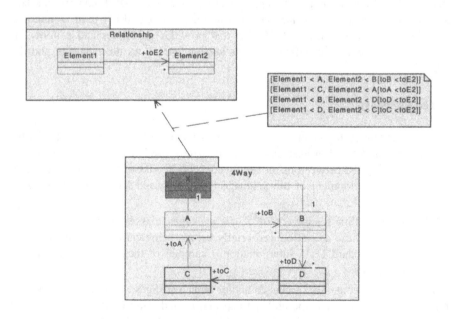

Fig. 1. Package Import

A generalisation arrow between packages denotes package generalisation. Package generalisation results in the contents of the package being specialised by the contents of the child class package. A renaming list can be attached to the generalisation arrow in a similar way to that used by import.

2.2 The MML Architecture and Patterns

The MML meta-model is specifically structured to provide a framework that can be readily used to construct precise definitions of families of modelling languages. To support this, a modular architecture is adopted, in which variation points are separated into packages. For example, MML includes packages for data types, extension mechanisms and constraints, all of which are extended from a single core package (see Fig. 2). The aim is that new languages can be rapidly constructed by changing or extending specific packages. For example, one could readily adapt the data types used by a specific modelling language by extending the data types package. If necessary, specific parts of the meta-model can be designated as mandatory, thereby ensuring cross language compatibility.

MML makes use of package generalisation to facilitate the construction of a layered framework of language definition components.

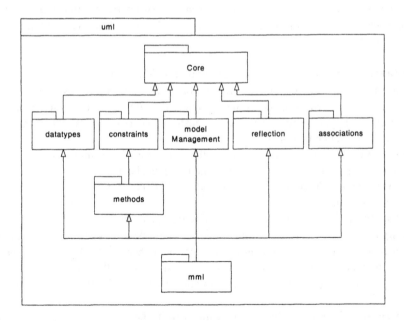

Fig. 2. The MML Architecture

MML also aims to identify patterns of language elements. These capture cross cutting structures and relationships that appear throughout meta-models. They include language definition patterns and a collection of language element patterns. The language definition pattern is used to structure the concrete syntax, abstract syntax and semantic elements of languages and to define mappings between them. This pattern is shown in Fig. 3.

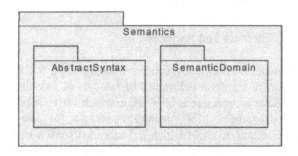

Fig. 3. The MML Language Definition Pattern

2.2.1 Language Element Patterns

The language element patterns capture common structural relationships between language elements. Six core patterns are shown in Fig. 4. A brief description of each pattern follows:

Instance: This pattern captures the semantic relationship found between types and their "instances". For example, instances of classes are objects. Note that in this pattern, abstract syntax concepts and semantic domain concepts are separated into different packages. Types are viewed as abstract syntax concepts, whilst instances belong to the semantic domain.

Containment: Elements may contain other elements. An example here is a class containing its attributes, or a package containing its classes.

Conformance: Elements conform to other elements; for instance, classes may conform to their parents.

Relationship: Many elements are related to other elements.

Comparable: Elements are comparable. For example a package can be compared with another package, or an object compared to another object. An element may be sub-equivalent to another element if they have a subset of the properties necessary for equivalence. If two elements are sub-equivalent to each other they are equivalent.

Inheritance: Elements may inherit features from their parents. All parents is the transitive closure of all parents of a elements. This pattern does not permit circular inheritance.

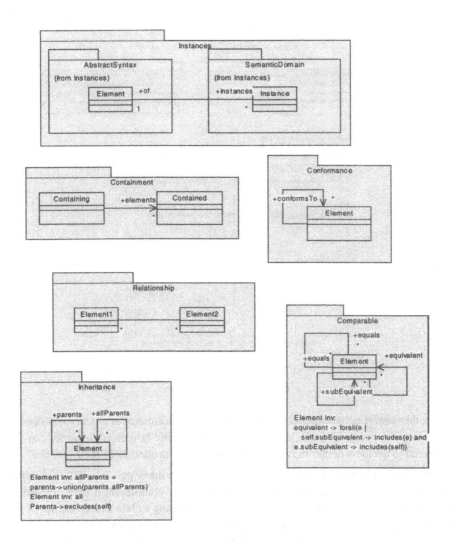

Fig. 4. Language Element Patterns

2.2.2 Composite Patterns

The core language element patterns can be combined to describe more complex patterns. The first of these is shown in Fig. 5. It describes the relationship between containers and their instances. A container has instances whose elements are instances of the elements of the container. The OCL constraint ensures that the relationship is commutative.

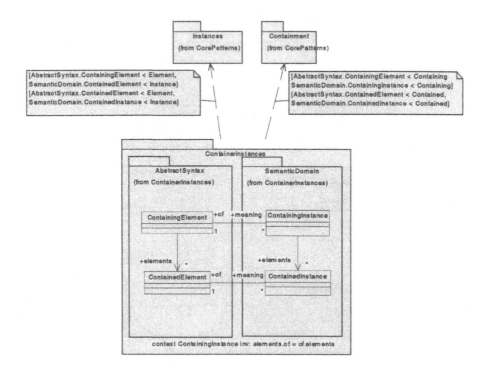

Fig. 5. Container Instances

Another useful pattern relates to conformance. Conformance is a general property that relates language elements of the same type. Many language elements can be compared to decide whether they are conformant to the properties of their parents.

Container conformance, as shown in Fig. 6, is one of many possible different kinds of conformance pattern. It states that two containers are conformant if their contained elements are conformant. As an example, consider treating a class as a container of its operations. The result of applying this pattern would be a rule for class containment that requires that for every operation belonging to a parent class, there must be an operation belonging to the child class that it is conformant to.

Finally, a possible static semantics for container conformance is described by the pattern shown in Fig. 7. This states that for an element to be conformant, its instances must be conformance to those of its parent. Here, conformance implies structural conformance, i.e. both the element and its instances must have the same structure as those of their parents.

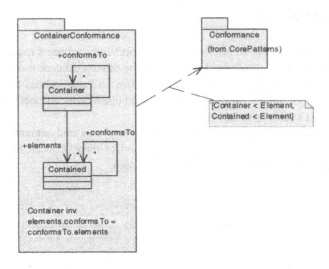

Fig. 6. Container Conformance

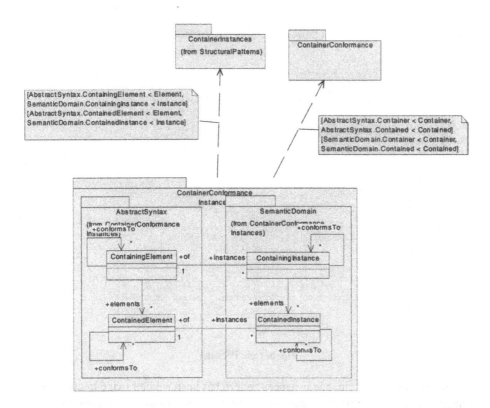

Fig. 7. Container Conformance Instances

3 The Core Package

The core package (see Fig. 8) provides the core modelling concepts required for meta-modelling in the MML. It is used here to illustrate the typical core modelling components of a static UML-like language. Note that we will not address the behavioural aspects of the core model (these will be described elsewhere). In Section 4, it will be extended with a static constraint language.

The core is divided into two packages: abstract syntax and semantic domain. As described above, an instances association is used to map between elements of the abstract syntax and elements of the semantic domain.

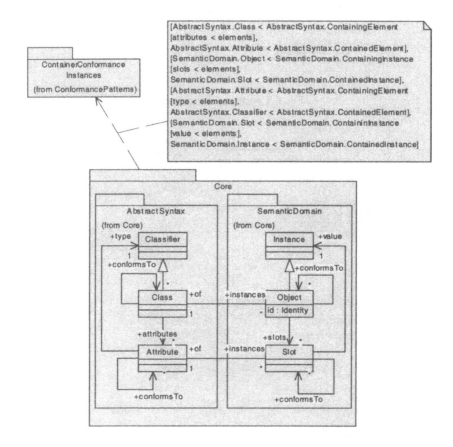

Fig. 8. Core Package

The container conformance instances pattern has been applied twice to construct a type/instance relationship for classes and attributes. The instances of a class are given by the collection of objects whose contents (slots) conform to the contents of the class (attributes). Objects and slots conform to the containership of class and attribute and are structurally conformant.

The effect of applying the patterns generates the following constraints:

[1] The slots of an object commute with the attributes of the object's class (from ContainerInstances):

> context Object inv: slots.of = of.attributes

[2] The value of a slot commutes with the type of the slot's attribute (from ContainerInstances):

> context Slot inv: value.of = of.type

A number of conformance constraints are also generated for classes, attributes, objects and slots. For example, a class conforms to another class if its instances (objects) conform to the instances of the parent.

4 Constraints

This section extends the core modeling concepts defined in section 3 with a simple static language for describing constraints. To support a family of constraint languages, the definition is structured to make a clear distinction between core concepts and language specific concepts.

The core constraints package (see Fig. 9) identifies concepts common to all object constraint languages. We assume that classifiers are associated with expressions. Expressions describe the *constraints* that must be evaluated on their instances. Expressions may also have sub-expressions and are associated with a collection of free variables. An important constraint that relates to free variables is that they are inherited by sub-expressions.

The static semantics of expressions are given by calculations. A calculation associates an expression and an environment (a set of variable bindings) with a value. The value is the result of evaluating the expression in the context of the binding. A distinguished variable, self, identifies the instance the expression is being evaluated against.

In the core constraints package, the pattern for container conformance is applied to classifiers, their expressions and their semantic domains: instances and calculations. This imposes properties of structural conformance and containership. The same properties also apply to expressions, their free variables, calculations and bindings. An implication is that the conformance of one expression to another is expressed in terms of substitutability of the values that are obtained from evaluating an expression. An expression is substitutable for another expression if the set of calculations, variable bindings and results satisfying the expression is a subset of those of its parent.

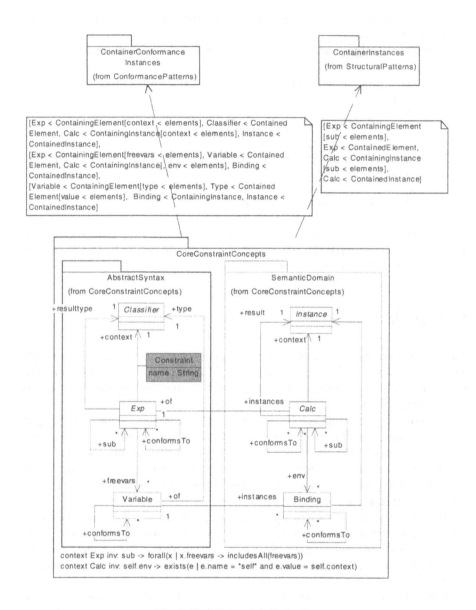

Fig. 9. Core Constraints Semantics

4.1 Language Specific Constraints

This section gives an example of an extension to the core constraint package (Fig. 10). It defines the core language expressions of a simple OCL-like profile for describing static constraints. These include logical expressions (and, not, equals, includes), slot references, variables and iterations. Note that most other constructs of an OCL-profile, for example or, collect, set union, could be easily defined in terms of the basic expressions defined here. This could be achieved by extension of translation (see Section 5).

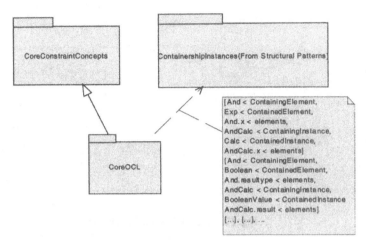

Fig. 10. OCL Language Extension

The abstract syntax for the core OCL package is shown in **Fig. 11**, whilst the corresponding semantic domain package is shown in Fig. 12. Applying the containership instances pattern to the core OCL package results in the appropriate instances associations and constraints being set up between each expression in the abstract syntax and its corresponding semantic domain element (note that not all the relevant substitutions are given in Fig. 10 for brevity). For example, the instances of an "And" expression will be "AndCalc", and so on.

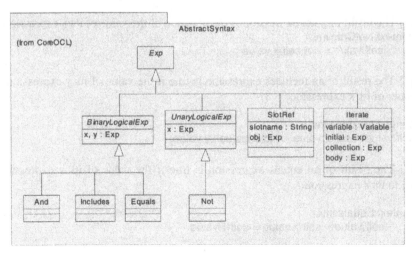

Fig. 11. Core OCL Abstract Syntax

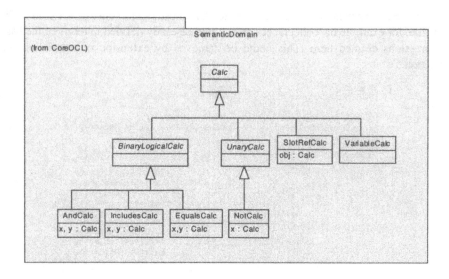

Fig. 12. Core OCL Semantic Domain

Finally, to complete the meta-model, a constraint is required for each calculation to describe its evaluation. For example, the result of an "And" expression is the conjunction of the value of its x and y expressions:

[1] And implies conjunction.
context AndCalc inv:
    self.value = self.x.value and self.y.value

Similar constraints are required for other calculations, for example:

[2] The result of a not expression is the negation of the value of its x expression.
context NotCalc inv:
    self.value = not self.x.value

[3] The result of an includes expression is true if the value of its y expression is a member of its x expression.

context Includes inv:
self.value = self.x.value ->includes(self.y.value)

[4] The result of an equals expression is true if the value of its y expression is equal to its x expression.

context Equals inv:
    self.value = self.x.value = self.y.value

[5] The result of a slot reference calculation is the value of the slot belonging to obj whose slotname is equal to the referenced slot name.

```
context SlotRefCalc inv:
      self.obj.value.slots -> exists(b |
                    b.value = self.value and b.name = self.exp.slotname)
```

[6] The result of evaluating a variable expression is the variable's binding.

```
context VariableCalc inv:
      self.env -> exists(e |
                    e.value = self.value and e.variable.name = self.exp.name)
```

A similar approach can be used to define the semantics for iterate, although the resulting constraints are too large to include here. The reader is referred to [Clark00] for an illustration of the approach.

4.2 Example

Fig. 13 gives a simple example of a constraint expressed as an instance of the core OCL meta-model. The expression "x > 5" is associated with a class A, which contains an attribute x of type Integer (we assume there is an appropriate package of data types and data values).

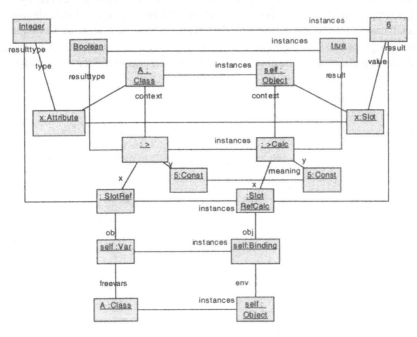

Fig. 13. Constraint Instance Example

An object satisfies the properties of A if:

- The object contains a slot corresponding to the attribute of A. This follows from the containership instances pattern.
- There is a calculation which evaluates the "x > 5" expression of A. This follows from the containership instances pattern, which ensures that any calculations associated with A conform to A's constraint expression.
- The result of comparing the value of the slot is greater than the constant "5" is true. This follows from the "greater than" evaluation constraint.

5 Profiles

This section describes two strategies that can be used to defining new profiles in MML. These strategies form an important part of the meta-modelling method (MMM). The first strategy, which we call the *extensional* strategy, involves extending appropriate core meta-model packages using package extension. This is the approach used in this paper. We identified core-modelling elements common to a number of constraint languages and extended their definition, gradually constructing a layered definition of a simple constraint language (a profile). Further extensions to this language can be described by additional packages. Fig. 14 illustrates how a family of constraint languages might be constructed by extending the core package.

The advantage of the extensional approach is that is intuitive – extending a language simply involves choosing an appropriate extension point and then defining the special cases. Furthermore, meta-models built in this way tend to have pleasing structural properties, for example one soon identifies a structure preserving relationship between elements in the abstract syntax and elements in the semantic domain.

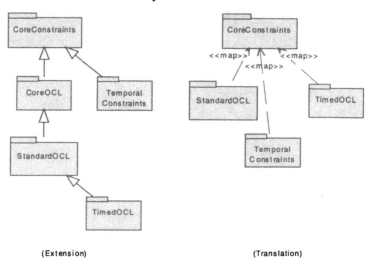

(Extension)   (Translation)

Fig. 14. Extension versus Translation

However, when it comes to implementation, the extensional approach suffers from weak interoperability. Consider two implemented profiles that extend a common core package. Tools that implement these profiles cannot readily share facilities for analysing properties of models because the relationship between the two models is based on the arbitrary extension of their profiles.

This leads to an alternative approach to profile construction, which we call the *translation* or *interpretative* approach (Fig. 14). Here, a common core language is defined with a minimal but expressive collection of modelling elements. Profiles are constructed by defining mappings from elements in the profile to elements in the core language. The key advantage of this approach is as follows - any facilities offered by a tool that implements the core language can be applied to any profile, provided that the profile is first translated into the core language. The trade-off here is that the core language must be sufficiently expressive to capture a wide variety of useful profile interpretations.

To support the definition of a family of constraint languages using the translation approach, a core constraint language must provide a minimal but expressive collection of logical expressions. For example, a core OCL-like constraint language should at least have the basic expressions of predicate and first-order logic, and arguably, higher order logics. Identifying the most appropriate expression set is not easy. Luckily, existing formal languages, many of which have been developed with minimal expression sets in mind, can guide us.

6 Conclusions

Over the next few years it is likely that an increasing number of UML profiles will be required. However, designing a profile from scratch is both time-consuming and inefficient. It ignores the significant amount of work invested in the development of other profiles. Instead, common variations between profiles must be identified and reused. A modular architecture should be designed in a way that allows new components of profiles to be readily plugged in to a common specification framework. The use of patterns to help identify common meta-modelling structures is essential if important cross cutting concerns such as conformance, modularity and consistency are to be properly addressed.

This paper has proposed one such framework for constraints based on the MMF. Constraint languages are likely to vary across profiles, and may even be shared. Constraint languages are also difficult to define from scratch, as they require a detailed knowledge of the principles of constraint language semantics. Thus, identifying core constraint language concepts is an essential step towards facilitating the development of families of constraint languages. This paper has defined such a core, and has described two approaches to viewing constraint language profiles as extensions or interpretations of the core.

References

[Warmer98] J.Warmer and A.Kleppe. *The Object Constraint Language: Precise Modeling with UML*. Addison-Wesley, 1998.

[Richters98] M.Richters and M.Gogolla. *On Formalising the UML Object Constraint Language*. In Tok Wang Ling, Sudha Ram and Mong Li Lee, editors, *Proc 17ᵗʰ Int. Conf. Conceptual Modeling (ER'98)*, volume 1507 of LNCS, pages 449-464, Springer, 1998.

[Kent99] S.Kent, S.Gaito, N.Ross. *A meta-model semantics for structural constraints in UML* In H.Kilov and B.Rumpe, editors, *Behavioural Specifications for Businesses and Systems*, Kluwer, 1999.

[Clark00a] A.Clark, S.Kent and J.Warmer. OCL Semantics FAQ, Workshop on the Object Constraint Language (OCL), Computing Laboratory, University of Kent, Canterbury, UK. Internet: http://www.cs.ukc.ac.uk/research/sse/oclws2k/index.html, March 2000.

[Evans00] A.Evans, S.Kent and B.Selic, editors, *Proc 3ʳᵈ Int. Conf. The Unified Modeling Language (<<UML>>2000)*, volume 1949 of LNCS, Springer, 2000.

[Cook00] S.Cook. *The UML Family: Profiles, Prefaces and Packages*. In [Evans00].

[Kleppe00]] A.Kleppe and J.Warmer. *Extending OCL to Include Actions*. In [Evans00].

[Knapman00a] J.Knapman. *Business- Oriented Constraint Language*. In [Evans00].

[Knapman00b] J.Knapman. *Statistical Constraints for EAI*. In [Evans00].

[OMG01] *Model Driven Architecture*. Available from http://www.omg.org/mda.

[Clark00b] A.Clark, A.Evans, S.Kent. *Rearchitecting UML as a Family of Language using a Precise OO Meta-Modelling Approach*. Available from http://www.puml.org/mmf, 2000.

[Clark01] A.Clark, A.Evans, S.Kent. *Engineering Modelling Languages: A Precise Meta-Modelling Approach*. Available from http://www.puml.org/mmf/langeng.ps, 2001.

[D'Souza98] D.D'Souza, A.Wills. *Object Components and Frameworks with UML: The Catalysis Approach*, Addison-Wesley, 1998.

A New Type Checking Approach for OCL Version 2.0 ?

Andy Schürr

Institute for Software Technology
University of the Federal Armed Forces, Munich
D-85577 Neubiberg, Germany
Andy.Schuerr@unibw-muenchen.de,
http://ist.unibw-muenchen.de/schuerr

Abstract. The Object Constraint Language OCL is an integral part of UML, the Unified Modeling Language standard. It has been added to Rational's UML core as a logic-based sublanguage for the definition of integrity constraints (invariants) on class diagrams as well as for the definition of pre- and postconditions of operations. Despite of the fact that OCL is called a statically typed language its type checking rules are not precisely defined in the UML standard version 1.3. Furthermore, they have certain deficiencies concerning the treatment of collection manipulating operations. This paper compares three different approaches for the definition of modified OCL type checking rules, selects one of these approaches as the most appropriate one and explains the new type checking rules for this approach in more detail. All presented proposals are based on our experiences with the design of a rather similar statically typed constraint language that is part of the graph transformation language PROGRES.

1 Introduction

The *object constraint language OCL* is an integral part of the Unified Modeling Language Standard UML [8] for the logic-based definition of class invariants or pre- and postconditions of operations [19]. In its current form OCL suffers from the same problems as many other parts of the UML standard: it possesses neither a precise static nor a precise dynamic semantics definition [14]. These are the reasons why groups of researchers are now active to refine and redesign parts of OCL in order to influence the definition of a new OCL version as part of the forthcoming UML 2.0 standard [5,13].

It is the purpose of this paper to apply our experiences with the development of the *graph transformation language PROGRES* to improve OCL. PROGRES is a visual, executable specification language that combines a subset of UML class diagrams for the definition of object structures with graph transformation rules for the definition of object structure manipulations and OCL-like path expressions for the definition of integrity constraints and queries [18].

The PROGRES *path expression sublanguage* is similar to OCL w.r.t. the following properties:

A. Clark and J. Warmer (Eds.): Object Modeling with the OCL, LNCS 2263, pp. 21–41, 2002.
© Springer-Verlag Berlin Heidelberg 2002

- It combines arithmetic expressions, predicate logic formulas and so forth with path expressions for navigation along associations.
- It may be used for the definition of integrity constraints attached to a single class of objects and for the definition of pre- and postconditions of operations.
- It is therefore related to UML-like class diagrams and object manipulating operations in the same way as OCL.
- It distinguishes between partially defined and always defined expressions as well as between single object and collection returning path expressions, too.

On the other hand, there exists a long list of significant differences between PROGRES path expressions and OCL:

1. PROGRES path expressions have a well-defined set of type checking rules expressed as predicate logic formulas that avoid some type checking problems of OCL version 1.3.
2. Furthermore, PROGRES has a precisely defined dynamic semantics based on nonmonotonic reasoning and fixpoint theory.
3. Its dynamic semantics definition distinguishes between terminating computations that return the undefined result nil and nonterminating computations with unknown results.
4. Partially defined Boolean expressions, which caused the introduction of a three-valued logic in OCL, are disallowed; this is due to our experience that a three-valued logic often leads to rather unexpected results.
5. Functional abstraction of ordinary expressions and path expressions is supported by using different syntactic constructs.
6. Operators for the definition of default values (for partially defined subexpressions), building the transitive closure, conditional iteration etc. are available that are missing in OCL.
7. The OCL-like textual path expression sublanguage of PROGRES is complemented by a graphical sublanguage which is closely related to the structural part of UML collaboration diagrams.
8. Attributed associations, n-ary associations, bags and sequences are not supported, despite of the fact that PROGRES users often complain about the lack of these OCL features.

As a consequence, it was quite tempting to start a research project which refines the wide-spread OCL standard based on our experiences with the more or less unknown specification language PROGRES. First results concerning the addition of new operators to OCL and a visual sublanguage based on UML collaboration diagrams are presented in [16] and will not be repeated here. In the following we will focus our interest on the first topic mentioned above, i.e. the construction of appropriate *OCL type checking rules* based on our experiences in this area, the vast body of knowledge about type checking polymorphic specification and programming languages in general [2,3], and a recently published paper about the OCL language's type system [4]. This paper presents a precise definition of the OCL type checking rules for the first time, but offers no solutions for the problems addressed in this contribution concerning the treatment of operations on collections (sets) of different types.

Our discussion of the addressed type checking problems is based on previously published results in a workshop proceedings [17]. For sake of completeness these results will be repeated here (in more detail). Furthermore, these results will be used in a modified form for the first time to define a set of type-checking rules for a representative subset of OCL.

The rest of this chapter is organized as follows: Section 2 explains the problems with the currently valid version of the OCL type checking rules for collection operators like **union**, `intersection`, and `includesAll`. Furthermore, it shows that variants of these problems affect the type checking rules for the comparison of objects or collections of objects, too.

Section 3 presents a straight-forward solution for the problems explained in Section 2 that follows the lines of the type checking approach invented for the predicate-logic-based language LOGIN [2]. This solution relies on the fact that class hierarchies have to be lattices, i.e. that any pair of classes possesses at most one smallest common superclass and at most one greatest common subclass (`OclAny` or `OclNil` in the worst case).

Section 4 presents a slightly different solution for the presented type checking problems that works with the powerset of all OCL types and avoids thereby the restriction of class hierarchies to lattices. Type checking based on sets of types is an already established approach, too. It is for instance used to define the type checking rules of the language TyCOON [12]. Both solutions of the type checking problem are closely related to each other; it is always possible to transform a given class hierarchy into a (for the programmer hidden) lattice that can be used for type checking purposes [1]. The additional classes of this lattice represent the needed nonsingleton sets of the type checking approach presented in Section 4.

Unfortunately, both approaches are too complex for the average OCL user who does not want to care about class lattices or sets of types. Therefore, Section 5 presents yet another solution that (1) works for all kinds of class hierarchies, (2) returns the same results as the type checking rules of the OCL standard version 1.3 as long as the standard rules do not reject a given OCL expression (and vice versa), and (3) simply determines a more general supertype where the type checking rules of Section 4 process nonsingleton sets of types. It is our opinion that this type checking approach constitutes the proper compromise between the restrictiveness and simplicity of the type checking rules of the OCL standard and the expressiveness and complexity of the solutions presented in Section 3 and 4 of this contribution.

Section 6 demonstrates for a core subset of OCL how the type checking approach introduced in Section 5 may be used to define the type checking rules for OCL version 2.0. Based on the examples presented here it is rather straight-forward to define the missing type checking rules for the rest of OCL, too.

Finally, Section 7 summarizes the presented three new OCL type checking approaches and discusses planned future work activities.

2   Problems with Type Checking OCL Expressions

We believe that the implicitely defined type checking rules for OCL version 1.3 in
[8] often return unwanted results and should be changed in the future version 2.0.
Let us assume that the OCL types (classes) Employee (of our University) and
Student are subtypes of Person as shown in Fig. 1. Furthermore, let us assume
that an OCL expression <T>Expr computes an object which is a member (direct
or indirect instance) of the type <T>, and that an OCL expression <T>SExpr
computes a set of members of the type <T>. Using these writing conventions
we know that EmployeeExpr returns a member of type Employee (an instance
of type Employee itself or an instance of Professor or Assistant), whereas
StudentSExpr returns a set of members of type Student.

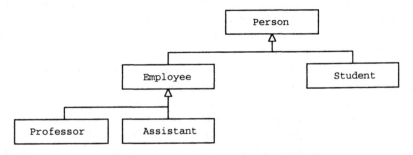

Fig. 1. A simple version of the running example.

Furthermore, we assume that

- the functor Eval[Expr] *evaluates* the given OCL expression and returns
  either an undefined result Nil or a single element or a collection of elements
  if provided with an additional environment parameter for the regarded object
  structure, used parameter values, etc.,
- the functor Type[Expr] determines a unique *static type* of the regarded
  expression or issues a type checking error by returning an undefined type
  which we call OclNil,
- the actual type of any element computed by Eval[Expr] always *conforms
  to* the static type returned by Type[Expr],
- the set of all expressions with type OclNil is a (decidable) subset of the set
  of expressions with an undefined value Nil,
- and that Type[Expr] is the most specific type w.r.t. the "conforms to" partial order known at compile time that fulfills the other requirements mentioned above.

The static type of an OCL expression may be modeled as a tuple of the
following form:
Type[Expr] = (Type[Expr].Sort, Type[Expr].Name) ∈ *Sort* × *Name*
where

$Sort = \{\texttt{simple}, \texttt{partial}, \texttt{collection}, \texttt{bag}, \texttt{set}, \texttt{sequence}\}$

$Name = BasicTypes \cup Classifiers \cup \{\texttt{OclAny}, \texttt{OclNil}\}$

$BasicTypes = \{\texttt{Real}, \texttt{Integer}, \texttt{String}, \texttt{Boolean}\}$

$Classifiers = $ the set of all classifiers of the related class diagram(s)

This representation of OCL types is not totally consistent with the OCL standard because of the addition of a "smallest" type OclNil that represents always undefined or illegal (wrong typed) expressions and the introduction of **partial** expressions. The standard is rather vague concerning the treatment of expressions which either return a single well-defined element or an undefined result as e.g. the navigation to an association end with multiplicity 0..1. It is unclear whether such a *partial expression* has to be treated (1) like an expression that returns a single instance which may be nil, or (2) like an expression that returns a collection of results which contains no or one element.

All remaining details of the static type representation introduced above are consistent with the OCL standard. We distinguish between simple expressions that have a single well-defined element as value and collection expressions that return a collection of values. The value of a simple expression may either be an element of one of the four basic types Real,... or an object (instance) of a defined UML classifier. Collections of values are either ordered sequences or unordered sets or bags that may contain multiple occurrences of the same element. The type OclAny is used as the supertype of all possible types of simple expressions.

Based on these assumptions the following type hierarchy definition (type conformance) rules are introduced (cf. [19]):

- **Type1** conforms to **Type2**
  if **Type1.Sort** is compatible with **Type2.Sort** and **Type1.Name** is a subtype of **Type2.Name**.
- **Sort1** is compatible with **Sort2** if **Sort1** = **Sort2**.
- **Sort1** is compatible with **Sort2**
  if **Sort2** = **collection** and **Sort1** ∈ {bag, set, sequence}.
- **Sort1** is compatible with **Sort2**
  if **Sort1** = **partial** and **Sort2** = **sequence**[1].
- **Name1** is a subtype of **Name2** if **Name1** = **Name2**.
- Any type **Name** ∈ *BasicTypes* ∪ *Classifiers* is a subtype of OclAny.
- OclNil is a subtype of any type **Name** ∈ *BasicTypes* ∪ *Classifiers*.
- **Integer** is a subtype of **Real**.

---

[1] A partial expression is not compatible with a simple expression or a set expression or a bag expression for the following reasons: the OCL standard states that navigations along associations with multiplicity unequal to 1..1 always return a sequence of elements. However, it is tempting to require that partial expressions are compatible with any sort of collections and to permit simple expressions where partial expressions are allowed. But these rules would have the side effect that simple expressions may be used where collections are expected, i.e. destroy OCL's philosophy to distinguish between operations on simple values and operations on collections.

- **Name1** is a subtype of **Name2**
  if **Name1** and **Name2** are UML classifiers and **Name2** generalizes **Name1**.
- The "conforms to" relationship is a partial order.

The suggested treatment of OCL types disregards type and expression parameters of OCL operators for the following reasons: OCL offers some operators that require types as input or return types as their results. However, it is still unclear whether OCL has the intention to treat *types as real first-order objects* and whether its future versions will offer *all* needed operators for accessing all (meta layer) properties of OCL types (UML classifiers). Today available operators return the attributes, association ends, and operations for a given type as collections of strings. No means are available for retrieving the properties of these strings, i.e. for determining the type of an attribute or the parameter profile of an operation or the multiplicity of an association end. It makes therefore no sense to present a type system that distinguishes between first-order types of object instances and second-order types of type instances as long as these important details are not clarified.

Concerning the treatment of *expression parameters* of OCL operators the situation is as follows: An operator like **iterate** that applies a given expression parameter to a collection of elements simply requires that this expression parameter has the type **OCLExpression**. The fact that the expression parameter references variables defined by the surrounding **iterate** expression is not taken into account by the OCL type system. Therefore, we will not make any attempts to define parameter profiles for OCL operators like **iterate** themselves, but restrict our interest to type checking rules for expressions containing applied/expanded occurrences of these operators.

Based on these assumptions we are now able to explain some of the problems with the currently used type checking rules of OCL. Let us consider some set manipulating expressions such as

```
XSExpr->union(YSExpr)
```

which computes the union of a set of X members and a set of Y members and

```
XSExpr->intersection(YSExpr)
```

which computes the intersection of a set of X members and a set of Y members.

The signatures (parameter profiles) of the involved set operations have about the following form:

```
Set(T)->union(set2:Set(T))  : Set(T)
Set(T)->intersection(set2:Set(T))  : Set(T)
```

These signatures require for both set manipulating expressions that the actual type (name) X is bound to the formal parameter type T and that the type Y of the second parameter is therefore a subtype of X. The result type of both expressions is Set(X), i.e.

```
Type[XSExpr->union(YSExpr)] =
Type[XSExpr->intersection(YSExpr)] = (set,X)
```

This has the consequence that the OCL expressions

```
EmployeeSExpr->union(PersonSExpr) and
EmployeeSExpr->intersection(PersonSExpr)
```

are illegal (`Person` is not a subtype of `Employee`), whereas the expressions

```
PersonSExpr->union(EmployeeSExpr) and
PersonSExpr->intersection(EmployeeSExpr)
```

are legal and possess the static type (`set`,`Person`). These results are in contradiction to our intuition that

- the mathematical union or intersection of $S1$ and $S2$ should be equivalent to the union or intersection of $S2$ and $S1$,
- the union of a set of `Employee` members with a set of `Person` members is computable and returns a set of `Person` members in any case,
- the intersection of a set of `Employee` members and a set of `Person` members always returns a set of `Employee` members (and never a `Person` member which is not an `Employee` member).

Similar problems occur when we study the definition of the signatures of the operations `includes`, `includesAll`, and the identity test for two objects under the assumption that objects are direct instances of a single class[2]:

- `EmployeeSExpr->includes(StudentExpr)` tests whether the result computed by `StudentExpr` is an element of the set computed by `EmployeeSExpr`. Regarding the class hierarchy of Fig. 1 we know that this expression is always `false` due to the fact that `Employee` and `Student` do not possess a common subclass. Nevertheless this expression is legal w.r.t. the signature `collection(T)->includes(object:OclAny) : Boolean` of the `includes` operation.
- `EmployeeSExpr->includesAll(StudentExpr)` on the other hand is an illegal operation even if `Employee` and `Student` would possess a common subclass. This is due to the fact that `includesAll` possesses the signature `collection(T)->includesAll(c2: collection(T)) : Boolean`.
- For similar reasons `EmployeeExpr = StudentExpr` is a legal expression which always returns `false` w.r.t. the class hierarchy of Fig. 1,
- whereas `EmployeeSExpr = StudentSExpr` is illegal as long as `Student` is not a subtype of `Employee`.

As a consequence, the standard type checking rules *are not complete* w.r.t. the OCL language's dynamic semantics as required in [4]. Some reasonable OCL expressions with a well-defined dynamic semantics are illegal w.r.t. the standard type checking rules. Even worse, the given rules often return types which are too

---

[2] UML permits objects that are direct instances of more than one class. However, most if not all UML tools and UML users rely on the fact that objects are instances of a single class which does not change during an object's life time. Therefore, OCL should at least possess a more sophisticated type checking mode which makes use of this widespread assumption and disallows e.g. the comparison of expressions with unrelated static types.

general and they return different results for expressions which obviously have the same dynamic semantics.

Therefore, some OCL explanations already use a different interpretation for the signatures of OCL collection operations such as **union** and **intersection**. They require for expressions like

XSExpr->*someOperation*(YSExpr)

with *someOperation* ∈ {**union**, **intersection**, ...}

the existence of a (smallest) common supertype of X and Y which is used as parameter T of the involved signature (template)

set(T)->*someOperation*(set2 : Set(T)): Set(T).

Such a smallest common supertype always exists due to the fact that all non-collection types are subtypes of **OclAny**. At a first glance this interpretation of the OCL standard solves almost all problems mentioned above—as long as the multiple inheritance concept is not used.

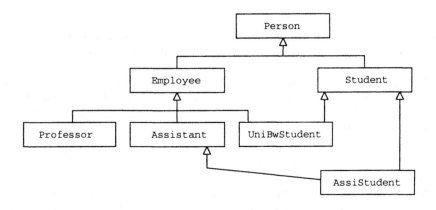

Fig. 2. A class hierarchy with multiple inheritance.

Fig. 2 presents one example of a UML class diagram that uses multiple inheritance. Both **Assi(stant)Student** and **UniBwStudent** are subtypes (subclasses) of **Employee** and **Student**. Probably such a class diagram is ill-designed[3] but it is legal. Regarding this class diagram we can explain our problems with the suggested new OCL type checking rules. Let us start with computing the types of the two expressions

AssiStudentSExpr->union(UniBwStudentSExpr)
EmployeeSExpr->intersection(StudentSExpr)

Using the new "smallest common supertype" rule we have to conclude that the union of the **AssiStudentSExpr** and the **UniBwStudentSExpr** has not a sin-

---

[3] For further details concerning a proper treatment of temporary object roles such as being a student or a professor the reader is referred to [10].

gle but two smallest common supertypes (set,Employee) and (set,Student) whereas the intersection of the EmployeeSExpr and the StudentSExpr has the most general type (set,Person). Both results are rather unwanted. In the case of the union expression we either have to work with a set of OCL types or we have to replace the type set {(set,Employee),(set,Student)} by the common supertype (set,Person). In the case of the intersection we have lost the information that all elements of the resulting set of Person elements are members of the type Employee *and* the type Student.

Similar problems occur, when we regard the (symmetric) difference of two collections or the inclusion or exclusion of single elements from collections. In many cases the standard OCL type checking rules as well as the suggested new type checking rules force the OCL user to add type casts at various places. Furthermore, the proposed type checking rules do not only return useless type information in many cases but still permit the construction of many useless expressions that could be recognized at compile time.

3   Type Checking with Type Lattices

It is possible to circumvent some of the type checking problems discussed in Section 2 by requiring that any two types have at most one smallest common supertype scs and at most one greatest common subtype gcs. These restrictions together with the existence of a greatest type (name) OclAny and a smallest type (name) OclNil ensure that all constructed type hierarchies are lattices (in the mathematical sense of the word).

Therefore, the class diagram of Fig. 2 is illegal, which maybe recognized by an incremental lattice checking algorithm as implemented in the PROGRES programming environment [18]. An automatically working completion algorithm adopted from [1] may be used to transform the class diagram of Fig. 2 into the class diagram of Fig. 3 by adding a single class EmplStudent and by redirecting some generalization relationships.

Relying on the automatically constructed class diagram of Fig. 3 we may introduce OCL type checking rules based on the following definitions of two binary functions scs and gcs on types:

- scs(t,t') computes *the unique* smallest common supertype of t and t'; it returns OclAny in the worst case.
- gcs(t,t') computes *the unique* greatest common subtype of t and t'; it returns OclNil in the worst case.

The following OCL type checking rules are still asymmetric w.r.t. the treatment of the *sort* of the first and the second argument of collection operations like union or intersection of sets in order to avoid any unnecessary inconsistencies with the currently valid OCL type checking rules. These rules require that the union of a set and a bag returns a set whereas the union of a bag and a set returns a set. It is worthwhile to discuss a modification of these rules such that the expression sort simple is compatible with partial and the expression sort

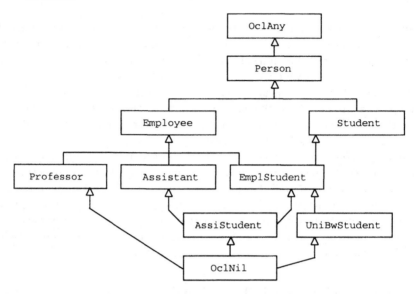

Fig. 3. Redesigned class hierarchy with lattice property.

set is compatible with bag. Based on these extensions the union of a set with a bag and a bag with a set would return a bag. Furthermore, the union of a set or bag expression with a simple or partial expression would be permitted, too; its result would be a set or bag, respectively.

Avoiding the just discussed extensions and sticking to the standard as close as possible we get the following type checking rules for union, intersection, and the identity operator = defined on simple elements and collections of elements:

1. Type[expr1->union(expr2)] :=
   (set,scs(Type[expr1].Name,Type[expr2].Name)),
   if Type[expr1].Sort = set and Type[expr2].Sort $\in$ {set,bag}.
2. Type[expr1->union(expr2)] :=
   (bag,scs(Type[expr1].Name,Type[expr2].Name)),
   if Type[expr1].Sort = bag and Type[expr2].Sort $\in$ {set,bag}.
3. Type[expr1->intersection(expr2)] :=
   (set,gcs(Type[expr1].Name,Type[expr2].Name),
   if Type[expr1].Sort = set and Type[expr2].Sort $\in$ {set,bag}.
4. Type[expr1->intersection(expr2)] :=
   (bag,gcs(Type[expr1].Name,Type[expr2].Name)),
   if Type[expr1].Sort = bag and Type[expr2].Sort $\in$ {set,bag}.
5. Type[expr1 = expr2] := (simple,Boolean),
   if gcs(Type[expr1].Name,Type[expr2].Name) $\neq$ OclNil
   and Type[expr1].Sort = Type[expr2].Sort $\neq$ collection.
6. Any expression without a matching rule is illegal. The same is true for expressions to which the type (S,OclNil) is assigned where S may be simple or partial or .... .

Applying these rules to the class diagram of Fig. 3 and some expressions introduced in Section 2 we get the following results:

Type[AssiStudentSExpr->union(UniBwStudentSExpr)] =
    (set,scs(AssiStudent,UniBwStudent)) = (set,EmplStudent)

and

Type[EmployeeSExpr->intersection(StudentSExpr)] =
    (set,gcs(Employee,Student)) = (set,EmplStudent)

Furthermore, the presented rules now reject expressions like

ProfessorExpr = AssistentExpr

due to the fact that Professor and Assistant have no (greatest) common subtype except of OclNil.

The main drawbacks of the presented solution are the requirements that type hierarchies have to be lattices and that objects are direct instances of a single type (class). These requirements often enforce the construction of better designed class hierarchies. However, our experiences show that it is difficult to convince OO modelers that type hierarchies should be lattices and to teach them how to transform a given type hierarchy into a lattice. Even if they are supported by tools which perform this task, they have difficulties to understand the output of such a transformation process, i.e. the needs for adding an exponential number of additional types in the worst case. Therefore, we present in the following section yet another variant of OCL type checking rules. These rules manipulate sets of OCL types instead of relying on the lattice property of class hierarchies.

4   Type Checking with Type Sets

One solution for avoiding the lattice restriction for type hierarchies is quite obvious: a hidden preprocessing phase checks the lattice property for the given UML class diagrams and adds the still needed intermediate classes without revealing their existence to the end user as already suggested in [1]. Whenever the type checking algorithm computes one of these intermediate types for a given OCL expression it displays its set of smallest user defined supertypes. From a theoretical point of view the lattice construction phase may even be omitted and the type checking rules may directly manipulate *sets of OCL types*. For this purpose the general "type checking axioms" of Section 2, which guide the design of our type checking rules, have to be modified as follows:

- the functor Eval[Expr] evaluates the given OCL expression and returns either an undefined result or a single element or a collection of elements (if provided with an additional environment parameter not considered here),
- the functor Type[Expr] determines a *set of* static types of the regarded expression or issues a type checking error by returning an *empty set of types*.
- the actual type of any element computed by Eval[Expr] conforms to *all static types* returned by Type[Expr],

- the type checking rules used for the definition of the functor Type assign *the empty set of types* to expressions with an always undefined value,
- and the type checking rules compute *the smallest set* of the most specific types w.r.t. the "conforms to" partial order that fulfills the requirements mentioned above.

Based on these assumptions the type checking rules for the operators union and intersection—restricted to arguments of sort set for simplicity reasons—have the following form:

Type[expr1->union(expr2)] := (set,rmSuper(TS))

where

TS = (allSuper(Type[expr1].Name) $\cap$ allSuper(Type[expr2].Name))

Furthermore,

Type[expr1->intersection(expr2)] := (set,rmSuper(T))

where

TS = allSuper(Type[expr1].Name) $\cup$ allSuper(Type[expr2].Name))

The used auxiliary functions rmSuper and allSuper are defined as follows using OCL and the functions directSupertypes and directSubtypes of the UML meta model:

```
allSuper(set) = set->union(directSupertypes.allSuper)
  -- allSuper computes the set of all direct and indirect
  -- supertypes of a set of types including the given set of
  -- types itself but without the most general type OclAny

rmSuper(set) =
  set->reject(directSubtypes->intersection(set)->notEmpty))
  -- rmSuper removes all types from set with direct subtypes
  -- in the set
```

Returning to our running example and the class diagram of Fig. 2 these new type checking rules work as follows:

Type[AssiStudentSExpr->union(UniBwStudentSExpr)] =
        (set,rmSuper(TS)) = (set,{Employee,Student})

where

TS = allSuper(AssiStudent) $\cap$ allSuper(UniBwStudent) =
    = {AssiStudent,Assistant,Employee,Student,Person} $\cap$
       {UniBwStudent,Employee,Student,Person}

Furthermore,

Type[EmployeeSExpr->intersection(StudentSExpr)] =
        (set,rmSuper(TS)) = (set,{Employee,Student})

where

TS = allSuper(Employee) $\cup$ allSuper(Student)
    = {Employee,Person} $\cup$ {Student,Person}

At a first glance the new type checking rules seem to be wrong for the following reasons: the type set of a union expression is computed by building the *intersection* of the types of its subexpressions whereas the type set of a intersection expression is computed by building the *union* of the types of its subexpressions. However, we have to keep in mind that an element of the union of two sets is a member of all the static types of the first argument *or* or a member of all the static types of the second argument but not an element of the union of all static types of both arguments in the general case. Therefore, we have to replace the set of types of the first and the second argument by the smallest set of *common* supertypes. For this purpose we (1) determine the supertypes of the types of the arguments, (2) build the intersection, and (3) remove all redundant supertypes of the resulting set of types.

Similarly, we know that any element in the intersection of two sets is a member of all static types of the first set *and* and that it is simultaneously a member of all static types of the second set. Therefore, it is save to compute the type set of an intersection by (1) determining the supertypes of the involved arguments, (2) building the union of the just constructed type sets, and (3) removing all redundant supertypes of the resulting set of types.

The main advantage of using type sets in type checking rules—instead of building first a hidden lattice—is related to the reason why the oclType operator of previous OCL versions has been removed in version 1.3. It has been removed because UML allows models where one object is a direct instance of more than one type (classifier). As a consequence, the oclType operator might return a set of types in the general case instead of always returning a single type as one might expect. The set-oriented type checking approach has no longer any problems with objects which are direct instances of more than one type. As a consequence it is possible to reintroduce the oclType operator together with other means for reflection.

The fact that objects may be direct instances of more than one type (classifier) had an important impact on the definition of the above introduced type checking rule. These rules do not make any attempt to compute sets of greatest common subtypes of the types of the regarded subexpressions. Therefore, the computed type set of the intersection expression

```
Type[EmployeeSExpr->intersection(StudentSExpr)] =
    (set,{Employee,Student}) ≠ (set,{EmplStudent})
```

is independent of the fact whether the class diagram of Fig. 2 or the class diagram of Fig. 3 is regarded. An object may be a member (direct instance) of both types (classes) Employee and Student without being a member of a subtype (subclass) of these two types (classes). Therefore, the object set of all members (extension) of EmplStudent is a proper subset of the intersection of the object sets (extensions) of all members of Employee and all members of Student in the general case.

5   Type Checking with Approximated Type Sets

The previously presented type checking solutions are either too restrictive or too complex to be useful for the average OCL user. The solution based on lattices enforces UML users to redesign their class hierarchies in certain cases, the solution based on sets of types is very unnatural for software developers familiar with the type checking rules of programming languages. Therefore, we have to find another solution with about the following properties:

- The new type checking rules accept more expressions with a well-defined dynamic semantics than the standard rules.
- If the standard OCL type checking rules and the rules of this section both accept an expression then the type checking rules defined here compute either the same type or a subtype of the "old" type.
- The new rules are identical to the rules presented in Section 3 as long as the regarded type hierarchies are lattices (after completion with OclAny and OclNil).
- The new rules approximate nonsingleton type sets computed by the rules of Section 4 by a unique smallest common supertype that is OclAny in the worst case.

Type checking rules that fulfill these properties may be defined as follows for the operators union and intersection (restricted to sets):

Type[expr1->union(expr2)] :=
    (set,scs*(Type[expr1].Name,Type[expr2].Name))
Type[expr1->union(expr2)] :=
    (set,gcs*(Type[expr1].Name,Type[expr2].Name))

where

scs*(T1,T2) := approximate(set of smallest common supertypes of T1,T2)
gcs*(T1,T2) := approximate(set of greatest common subtypes of T1,T2)
approximate({T}) := T
approximate({T1,T2} $\cup$ TSet) := approximate(scs*(T1,T2) $\cup$ TSet)

Having presented these rules we have to prove that their definitions are sensible. First of all we have to show that the evaluation of the just introduced recursively defined functions scs* and approximate terminates for all possible inputs. This is true for the following reasons: The operator scs* either determines a set of *proper* supertypes of its two type arguments or it returns one of the two type arguments (if one argument is a supertype of the other one). Based on the assumption that type hierarchies are finite and that the supertype (subtype) relationship is a partial order we know that the approximation process will finally terminate with returning OclAny in the worst case.

Furthermore, it is easy to show that the new rules fulfill the properties required above:

- The new rules accept all expressions accepted by the rules of Section 3, which were already more liberal than the type checking rules of the standard in some cases.

– The standard OCL type checking rules require that the type of the second argument of a union or intersection conforms to the type of its first argument. Therefore, the type of the first argument of a legal union expression is always the smallest common supertype of the types of both arguments whereas the type of the second argument of a legal intersection expression is always the greatest common subtype of the types of both arguments. As a consequence the new rules compute for the union the same type and for the intersection a subtype of the type computed by the standard rules.
– As long as the regarded UML class hierarchy is a lattice no approximation of type sets by the operator approximate is needed. Under these assumptions the rules defined here compute the same type as the rules of Section 3.

Applying the new type checking rules to some OCL expressions of Section 3 we expect therefore the following results for the class hierarchy of Fig. 3:

```
Type[AssiStudentSExpr->union(UniBwStudentSExpr)] =
    (set,EmplStudent)
Type[EmployeeSExpr->intersection(StudentSExpr)] =
    (set,EmplStudent)
```

Applying the new rules to the same expressions regarding the class hierarchy of Fig. 2 yields the following results:

```
Type[AssiStudentSExpr->union(UniBwStudentSExpr)] =
    (set,approximate({Employee,Student} = (set,Person)
Type[EmployeeSExpr->intersection(StudentSExpr)] =
    (set,approximate({AssiStudent,UniBwStudent} = (set,Person)
```

The approximations of sets of smallest common supertypes or greatest common subtypes are sometimes unprecise. The type checking rules of this section require in some cases "downcasts" where the type checking rules of Section 4 would accept an OCL expression as type safe. Using the type checking rules of Section 4 any operation defined for all members of type Employee or defined for all members of type Student may be applied to the union expression regarded above. On the contrary, the new type checking rules introduced in this section rule out the application of operations that are not defined for all members of the type Person.

A similar problem occurs when we regard the intersection defined above. We know that all elements of the result set are either members of AssiStudent or UniBwStudent. To be on the safe side we may therefore apply operations (features) to the computed set of elements which are defined for both types AssiStudent and UniBwStudent. These are the inherited features of the set of their smallest common superclasses, Employee and Student. Again the type checking rules of Section 4 would permit the application of all operations defined for Employee or Student, whereas the type checking rules of this section permit the application of operations defined for the type Person only. This is the price we have to pay for manipulating single type names instead of sets of type names if the regarded type hierarchies are not lattices. However, we believe that OCL users will not have any problems with the type checking rules of this section for the following reasons:

- The new type checking rules require a considerable smaller number of down-casts than the standard rules.
- OO programmers are used to solve type checking problems by inserting type casts if needed.
- Software developers are told to avoid multiple inheritance whenever possible, i.e. developed type hierarchies are very often trees, which are lattices after the addition of the smallest type `OclNil`.

6   More Type Checking Rules for OCL

Based on the type checking approach presented in the previous section we will now propose a complete set of *type checking rules for a core subset of OCL*. Again, we are avoiding mathematical symbols as far as possible[4] in order to make these rules readable for the average OCL user. However, it is a rather straightforward task to translate the rules given here into more formal notations which are usually used by experts for the definition of type theories.

Furthermore, we are not introducing an environment parameter which provides all needed details about regarded UML class diagrams and which binds variables of OCL expressions to their types. On the contrary,. we are simply assuming that

- `Type[navigation]` $:= (S,\mathtt{T})$, where T is the name of the involved classifier of the regarded binary association end and where

$S = $ `partial` if the multiplicity of the regarded association end is `0..1`,
$S = $ `simple` if the multiplicity is `1..1`, and
$S = $ `sequence`, otherwise.

- `Domain[navigation]` $:= \mathtt{T}$, where T is the name of the classifier of the opposite end of the regarded binary association end.
- `Type[var]` $:= (S,\mathtt{T})$
  if the variable var is declared as var: T with $S = $ `simple`
  or declared as var: $S(\mathtt{T})$ with $K \in \{\mathtt{set},\mathtt{bag},\mathtt{sequence},\mathtt{collection}\}$.

Based on these assumptions we are now able to introduce the rules for navigating along associations (operations of classifiers and attributes may be treated similarly), comparing elements or collections of elements, and building the **union** and **intersection** of collections of elements. Furthermore we will present the type checking rules for the rather complex **iteration** operation, for conditional expressions, and for the various forms of type casts in OCL. These constructs form a kind of OCL core. They hopefully give the reader a sufficiently precise impression of how the type checking rules for the rest of OCL look like.

---

[4] Steve Cook says in his foreword of the OCL book written by Jos Warmer and Anneke Kleppe that it was one of the most important design goals of OCL to avoid mathematical symbols in order to make it useful for a broad spectrum of software developers.

1. Type[e.navigation] := (S,T), where

    T = Type[navigation].Name
    S = simple if Type[navigation].Sort = Type[e].Sort = simple
    S = sequence if Type[e].Sort $\notin$ {simple,partial}
    S = sequence if Type[navigation].Sort $\notin$ {simple,partial}
    S = partial otherwise.

    if Domain[navigation] is a subtype of Type[e].Name.

    A navigational expression returns a single well-defined element only if it is applied to a simple expression and if the regarded association end has multiplicity 1..1. It returns a sequence of objects if either the expression returns already a collection of elements or if the regarded association end has neither the multiplicity 0..1 nor the multiplicity 1..1. It is a partial expression which returns either a well-defined element or a "defined undefined" value otherwise.

2. Type[e1 = e2] := (simple,Boolean), if

    gcs*(Type[e1].Name,Type[e2].Name) $\neq$ OclNil and if
    Type[e1].Sort = partial or if
    Type[e2].Sort = partial or if
    Type[e1].Sort = Type[e2].Sort $\neq$ collection

    It is a matter of debate whether the comparison of two partial expressions or the comparison of a partial expression with an always defined expression should be permitted. The OCL standard probably treats partial expressions like sequences. It disallows therefore the comparison of a partial expression with an always defined expression but permits the comparison of a partial expression with a sequence. From our point of view the most liberal solution allows the comparison of partial expressions with any sort of expressions by treating undefined values like empty bags, sequences, or sets if required.
    It is clear that the comparison of two expressions makes no sense if their types have no common subtype except of OclNil. In this case static analysis does already tell us that the comparison always delivers the result false. Furthermore, it is clear that the comparison of a simple expression with a collection or a set with a bag, etc. should be forbidden, thereby forcing the OCL user to insert conversions from sets to bags, ... explicitly.

3. Type[e1->union(e2)] := (S,T), where
    T = scs*(Type[e1].Name,Type[e2].Name)
    S = Type[e1].Sort = set if Type[e2].Sort $\in$ {set,bag}
    S = Type[e1].Sort = bag if Type[e2].Sort $\in$ {set,bag}

    The type checking rule for the union of sets or bags should be clear based on the explanations of the previous sections. Please note that OCL implicitly adds conversion functions where needed. If the first argument of the union of two expressions has the sort set and the second expression has the sort bag then the second argument is implicitly converted into a set. The same is true if the words set and bag are exchanged in the previous sentence.

4. `Type[e1->intersection(e2)]` := (S,T), where
T = `gcs*(Type[e1].Name,Type[e2].Name)`
S = `Type[e1].Sort` = `set` if `Type[e2].Sort` $\in$ {`set`,`bag`}
S = `Type[e1].Sort` = `bag` if `Type[e2].Sort` $\in$ {`set`,`bag`}

The type checking rule for the `intersection` of sets or bags should be clear based on the explanations of the previous sections.

5. `Type[coll->iterate(e: T1; r: T2 = e1 | e2)]` := ST, where
ST = `Type[r]` if
`Type[coll].Name` is subtype of `Type[e].Name` and
`Type[coll].Sort` $\neq$ `simple` and `Type[e].Sort` = `simple` and
`Type[e1]` conforms to `Type[r]` and `Type[e2]` conforms to `Type[r]`.

The type checking rule for the `iteration` operator is rather straightforward if we regard its dynamic semantics definition. The operator assigns the value of the expression `exp1` to the accumulator variable `r` of type T2. Furthermore, it assigns one element of the given collection `coll` after the other to the loop variable `e` of type T1. Based on the just computed value of the variable `r` and the variable `e` it evaluates the expression `exp2` and assigns the new determined value again to the variable `r`. This process is repeated until all elements of the collection have been assigned to variable `e`.

It is unclear whether it makes sense to apply the `iteration` operator to a partial expression which either returns a single element or the undefined value. The rule introduced here tolerates such a situation based on the assumption that partial expressions and sequences are treated similarly.

6. `Type[if b then e1 else e2 endif]` := (S,T), where
T = `scs*(Type[e1].Name,Type[e2].Name)` if
`Type[b]` = (`simple`, `Boolean`)
S = `Type[e1].Sort` if `Type[e2].Sort` compatible with `Type[e1].Sort`
S = `Type[e2].Sort` if `Type[e1].Sort` compatible with `Type[e2].Sort`
S = `collection` otherwise

The OCL standard states that the type of the result of an `if-then-else` expression is the type of the subexpression of its then-branch *and* its else-branch. It does not explain the meaning of the word "and" in this case. The type checking rule above chooses a rather liberal interpretation of the word "and" where any combination of sorts of subexpressions `e1` and `e2` is permitted. The sort of the resulting expression is `collection` in the worst case. The most restrictive interpretation of the word "and" would require that `Type[e1].Sort` = `Type[e2].Sort`.

7. `Type[e.oclIsTypeOf(TName)]` := (`simple`,`Boolean`), where
`TName` conforms to `Type[e].Name` and
`TName` $\in$ *Classifier* and `Type[e].Sort` = `simple`

The operator `oclIsTypeOf` may be applied to any expression which returns a single object. It checks whether this object is a direct *instance* of the given type `TName` and returns the appropriate boolean result.

8. `Type[e.oclIsKindOf(TName)]` := (simple,Boolean), where

   `gcs*(Type[e].Name,TName)` $\neq$ `OCLNil` and
   `Type[e].Name` does not conform to `TName` and
   `TName` $\in$ *Classifier* and `Type[e].Sort` = `simple`

   The operator `oclIsKindOf` may be applied to any expression which returns a single object. It checks whether this object is a *member* of the given type `TName` and returns the appropriate boolean result. It makes therefore no sense to write down an `oclIsKindOf` expression where static type analysis is already able to guarantee that the computed object has a type which conforms to `TName`.

9. `Type[e.oclAsTypeOf(TName)]` := (partial,T), where

   T = `gcs*(Type[e].Name,TName)` if
   `Type[e].Name` does not conform to `TName` and if
   `TName` $\in$ *Classifier* and `Type[e].Sort` = `simple`

   The operator `oclAsTypeOf` may be applied to any expression which returns a single object. It returns the given object if it is a member of the type `TName` it returns the undefined value otherwise. It makes therefore no sense to write down an `oclAsTypeOf` expression where static type analysis is already able to guarantee that the computed object has a type which conforms to `TName`.

Note that the type checking rules introduced above do not cover all possible combinations of the types of the subexpressions of a regarded expression. It is a matter of debate whether a default rule should be added that "fires" if no other type checking rules are applicable and assigns the type (...,`OclNil`) to a subexpression with an otherwise undefined type. We have made the experience that the introduction of such a default type, which is compatible with any other type, allows us to type check expressions with ill-defined subexpressions without generating too many misleading error messages. In any case, a type checking tool has to generate an error message if it encounters an expression with an undefined type or with a type equal to (...,`OclNil`).

7 Conclusions and Future Work

In the previous sections we discussed some OCL type checking problems and presented three different solutions for these problems. The first solution relies on the construction of type hierarchies where any pair of types possesses (at most) one smallest common supertype and (at most) one greatest common subtype. Furthermore, it assumes that objects are direct instances of a single type (class). The second solution avoids these restrictions. It uses sets of types as extensional representations for missing uniquely defined supertypes or subtypes. Due to the fact that its accompanying type checking rules are too complex to be useful in practice a third solution has been developed. It makes no assumptions concerning the structure of a regarded type hierarchy and computes a single type for any legal OCL expression (instead of a set of types).

Compared with the currently valid type checking rules of the OCL standard, the proposed new rules have the following advantages:

- They accept reasonable expressions such as S1->union(S2), where the type of S1 conforms to the type of S2 but not vice versa which are rejected nowadays.
- They reject useless expressions such as S1->intersection(S2) or S1 = S2 where the type of S1 and the type of S2 do not possess a common subtype which are accepted nowadays.
- They compute more specific types for collection manipulating expressions such as S1->intersection(S2) where the type of S2 conforms to the type of S1 (the new rules return the type of S2 instead of the type of S1).

However, many important questions concerning the OCL standard version 1.3 still have to be addressed:

- The dynamic semantics of partially defined expressions is more or less undefined.
- The same is true for the transitive closure of associations if the regarded association is not a partial order.
- The available means for reflection (operations which determine the type of an object, the attributes of a type, etc.) do not possess any precisely defined type checking rules.
- ...

It is the subject for future work to fix the dynamic semantics definition of OCL and to write down a complete set of OCL type checking rules based on the proposed OCL meta model in [14]. These new type checking rules should become an accepted part of the forthcoming OCL standard version 2.0. Furthermore, they should be implemented as part of already existing OCL toolkits such as the Dresden OCL compiler [11] or the OCL toolkit from Bremen [15].

References

1. H. Ait-Kaci, R. Boyer, P. Lincoln, and R. Nasr. Efficient implementation of lattice operations. *ACM Transactions on Programming Languages and Systems*, 19(2):106–190, 1987.
2. H. Ait-Kaci and R. Nasr. Integrating data type inheritance into logic programming. In M.P. Atkinson, P. Buneman, and R. Morrison, editors, *Data Types and Persistence*, pages 121–136. Springer Verlag, Berlin, 1989.
3. L. Cardell and P. Wegner. On understanding types, data abstraction and polymorphism. *ACM Computing Surveys*, 17(4):471–522, 1985.
4. T. Clark. Typechecking UML static model. In *[9]*, pages 503–517, 1999.
5. St. Cook, A. Kleppe, and R. Mitchell et al. The Amsterdam manifesto on OCL. Technical report, 2000. http://www.trireme.com/amsterdam/manifesto-1-5.pdf (visited: 11/07/2000).

6. H. Ehrig, G. Engels, H.-J. Kreowski, and G. Rozenberg, editors. *Handbook of Graph Grammars and Computing by Graph Transformation: Applications, Languages, and Tools*, volume 2. World Scientific, Singapore, 1999.
7. A. Evans and St. Kent, editors. *Proc. 3rd Int. Conf. Unified Modeling Language (UML'2000)*, volume 1939 of *Lecture Notes in Computer Science*, Berlin, 2000. Springer Verlag.
8. UML Revision Task Force. OMG unified modeling language specification v. 1.3, document ad/99-06-08. Technical report, Object Management Group, 2000. http://www.omg.org/uml/ (visited: 07/11/2000).
9. R. France and B. Rumpe, editors. *Proc. 2nd Int. Conf. Unified Modeling Language (UML'99)*, volume 1723 of *Lecture Notes in Computer Science*, Berlin, 1999. Springer Verlag.
10. Martin Hitz and Gerti Kappel. *UML@Work - Von der Analyse zur Realisierung*. dpunkt.lehrbuch. dpunkt.verlag, Heidelberg, 1998.
11. H. Hussmann, B. Demuth, and F. Finger. Modular architecture for a toolset supporting OCL. In *[7]*, pages 278–293, 2000.
12. Jörg-Volker Müller. *Entwurf einer objektorientierten Programmiersprache mit statischem Typkonzept und Parallelität*. Shaker Verlag, Aachen, 1994.
13. The precise UML group. PUML home page. Technical report, 2000. http://www.cs.york.ac.uk/puml/ (visited: 11/07/2000).
14. M. Richters and M. Gogolla. A metamodel for OCL. In *[9]*, pages 156–171, 1999.
15. M. Richters and M. Gogolla. Validating UML models and OCL constraints. In *9*, pages 265–277, 2000.
16. Andy Schürr. Adding graph transformation concepts to uml's constraint language ocl. In J. Padberg, editor, *appears in: Proc. UNIGRA Satellite Workshop of ETAPS 2001*, Amsterdam, 2001. Elsevier Science Publ.
17. Andy Schürr. New type checking rules for OCL (collection) expressions. 2001.
18. Andy Schürr, Andreas J. Winter, and Albert Zündorf. PROGRES: Language and environment. In *[6]*, pages 487–550. 1999.
19. J. Warmer and A. Kleppe. *OCL: The Object Constraint Language - Precise Modeling with UML*. Addison Wesley, New York, 1999.

OCL: Syntax, Semantics, and Tools

Mark Richters and Martin Gogolla

University of Bremen, FB 3, Computer Science Department
Postfach 330440, D-28334 Bremen, Germany
{mr|gogolla}@informatik.uni-bremen.de,
http://www.db.informatik.uni-bremen.de

Abstract. The Object Constraint Language OCL allows to formally specify constraints on a UML model. We present a formal syntax and semantics for OCL based on set theory including expressions, invariants and pre- and postconditions. A formal foundation for OCL makes the meaning of constraints precise and helps to eliminate ambiguities and inconsistencies. A precise language definition is also a prerequisite for implementing CASE tools providing enhanced support for UML models and OCL constraints. We give a survey of some OCL tools and discuss one of the tools in some more detail. The design and implementation of the USE tool supporting the validation of UML models and OCL constraints is based on the formal approach presented in this paper.

1 Introduction

The Unified Modeling Language (UML) [4,19,26] is a widely accepted standard for object-oriented modeling. The UML notation is largely based on diagrams. However, for certain aspects of a design, diagrams often do not provide the level of conciseness and expressiveness that a textual language can offer. Thus, textual annotations are frequently used to add details to a design. A special class of annotations are constraints that impose additional restrictions on a model. For this purpose, the Object Constraint Language (OCL) [18,28] provides a framework for specifying constraints on a model in a formal way. OCL is a textual constraint language with a notational style similar to common object-oriented languages. OCL expressions are declarative and side effect-free. The language allows the modeler to specify constraints on a conceptual level helping to abstract from lower level implementation details.

Although designed to be a formal language, experience with OCL has shown that the language definition is not precise enough. Various authors have pointed out language issues related to ambiguities, inconsistencies or open interpretations [7,11,12]. In this paper, we present a formal foundation for OCL defining the abstract syntax and the semantics of OCL expressions, invariants, and pre- and postconditions. A formalization of OCL improves the language and helps to gain a more precise understanding of UML models and their interpretation. In our view, a precise language definition is also a prerequisite for implementing CASE tools providing enhanced support for UML models and OCL constraints.

A. Clark and J. Warmer (Eds.): Object Modeling with the OCL, LNCS 2263, pp. 42–68, 2002.
© Springer-Verlag Berlin Heidelberg 2002

We give a brief survey of OCL tools and discuss one of the tools in some more detail.

There are various different approaches in related work addressing formal aspects of OCL. A semantics for OCL without pre- and postconditions was first given in [22]. A graph-based semantics for OCL was developed by translating OCL constraints into expressions over graph rules [5]. A formal semantics was also provided by a mapping from OCL to a temporal logic [9]. An OCL extension to support temporal operators is proposed in [20]. The expressive power of OCL in terms of navigability and computability is discussed in [16]. Metamodels for OCL [1,23] follow the metamodeling approach used in the UML standard. An approach for generating OCL constraints based on design patterns is described in [2]. Recently, a need for OCL features allowing behavioral constraints on occurrences of events, signals, and operation calls has been emphasized [15,27].

The paper is structured as follows. Section 2 introduces a short example illustrating the application of OCL for specifying constraints. Section 3 defines UML object models and states providing the context for OCL. In Section 4, we briefly summarize the abstract syntax and semantics of OCL expressions which was first introduced in [22]. In addition to [22], we formally define the OCL notion of a context. Section 5 defines the syntax and semantics of pre- and postconditions. We explain the various additional syntactic possibilities and keywords like result, isOclNew, and @pre that may appear in postconditions. OCL tool support is discussed in Section 6. Section 7 presents some conclusions.

2   Specifying OCL Constraints

OCL is a textual language that allows to specify additional constraints on a UML model. A model always provides the context for constraints. Figure 1 shows a class diagram modeling employees, departments, and projects. Attributes like name, age, and salary represent properties that are common among all objects of a class. The operation raiseSalary can be invoked on employee objects. This is the only operation in our model to keep the example small. The operation signature defines a parameter and a return value of type Real. Relationships between the classes are modeled as associations WorksIn, WorksOn, and Controls.

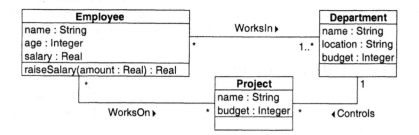

Fig. 1. UML class diagram of example model

OCL can be used to specify constraints concerning the static structure and the behavior of a system. Invariants are static structure constraints. An invariant is a condition that "must be true for all instances of that type at any time" [18, p. 7-6]. For example, the following invariant requires all department objects to have a non-negative budget.

```
context Department inv:
  self.budget >= 0
```

More complex constraints can be built by navigating along the associations between classes, for example:

```
-- Employees working on more projects than other employees
-- of the same department get a higher salary.
context Department inv:
  self.employee->forAll(e1, e2 |
    e1.project->size > e2.project->size
      implies e1.salary > e2.salary)
```

The forAll expression asserts a condition for each pair of employee objects working at the same department. The expression e1.project yields the set of projects the employee e1 is working on. The OCL standard operation size determines the cardinality of that set. Role names like project and employee at the ends of associations are omitted in Figure 1. If no role name is given, the default in UML is to use the class name starting with a lowercase letter.

The behavioral interface of objects is defined by operations. Constraints on the behavior are specified in OCL by means of pre- and postconditions. Such a constraint defines a contract that an implementation of the operation has to fulfill [17]. It also provides the possibility for verifying the correctness of an implementation, e.g., in the style of Hoare logic [13].

```
-- If the amount is positive, raise
-- the salary by the given amount
context Employee::raiseSalary(amount : Real) : Real
  pre:  amount > 0
  post: self.salary = self.salary@pre + amount
        and result = self.salary
```

Pre- and postconditions will be discussed in detail in Section 5. In the next two sections, we will first discuss object models and simple OCL expressions that may appear in invariants. The definition for simple expressions is later extended to incorporate additional features that may appear only in postconditions.

3   Object Models and States

OCL expressions refer to various elements of a UML model. We therefore define an object model $\mathcal{M}$ to contain basically those elements of UML that are relevant for use with OCL. An object model

$$\mathcal{M} = (\text{CLASS}, \text{ATT}_c, \text{OP}_c, \text{ASSOC}, \text{associates}, \text{roles}, \text{multiplicities}, \prec)$$

contains elements found in class diagrams. We only give an informal description of the components of an object model here. Examples in parentheses refer to the model shown in Figure 1. More details can be found in [22].

- CLASS is a set of class names (CLASS = {*Employee, Department, Project*}).
- ATT_c is a set of operation signatures for functions mapping an object of class c to an associated attribute value
  ($\text{ATT}_{\text{Employee}}$ = {name : *Employee* $\rightarrow$ *String*, ... }).
- OP_c is a set of signatures for user-defined operations of a class c without side effects (these are tagged *isQuery* in a UML model, our example does not have any).
- ASSOC is a set of association names
  (ASSOC = {WorksIn, WorksOn, Controls}).

  - associates is a function mapping each association name to a list of participating classes (associates : WorksIn $\mapsto$ ⟨*Employee, Department*⟩).
  - roles is a function assigning each end of an association a role name (roles : WorksIn $\mapsto$ ⟨*employee, department*⟩).
  - multiplicities is a function assigning each end of an association a multiplicity specification (multiplicities : WorksIn $\mapsto$ ⟨$\mathbb{N}_0, \mathbb{N}$⟩).

- $\prec$ is a partial order on CLASS reflecting the generalization hierarchy of classes (there is no generalization used in our example, therefore $\prec = \emptyset$).

The interpretation of an object model is the set of possible system states. A system state includes objects, links and attribute values. A system may be in different states as it changes over time. Therefore, a system state is also called a snapshot of a running system. With respect to OCL, we can, in many cases, concentrate on a single system state given at a discrete point in time. For example, a system state provides the complete context for the evaluation of class invariants. For pre- and postconditions, however, it is necessary to consider two consecutive states (see Section 5).

A single system state for an object model $\mathcal{M}$ is a structure $\sigma(\mathcal{M}) = (\sigma_{\text{CLASS}}, \sigma_{\text{ATT}}, \sigma_{\text{ASSOC}})$ where the finite sets $\sigma_{\text{CLASS}}(c)$ contain all objects of a class $c \in$ CLASS currently existing in the system state, functions σ_{ATT} assign attribute values to each object, and the finite sets $\sigma_{\text{ASSOC}}(as)$ contain links connecting objects for each association $as \in$ ASSOC.

4   OCL Expressions

The definition of OCL expressions is based upon a signature $\Sigma_{\mathcal{M}} = (T_{\mathcal{M}}, \leq, \Omega_{\mathcal{M}})$ for an object model $\mathcal{M}$ providing a set of types $T_{\mathcal{M}}$, a relation $\leq$ on types reflecting the type hierarchy, and a set of operations $\Omega_{\mathcal{M}}$. The signature contains the initial set of syntactic elements upon which we build the expression syntax.

For example, the signature for the model in Fig. 1 is

$$\Sigma_{\mathcal{M}} = (\{Employee, Department, Project, Integer, Real, Set(Project), \dots\},$$
$$\{Integer \leq Real, \dots\},$$
$$\{+ : Integer \times Integer \to Integer,$$
$$\text{name} : Employee \to String,$$
$$\text{project} : Employee \to Set(Project), \dots\}) \ .$$

The set of types $T_{\mathcal{M}}$ includes type expressions for constructing the OCL collection types $Collection(t)$, $Set(t)$, $Sequence(t)$, and $Bag(t)$ which are parameterized by an element type t. Note that $\Omega_{\mathcal{M}}$ only includes signatures of side effect-free operations such as standard arithmetic, attribute access and navigation by role names. These operations are intended to be available as part of side effect-free OCL expressions, for example, in invariants. The operation raise-Salary in class $Employee$ is expected to cause side effects to the system state and is therefore not included in the signature.

A semantics for a data signature $\Sigma_{\mathcal{M}}$ is a mapping associating each type $t \in T_{\mathcal{M}}$ with a domain $I(t)$ and each operation $\omega : t_1 \times \cdots \times t_n \to t \in \Omega_{\mathcal{M}}$ with a function $I(\omega)(\sigma) : I(t_1) \times \cdots \times I(t_n) \to I(t)$. The parameter σ denotes a system state with a set of objects, their attribute values and association links. It is required for evaluating attribute access and navigation operations.

4.1   Syntax of Expressions

We define the syntax of expressions inductively so that more complex expressions are recursively built from simple structures. For each expression the set of free occurrences of variables is also defined. The latter is necessary for determining the scope of a variable and the possible context of an expression as discussed in Section 4.3.

Definition 1 (Syntax of expressions)
Let $\Sigma_{\mathcal{M}} = (T_{\mathcal{M}}, \leq, \Omega_{\mathcal{M}})$ be a data signature over an object model $\mathcal{M}$. Let $\text{Var} = \{Var_t\}_{t \in T_{\mathcal{M}}}$ be a family of variable sets where each variable set is indexed by a type t. The syntax of expressions over the signature $\Sigma_{\mathcal{M}}$ is given by a set $\text{Expr} = \{Expr_t\}_{t \in T_{\mathcal{M}}}$ and a function free : $\text{Expr} \to \mathcal{F}(\text{Var})$ defined as follows.

i. If $v \in Var_t$ then $v \in Expr_t$ and $\text{free}(v) := \{v\}$.

ii. If $v \in Var_{t_1}, e_1 \in Expr_{t_1}, e_2 \in Expr_{t_2}$ then **let $v = e_1$ in e_2** $\in Expr_{t_2}$ and $\text{free}(\text{let } v = e_1 \text{ in } e_2) := \text{free}(e_2) - \{v\}$.

iii. If $\omega : t_1 \times \cdots \times t_n \to t \in \Omega_{\mathcal{M}}$ and $e_i \in Expr_{t_i}$ for all $i = 1, \dots, n$ then $\omega(e_1, \dots, e_n) \in Expr_t$ and $\text{free}(\omega(e_1, \dots, e_n)) := \text{free}(e_1) \cup \cdots \cup \text{free}(e_n)$.

iv. If $e_1 \in Expr_{\text{Boolean}}$ and $e_2, e_3 \in Expr_t$ then **if e_1 then e_2 else e_3 endif** $\in Expr_t$ and $\text{free}(\text{if } e_1 \text{ then } e_2 \text{ else } e_3 \text{ endif}) := \text{free}(e_1) \cup \text{free}(e_2) \cup \text{free}(e_3)$.

v. If $e \in \text{Expr}_t$ and $t' \leq t$ or $t \leq t'$ then $(e \text{ asType } t') \in \text{Expr}_{t'}$,
$(e \text{ isTypeOf } t') \in \text{Expr}_{\text{Boolean}}$, $(e \text{ isKindOf } t') \in \text{Expr}_{\text{Boolean}}$ and
free$((e \text{ asType } t')) := \text{free}(e)$, free$((e \text{ isTypeOf } t')) := \text{free}(e)$,
free$((e \text{ isKindOf } t')) := \text{free}(e)$.

vi. If $e_1 \in \text{Expr}_{Collection(t_1)}$, $v_1 \in \text{Var}_{t_1}$, $v_2 \in \text{Var}_{t_2}$, and $e_2, e_3 \in \text{Expr}_{t_2}$ then
$e_1 \rightarrow \textbf{iterate}(v_1; v_2 = e_2 \mid e_3) \in \text{Expr}_{t_2}$ and
free$(e_1 \rightarrow \text{iterate}(v_1; v_2 = e_2 \mid e_3)) := (\text{free}(e_1) \cup \text{free}(e_2) \cup \text{free}(e_3)) - \{v_1, v_2\}$.

An expression of type t' is also an expression of a more general type t. For all
$t' \leq t$: if $e \in \text{Expr}_{t'}$ then $e \in \text{Expr}_t$.   □

A variable expression (i) refers to the value of a variable. Variables (including
the special variable self) may be introduced by the context of an expression,
as part of an iterate expression, and by a let expression. Let expressions (ii) do
not add to the expressiveness of OCL but help to avoid repetitions of common
sub-expressions. Operation expressions (iii) apply an operation from $\Omega_{\mathcal{M}}$. The
set of operations includes:

- predefined data operations: +, -, *, <, >, size, max
- attribute operations: self.age, e.salary
- side effect-free operations defined by a class
- navigation by role names: e.employee
- constants: 25, 'aString'

As demonstrated by the examples, an operation expression may also be written in OCL path syntax as $e_1.\omega(e_2, \ldots, e_n)$. This notational style is common in
many object-oriented languages. It emphasizes the role of the first argument as
the "receiver" of a "message". If e_1 denotes a collection value, an arrow symbol
is used in OCL instead of the period: $e_1 \rightarrow \omega(e_2, \ldots, e_n)$. Collections may be
bags, sets, or lists. An if-expression (iv) provides an alternative selection of two
expressions depending on the result of a condition given by a boolean expression.

An asType expression (v) can be used in cases where static type information
is insufficient. It corresponds to the oclAsType operation in OCL and can
be understood as a cast of a source expression to an equivalent expression of a
(usually) more specific target type. The target type must be related to the source
type, that is, one must be a subtype of the other. The isTypeOf and isKindOf
expressions correspond to the oclIsTypeOf and oclIsKindOf operations,
respectively. An expression $(e \text{ isTypeOf } t')$ can be used to test whether the type
of the value resulting from the expression e has the type t' given as argument.
An isKindOf expression $(e \text{ isKindOf } t')$ is not as strict in that it is sufficient for
the expression to become true if t' is a supertype of the type of the value of e.
Note that OCL defines these type casts and tests as operations with parameters
of type $OclType$. In contrast to OCL, we technically define them as first class
expressions which has the benefit that we do not need the metatype $OclType$.
Thus the type system is kept simple while preserving compatibility with standard
OCL syntax. A related discussion about the removal of OCL metatypes can be
found in the paper by Rumpe in this proceedings.

An iterate expression (vi) is a general loop construct which evaluates an argument expression e_3 repeatedly for all elements of a collection which is given by a source expression e_1. Each element of the collection is bound in turn to the variable v_1 for each evaluation of the argument expression. The argument expression e_3 may contain the variable v_1 to refer to the current element of the collection. The result variable v_2 is initialized with the expression e_2. After each evaluation of the argument expression e_3, the result is bound to the variable v_2. The final value of v_2 is the result of the whole expression. The iterate construct is probably the most important kind of expression in OCL. We will shortly see how other OCL constructs can be equivalently defined in terms of an iterate expression.

4.2   Semantics of Expressions

The semantics of expressions is made precise in the following definition. A context for evaluation is given by an environment $\tau = (\sigma, \beta)$ consisting of a system state σ and a variable assignment $\beta : \mathrm{Var}_t \to I(t)$. A system state σ provides access to the set of currently existing objects, their attribute values, and association links between objects. A variable assignment β maps variable names to values.

Definition 2 (Semantics of expressions)
Let Env be the set of environments $\tau = (\sigma, \beta)$. The semantics of an expression $e \in \mathrm{Expr}_t$ is a function $I[\![e]\!] : \mathrm{Env} \to I(t)$ that is defined as follows.

i. $I[\![v]\!](\tau) = \beta(v)$.

ii. $I[\![\text{let } v = e_1 \text{ in } e_2]\!](\tau) = I[\![e_2]\!](\sigma, \beta\{v/I[\![e_1]\!](\tau)\})$.

iii. $I[\![\omega(e_1, \ldots, e_n)]\!](\tau) = I(\omega)(\tau)(I[\![e_1]\!](\tau), \ldots, I[\![e_n]\!](\tau))$.

iv. $I[\![\text{if } e_1 \text{ then } e_2 \text{ else } e_3 \text{ endif}]\!](\tau) = \begin{cases} I[\![e_2]\!](\tau) & \text{if } I[\![e_1]\!](\tau) = \text{true}, \\ I[\![e_3]\!](\tau) & \text{if } I[\![e_1]\!](\tau) = \text{false}, \\ \bot & \text{otherwise.} \end{cases}$

v. $I[\![(e \text{ asType } t')]\!](\tau) = \begin{cases} I[\![e]\!](\tau) & \text{if } I[\![e]\!](\tau) \in I(t'), \\ \bot & \text{otherwise.} \end{cases}$

$I[\![(e \text{ isTypeOf } t')]\!](\tau) = \begin{cases} \text{true} & \text{if } I[\![e]\!](\tau) \in I(t') - \bigcup_{t'' < t'} I(t''), \\ \text{false} & \text{otherwise.} \end{cases}$

$I[\![(e \text{ isKindOf } t')]\!](\tau) = \begin{cases} \text{true} & \text{if } I[\![e]\!](\tau) \in I(t'), \\ \text{false} & \text{otherwise.} \end{cases}$

vi. $I[\![e_1 \to \text{iterate}(v_1; v_2 = e_2 \mid e_3)]\!](\tau) = I[\![e_1 \to \text{iterate}'(v_1 \mid e_3)]\!](\tau')$ where $\tau' = (\sigma, \beta')$ and $\tau'' = (\sigma, \beta'')$ are environments with modified variable assignments

$$\beta' := \beta\{v_2/I[\![e_2]\!](\tau)\}$$
$$\beta'' := \beta'\{v_2/I[\![e_3]\!](\sigma, \beta'\{v_1/x_1\})\}$$

and iterate' is defined as:[1]

---

[1] The constructor operations $\mathrm{mkSequence}_t, \mathrm{mkBag}_t$, and mkSet_t are in $\Omega_\mathcal{M}$ and provide the abstract syntax for collection literals like `Set{1,2}` in concrete OCL syntax.

a) If $e_1 \in \mathrm{Expr}_{Sequence(t_1)}$ then $I[\![\, e_1 \to \mathrm{iterate}'(v_1 \mid e_3)\,]\!](\tau') =$

$$
\begin{cases}
I[\![\, v_2\,]\!](\tau') \\
\quad \text{if } I[\![\, e_1\,]\!](\tau') = \langle\rangle, \\
I[\![\, \mathrm{mkSequence}_{t_1}(x_2, \ldots, x_n) \to \mathrm{iterate}'(v_1 \mid e_3)\,]\!](\tau'') \\
\quad \text{if } I[\![\, e_1\,]\!](\tau') = \langle x_1, \ldots, x_n \rangle.
\end{cases}
$$

b) If $e_1 \in \mathrm{Expr}_{Set(t_1)}$ then $I[\![\, e_1 \to \mathrm{iterate}'(v_1 \mid e_3)\,]\!](\tau') =$

$$
\begin{cases}
I[\![\, v_2\,]\!](\tau') \\
\quad \text{if } I[\![\, e_1\,]\!](\tau') = \emptyset, \\
I[\![\, \mathrm{mkSet}_{t_1}(x_2, \ldots, x_n) \to \mathrm{iterate}'(v_1 \mid e_3)\,]\!](\tau'') \\
\quad \text{if } I[\![\, e_1\,]\!](\tau') = \{x_1, \ldots, x_n\}.
\end{cases}
$$

c) If $e_1 \in \mathrm{Expr}_{Bag(t_1)}$ then $I[\![\, e_1 \to \mathrm{iterate}'(v_1 \mid e_3)\,]\!](\tau') =$

$$
\begin{cases}
I[\![\, v_2\,]\!](\tau') \\
\quad \text{if } I[\![\, e_1\,]\!](\tau') = \emptyset, \\
I[\![\, \mathrm{mkBag}_{t_1}(x_2, \ldots, x_n) \to \mathrm{iterate}'(v_1 \mid e_3)\,]\!](\tau'') \\
\quad \text{if } I[\![\, e_1\,]\!](\tau') = \{\!\{x_1, \ldots, x_n\}\!\}.
\end{cases}
$$

$\square$

The semantics of a variable expression (i) is the value assigned to the variable. A let expression (ii) results in the value of the sub-expression e_2. Free occurrences of the variable v in e_2 are bound to the value of the expression e_1. An operation expression (iii) is interpreted by the function associated with the operation. Each argument expression is evaluated separately. The result of an if-expression (iv) is given by the then-part if the condition is true. If the condition is false, the else-part is the result of the expression. The result of a cast expression (v) using asType is the value of the expression, if the value lies within the domain of the specified target type, otherwise it is undefined. A type test expression with isTypeOf is true if the expression value lies exactly within the domain of the specified target type without considering subtypes. An isKindOf type test expression is true if the expression value lies within the domain of the specified target type *or* one of its subtypes. An iterate expression (vi) loops over the elements of a collection and allows the application of a function to each collection element. The function results are successively combined into a value that serves as the result of the whole iterate expression. This kind of evaluation is also known in functional style programming languages as *fold* operation.

One must be careful when using iterate expression on sets and bags. For sets and bags as source collection there may be expressions where the result of the whole iterate expression depends on the order in which collection elements are selected for application. The following expression concatenates the names of all employees working on a project. However, the names in the resulting string may appear in any order, because it is unspecified in which order the elements in the set p.employee are applied.

```
p.employee->iterate(e : Employee;
   names : String = '' | names.concat(e.name))
```

A number of important OCL constructs such as exists, forAll, select, reject, collect, and isUnique are defined in terms of iterate expressions. In [18] the intended semantics of these expressions is given by postconditions with iterate-based expressions. The following schema shows how these expressions can be translated to equivalent iterate expressions. A similar translation is given in [6].

$$I[\![\, e_1 \to \mathrm{exists}(v_1 \mid e_3)\,]\!](\tau) =$$
$$\quad I[\![\, e_1 \to \mathrm{iterate}(v1; v2 = \mathrm{false} \mid v_2 \text{ or } e_3)\,]\!](\tau)$$

$$I[\![\, e_1 \to \mathrm{forAll}(v_1 \mid e_3)\,]\!](\tau) =$$
$$\quad I[\![\, e_1 \to \mathrm{iterate}(v1; v2 = \mathrm{true} \mid v_2 \text{ and } e_3)\,]\!](\tau)$$

$$I[\![\, e_1 \to \mathrm{select}(v_1 \mid e_3)\,]\!](\tau) =$$
$$\quad I[\![\, e_1 \to \mathrm{iterate}(v1; v2 = e_1 \mid$$
$$\qquad \text{if } e_3 \text{ then } v_2 \text{ else } v_2 \to \mathrm{excluding}(v_1) \text{ endif})\,]\!](\tau)$$

$$I[\![\, e_1 \to \mathrm{reject}(v_1 \mid e_3)\,]\!](\tau) =$$
$$\quad I[\![\, e_1 \to \mathrm{iterate}(v1; v2 = e_1 \mid$$
$$\qquad \text{if } e_3 \text{ then } v_2 \to \mathrm{excluding}(v_1) \text{ else } v_2 \text{ endif})\,]\!](\tau)$$

$$I[\![\, e_1 \to \mathrm{collect}(v_1 \mid e_3)\,]\!](\tau) =$$
$$\quad I[\![\, e_1 \to \mathrm{iterate}(v1; v2 = \mathrm{mkBag}_{type\text{-}of\text{-}e_3} \mid$$
$$\qquad v_2 \to \mathrm{including}(v_1))\,]\!](\tau)$$

$$I[\![\, e_1 \to \mathrm{isUnique}(v_1 \mid e_3)\,]\!](\tau) =$$
$$\quad I[\![\, e_1 \to \mathrm{iterate}(v1; v2 = \mathrm{true} \mid$$
$$\qquad v_2 \text{ and } e_1 \to \mathrm{count}(v_1) = 1)\,]\!](\tau)$$

4.3   Expression Context

An OCL expression is always written in some syntactical context. Since the primary purpose of OCL is the specification of constraints on a UML model, it is obvious that the model itself provides the most general kind of context. In our approach, the signature Σ_M contains types (e.g., object types) and operations (e.g., attribute operations) that are imported from a model, thus providing a context for building expressions that depend on the elements of a specific model.

On a much smaller scale, there is also a notion of context in OCL that simply introduces variable declarations. This notion is closely related to the syntax for constraints written in OCL. A context clause declares variables in invariants, and parameters in pre- and postconditions. The following example declares a variable e which is subsequently used in an invariant expression.

```
context e : Employee inv:
    e.age > 18
```

The next example declares a parameter amount which is used in a pre- and postcondition specification.

```
context Employee::raiseSalary(amount : Real) : Real
   pre:   amount > 0
   post: self.salary = self.salary@pre + amount
         and result = self.salary
```

Here we use the second meaning of context, that is, a context provides a set of variable declarations. The more general meaning of context is already subsumed by our concept of a signature as described above. A similar distinction between *local* and *global* declarations is also made in [8]. In their paper, the authors extend the OCL context syntax to include global declarations and outline a general approach to derive declarations from information on the UML metamodel level.

A *context for an invariant* (corresponding to the nonterminal classifierContext in the OCL grammar [18]) is a declaration of variables. The variable declaration may be implicit or explicit. In the implicit form, the context is written as

```
context C inv:
   <expression>
```

In this case, the <expression> may use the variable self of type C as a free variable. In the explicit form, the context is written as

```
context v₁ : C₁,..., vₙ : Cₙ inv:
   <expression>
```

The <expression> may use the variables $v_1, \ldots, v_n$ of types $C_1, \ldots, C_n$ as free variables. The OCL grammar actually only allows the explicit declaration of at most one variable in a classifierContext. This restriction seems unnecessarily strict. Having multiple variables is especially useful for constraints specifying key properties of attributes. The example (taken from [18, p. 7-18])

```
context Person inv:
   Person.allInstances->forAll(p1, p2 |
     p1 <> p2 implies p1.name <> p2.name)
```

could then be just written as:

```
context p1, p2 : Person inv:
   p1 <> p2 implies p1.name <> p2.name
```

A *context for a pre-/postcondition* (corresponding to the nonterminal operationContext in the OCL grammar) is a declaration of variables. In this case, the context is written as

```
context C :: op(p₁ : T₁,..., pₙ : Tₙ) : T
   pre:  P
   post: Q
```

This means that the variable `self` (of type C) and the parameters $p_1, \ldots, p_n$ may be used as free variables in the precondition P and the postcondition Q. Additionally, the postcondition may use `result` (of type T) as a free variable. The details are explained in Section 5.

An *invariant* is an expression with boolean result type and a set of (explicitly or implicitly declared) free variables $v_1 : C_1, \ldots, v_n : C_n$ where $C_1, \ldots, C_n$ are classifier types. An invariant

> **context** $v_1 : C_1, \ldots, v_n : C_n$ **inv**:
>   <expression>

is equivalent to the following expression without free variables that must be valid in all system states.

> C_1.allInstances->forAll(v_1 : C_1 |
>   ...
> C_n.allInstances->forAll(v_n : C_n |
>   <expression>
>   )
>   ...
>)

5   Pre- and Postconditions

The definition of expressions in Section 4 is sufficient for invariants and queries where we have to consider only single system states. For pre- and postconditions, there are additional language constructs in OCL which enable references to the system state before the execution of an operation and to the system state that results from the operation execution. The general syntax of an operation specification with pre- and postconditions is defined as

> **context** $C :: \mathrm{op}(p_1 : T_1, \ldots, p_n : T_n)$
>   **pre**: P
>   **post**: Q

First, the context is determined by giving the signature of the operation for which pre- and postconditions are to be specified. The operation op which is defined as part of the classifier C has a set of typed parameters $\mathrm{PARAMS}_{op} = \{p_1, \ldots, p_n\}$. The UML model providing the definition of an operation signature also specifies the direction kind of each parameter. We use a function *kind* : $\mathrm{PARAMS}_{op} \to \{\mathrm{in}, \mathrm{out}, \mathrm{inout}, \mathrm{return}\}$ to map each parameter to one of these kinds. Although UML makes no restriction on the number of return parameters, there is usually only at most one return parameter considered in OCL which is referred to by the keyword `result` in a postcondition. In this case, the signature is also written as $C :: \mathrm{op}(p_1 : T_1, \ldots, p_{n-1} : T_{n-1}) : T$ with T being the type of the `result` parameter.

The precondition of the operation is given by an expression P, and the postcondition is specified by an expression Q. P and Q must have a boolean result type. If the precondition holds, the contract of the operation guarantees that the postcondition is satisfied after completion of op. Pre- and postconditions form a pair. A condition defaults to true if it is not explicitly specified.

Note that in the previous section, we have talked about side effect-free operations. Now we are discussing operations that usually have side effects. Table 1 summarizes different kinds of operations in UML. Operations in the table are classified by the existence of a return parameter in the signature, whether they are declared as being side effect-free (with the tag *isQuery* in UML), the state before and after execution, and the languages in which (1) the operation body can be expressed (Body), and (2) the operation may be called (Caller).

Table 1. Different kinds of operations in UML

Return value	side effect-free	States	Body	Caller
no	no	pre-state $\neq$ post-state allowed	AL	AL
yes	no	pre-state $\neq$ post-state allowed	AL	AL
yes	yes	pre-state = post-state required	OCL	OCL, AL

The first row of the table describes operations without a return value. These are used to specify side effects on a system state. Therefore, the post-state usually differs from the state before the operation call. Since specifying side effects is out of the scope of OCL expressions, the body of the operation must be expressed in some kind of *Action Language* (AL). Furthermore, the operation cannot be used without restriction as part of an OCL expression because all operations in an OCL expression must be tagged *isQuery*. The same arguments apply to operations with a return value that are listed in the second row. The third kind of operations are those operations which may be used in OCL without restrictions. Because their execution does not have side effects, the pre- and post-states are always equal. Often, the body of the operation can be specified with an OCL expression. It might be desirable for an action language to make use of these kinds of operations by including OCL as a sub-language.

5.1 Motivating Example

Before we give a formal definition of operation specifications with pre- and post-conditions, we demonstrate the fundamental concepts by means of an example. Figure 2 shows a class diagram with two classes A and B that are related to each other by an association R. Class A has an operation op() but no attributes. Class B has an attribute c and no operations. The implicit role names a and b at the association ends allow navigation in OCL expressions from a B object to the associated A object and vice versa.

Figure 3 shows an example for two consecutive states of a system corresponding to the given class model. The object diagrams show instances of classes A and B and links of the association R. The left object diagram shows the state

Fig. 2. Example class diagram

before the execution of an operation, whereas the right diagram shows the state after the operation has been executed. The effect of the operation can be described by the following changes in the post-state: (1) the value of the attribute c in object b_1 has been incremented by one, (2) a new object b_2 has been created, (3) the link between a and b_1 has been removed, and (4) a new link between a and b_2 has been established.

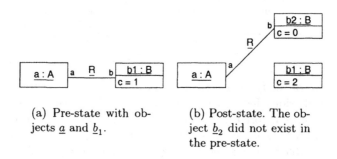

(a) Pre-state with objects a and b_1.

(b) Post-state. The object b_2 did not exist in the pre-state.

Fig. 3. Object diagrams showing a pre- and a post-state

For the following discussion, consider the OCL expression a.b.c where a is a variable denoting the object a. The expression navigates to the associated object of class B and results in the value of the attribute c. Therefore, the expression evaluates to 1 in the pre-state shown in Figure 3(a).

As an example of how the OCL modifier @pre may be used in a postcondition to refer to properties of the previous state, we now look at some variations of the expression a.b.c that may appear as part of a postcondition. For each case, the result is given and explained.

- a.b.c = 0
  Because the expression is completely evaluated in the post-state, the navigation from a leads to the b_2 object. The value of the attribute c of b_2 is 0 in Figure 3(b).
- a.b@pre.c = 2
  This expression refers to both the pre- and the post-state. The previous value of a.b is a reference to object b_1. However, since the @pre modifier only applies to the expression a.b, the following reference to the attribute c is

evaluated in the post-state of $\underline{b}_1$, even though $\underline{b}_1$ is not connected anymore to $\underline{a}$. Therefore, the result is 2.

- a.b@pre.c@pre = 1

  In this case, the value of the attribute c of object $\underline{b}_1$ is taken from the pre-state. This expression is semantically equivalent to the expression a.b.c in a precondition.

- a.b.c@pre = $\perp$

  The expression a.b evaluated in the post-state yields a reference to object $\underline{b}_2$ which is now connected to $\underline{a}$. Since $\underline{b}_2$ has just been created by the operation, there is no previous state of $\underline{b}_2$. Hence, a reference to the previous value of attribute c is undefined.

Note that the @pre modifier may only be applied to operations not to arbitrary expressions. An expression such as (a.b)@pre is syntactically illegal.

OCL provides the standard operation oclIsNew for checking whether an object has been created during the execution of an operation. This operation may only be used in postconditions. For our example, the following conditions indicate that the object $\underline{b}_2$ has just been created in the post-state and $\underline{b}_1$ already existed in the pre-state.

- a.b.oclIsNew = true
- a.b@pre.oclIsNew = false

5.2   Syntax and Semantics of Postconditions

All common OCL expressions can be used in a precondition P. Syntax and semantics of preconditions are defined exactly like those for plain OCL expressions in Section 4. Also, all common OCL expressions can be used in a postcondition Q. Additionally, the @pre construct, the special variable result, and the operation oclIsNew may appear in a postcondition. In the following, we extend Definition 1 for the syntax of OCL expressions to provide these additional features.

Definition 3 (Syntax of expressions in postconditions)

Let op be an operation with a set of parameters $\mathrm{PARAMS_{op}}$. The set of parameters includes at most one parameter of kind "return". The basic set of expressions in postconditions is defined by repeating Definition 1 while substituting all occurrences of Expr_t with $\mathrm{Post\text{-}Expr}_t$. Furthermore, we define that

- Each non-return parameter $p \in \mathrm{PARAMS_{op}}$ with a declared type t is available as variable: $p \in \mathrm{Var}_t$.
- If $\mathrm{PARAMS_{op}}$ contains a parameter of kind "return" and type t then result is a variable: $\mathrm{result} \in \mathrm{Var}_t$.
- The operation oclIsNew : $c \to$ *Boolean* is in $\Omega_\mathcal{M}$ for all object types $c \in T_\mathcal{M}$.

The syntax of expressions in postconditions is extended by the following rule.

vii. If $\omega : t_1 \times \cdots \times t_n \to t \in \Omega_\mathcal{M}$ and $e_i \in$ Post-Expr$_{t'}$ for all $i = 1, \ldots, n$ then
$\omega_{@\mathrm{pre}}(e_1, \ldots, e_n) \in$ Post-Expr$_t$.

$\square$

All general OCL expressions may be used in a postcondition. Moreover, the basic rules for recursively constructing expressions do also apply. Operation parameters are added to the set of variables. For operations with a return type, the variable result refers to the operation result. The set of operations is extended by oclIsNew which is defined for all object types. Operations $\omega_{@\mathrm{pre}}$ are added for allowing references to the previous state (vii). The rule says that the @pre modifier may be applied to all operations, although, in general, not all operations do actually depend on a system state (for example, operations on data types). The result of these operations will be the same in all states. Operations which do depend on a system state are, e.g., attribute access and navigation operations.

For a definition of the semantics of postconditions, we will refer to *environments* describing the previous state and the state resulting from executing the operation. An environment $\tau = (\sigma, \beta)$ is a pair consisting of a system state σ and a variable assignment β (see Section 4.2). The necessity of including variable assignments into environments will be discussed shortly. We call an environment $\tau_{\mathrm{pre}} = (\sigma_{\mathrm{pre}}, \beta_{\mathrm{pre}})$ describing a system state and variable assignments before the execution of an operation a *pre-environment*. Likewise, an environment $\tau_{\mathrm{post}} = (\sigma_{\mathrm{post}}, \beta_{\mathrm{post}})$ after the completion of an operation is called a *post-environment*.

Definition 4 (Semantics of postcondition expressions)
Let Env be the set of environments. The semantics of an expression $e \in$ Post-Expr$_t$ is a function $I[\![e]\!]$: Env $\times$ Env $\to I(t)$. The semantics of the basic set of expressions in postconditions is defined by repeating Definition 2 while substituting all occurrences of Expr$_t$ with Post-Expr$_t$. References to $I[\![e]\!](\tau)$ are replaced by $I[\![e]\!](\tau_{\mathrm{pre}}, \tau_{\mathrm{post}})$ to include the pre-environment. Occurrences of τ are changed to τ_{post} which is the default environment in a postcondition.

- For all $p \in$ PARAMS$_{\mathrm{op}}$: $I[\![p]\!](\tau_{\mathrm{pre}}, \tau_{\mathrm{post}}) = \beta_{\mathrm{post}}(p)$.
  - Input parameters may not be modified by an operation:
    $\mathrm{kind}(p) = \mathrm{in}$ implies $\beta_{\mathrm{pre}}(p) = \beta_{\mathrm{post}}(p)$.
  - Output parameters are undefined on entry:
    $\mathrm{kind}(p) = \mathrm{out}$ implies $\beta_{\mathrm{pre}}(p) = \bot$.
- $I[\![\mathrm{result}]\!](\tau_{\mathrm{pre}}, \tau_{\mathrm{post}}) = \beta_{\mathrm{post}}(\mathrm{result})$.
- $I[\![\mathrm{oclIsNew}]\!](\tau_{\mathrm{pre}}, \tau_{\mathrm{post}})(\underline{c}) = \begin{cases} \mathrm{true} & \text{if } \underline{c} \notin \sigma_{\mathrm{pre}}(c), \\ \mathrm{false} & \text{otherwise.} \end{cases}$

vii. $I[\![\omega_{@\mathrm{pre}}(e_1, \ldots, e_n)]\!](\tau_{\mathrm{pre}}, \tau_{\mathrm{post}}) =$
$I(\omega)(\tau_{\mathrm{pre}})(I[\![e_1]\!](\tau_{\mathrm{pre}}, \tau_{\mathrm{post}}), \ldots, I[\![e_n]\!](\tau_{\mathrm{pre}}, \tau_{\mathrm{post}}))$

$\square$

Standard expressions are evaluated as defined in Definition 2 with the post-environment determining the context of evaluation. Input parameters do not change during the execution of the operation. Therefore, their values are equal in the pre- and post-environment. The value of the `result` variable is determined by the variable assignment of the post-environment. The `oclIsNew` operation yields true if an object did not exist in the previous system state. Operations referring to the previous state are evaluated in context of the pre-environment (vii). Note that the operation arguments may still be evaluated in the post-environment. Therefore, in a nested expression, the environment only applies to the current operation, whereas deeper nested operations may evaluate in a different environment.

With these preparations, the semantics of an operation specification with pre- and postconditions can be precisely defined as follows. We say that a precondition P *satisfies* a pre-environment τ_{pre} – written as $\tau_{\mathrm{pre}} \models P$ – if the expression P evaluates to true according to Definition 2. Similarly, a postcondition Q satisfies a pair of pre- and post-environments, if the expression Q evaluates to true according to Definition 4:

$$\tau_{\mathrm{pre}} \models P \quad \text{iff} \quad I[\![P]\!](\tau_{\mathrm{pre}}) = \text{true}$$
$$(\tau_{\mathrm{pre}}, \tau_{\mathrm{post}}) \models Q \quad \text{iff} \quad I[\![Q]\!](\tau_{\mathrm{pre}}, \tau_{\mathrm{post}}) = \text{true}$$

Definition 5 (Semantics of operation specifications)
The semantics of an operation specification is a set $R \subseteq \text{Env} \times \text{Env}$ defined as

$$I[\![\ \textbf{context} \ \ C :: \mathrm{op}(p_1 : T_1, \ldots, p_n : T_n)$$
$$\textbf{pre:} \ \ P$$
$$\textbf{post:} \ \ Q \ ] \ = \ R$$

where R is the set of all pre- and post-environment pairs such that the pre-environment τ_{pre} satisfies the precondition P and the pair of both environments satisfies the postcondition Q:

$$R = \{(\tau_{\mathrm{pre}}, \tau_{\mathrm{post}}) \mid \tau_{\mathrm{pre}} \models P \wedge (\tau_{\mathrm{pre}}, \tau_{\mathrm{post}}) \models Q\}$$

□

The satisfaction relation for Q is defined in terms of both environments since the postcondition may contain references to the previous state. The set R defines all legal transitions between two states corresponding to the effect of an operation. It therefore provides a framework for a correct implementation.

Definition 6 (Satisfaction of operation specifications)
An operation specification with pre- and postconditions is satisfied by a program S in the sense of total correctness if the computation of S is a total function $f_S : \mathrm{dom}(R) \to \mathrm{im}(R)$ and $\mathrm{graph}(f_S) \subseteq R$.

□

In other words, the program S accepts each environment satisfying the precondition as input and produces an environment that satisfies the postcondition. The definition of R allows us to make some statements about the specification. In general, a reasonable specification implies a non-empty set R allowing one or more different implementations of the operation. If $R = \emptyset$, then there is obviously no implementation possible. We distinguish two cases: (1) no environment satisfying the precondition exists, or (2) there are environments making the precondition true, but no environments do satisfy the postcondition. Both cases indicate that the specification is inconsistent with the model. Either the constraint or the model providing the context should be changed. A more restrictive definition might even prohibit the second case.

5.3   Examples

Consider the operation raiseSalary from the example in Section 2. The operation raises the salary of an employee by a certain amount and returns the new salary.

```
context Employee::raiseSalary(amount : Real) : Real
  pre:  amount > 0
  post: result = self.salary
  post: self.salary = self.salary@pre + amount
```

The precondition only allows positive values for the amount parameter. The postcondition is specified as two parts which must both be true after executing the operation. This could equivalently be rephrased into a single expression combining both parts with a logical *and*. The first postcondition specifies that the result of the operation must be equal to the salary in the post-state. The second postcondition defines the new salary to be equal to the sum of the old salary and the amount parameter. All system states making the postcondition true, after a call to raiseSalary has completed, satisfy the operation specification.

The above example gives an exclusive specification of the operation's effect. The result is uniquely defined by the postconditions. Compare this with the next example giving a much looser specification of the result.

```
context Employee::raiseSalary(amount : Real) : Real
  pre:  amount > 0
  post: result > self.salary@pre
```

The result may be any value greater than the value of the salary in the previous state. Thus, the postcondition does not even prevent the salary from being decreased. However, what the example should make clear, is that there may not only exist many post-states but also many bindings of the result variable satisfying a postcondition. This is the reason why we have to consider both the system state *and* the set of variable bindings for determining the environment of an expression in a postcondition.

The following example shows the evaluation of the expression a.b@pre.c. An informal explanation was given in Section 5.1. With the previous syntax and semantics definitions, we are now able to give a precise meaning to this expression. Numbers in parentheses at the right of the transformations show which rule of Definition 4 (and Definition 2) has been applied in each step.

$$
\begin{aligned}
I[\![\, c(b_{@\mathrm{pre}}(a))\,]\!](\tau_{\mathrm{pre}}, \tau_{\mathrm{post}}) \\
&= I(c)(\tau_{\mathrm{post}})(I[\![\, b_{@\mathrm{pre}}(a)\,]\!](\tau_{\mathrm{pre}}, \tau_{\mathrm{post}})) && \text{(iii)} \\
&= I(c)(\tau_{\mathrm{post}})(I(b)(\tau_{\mathrm{pre}})(I[\![\, a\,]\!](\tau_{\mathrm{pre}}, \tau_{\mathrm{post}}))) && \text{(vii)} \\
&= I(c)(\tau_{\mathrm{post}})(I(b)(\tau_{\mathrm{pre}})(\beta(a))) && \text{(i)} \\
&= I(c)(\tau_{\mathrm{post}})(I(b)(\tau_{\mathrm{pre}})(\underline{a})) \\
&= I(c)(\tau_{\mathrm{post}})(\underline{b}_1) \\
&= 2
\end{aligned}
$$

6 OCL Tools

There are many CASE tools supporting drawing of UML diagrams and features like code generation and reverse engineering. However, support for OCL and semantic analysis of models is rarely found in these tools.

There are several tasks related to OCL for which tool support seems beneficial. For example, syntax checking of constraints helps in writing syntactically correct expressions. The next step could be an interpreter enabling the evaluation of expressions. Given a snapshot of a system, it could check the correctness of the snapshot with respect to the constraints. An alternative way for checking constraints is based on code generation. OCL expressions are transformed into statements of the implementation language. The generated code is responsible for detecting constraint violations.

A comprehensive list enumerating the most important kinds of tools supporting OCL is given in [14]. The authors distinguish between tools doing (1) syntactical analysis, (2) type checking, (3) logical consistency checking, (4) dynamic invariant validation, (5) dynamic pre-/postcondition validation, (6) test automation, and (7) code verification and synthesis. The following (incomplete) list gives an overview of some OCL tools.

- Probably the first available tool for OCL was a parser developed by the OCL authors at IBM (and now maintained at Klasse Objecten). The parser is automatically generated from the grammar given in [18].
- An OCL toolset is being developed at the TU Dresden [14]. Part of the toolset is an OCL compiler [10] that also has been integrated with the open source CASE tool Argo/UML [25].
- An OCL interpreter is described in [29]. It is partly based on an OCL metamodel describing the abstract syntax of OCL as a UML model [23].
- A commercial tool named ModelRun [3] provides validation of invariants against snapshots.
- The USE tool [21,24] allows validation of OCL constraints by checking snapshots of a system. The tool also provides support for an analysis of constraints.

Table 2 compares the tools with respect to the features they support. The table only gives a rough indication about what is provided by a specific tool. However, what can clearly be seen is that logical consistency checking and code verification are features that currently none of the tools we considered here offers.

Table 2. Some OCL tools and the features they support.

Feature	Tool				
	IBM Parser	Dresden OCL Toolkit	TU Munich	ModelRun	USE
(1) syntactical analysis	•	•	•	•	•
(2) type checking	–	•	•	•	•
(3) logical consis-tency checking	–	–	–	–	–
(4) dynamic invari-ant validation	–	–	•	•	•
(5) dynamic pre-/post-condition validation	–	–	–	–	•
(6) test automation	–	–	–	–	•
(7) code verification and synthesis	–	–	–	–	–

6.1   The USE Tool

In this section, we present a tool for validating UML models and OCL constraints based on the formal syntax and semantics of OCL and UML models given earlier in this paper. The USE tool [21,24] has an interpreter for OCL expressions and a facility for animating snapshots of a system. Different snapshots can be interactively generated and checked against the invariants specified as part of a model.

The goal of model validation is to achieve a good design before implementation starts. There are many different approaches to validation: simulation, rapid prototyping, etc. In this context, we consider validation by generating snapshots as prototypical instances of a model and comparing them against the specified model. This approach requires very little effort from developers since models can be directly used as input for validation. Moreover, snapshots provide immediate feedback and can be visualized using the standard notation of UML object diagrams – a notation most developers are familiar with.

The result of validating a model can lead to several consequences with respect to the design. First, if there are reasonable snapshots that do not fulfill the constraints, this may indicate that the constraints are too strong or the model is not adequate in general. Therefore, the design must be revisited, e.g., by relaxing the constraints to include these cases. On the other hand, constraints may be too weak, therefore allowing undesirable system states. In this case, the constraints must be changed to be more restrictive. Still, one has to be careful about the fact that a situation in which undesirable snapshots are detected during validation and desired snapshots pass all constraints does not allow a general statement about the correctness of a specification in a formal sense. It only says that the model is correct with respect to the analyzed system states. However, some advantages of validation in contrast to a formal verification are the possibility to validate non-formal requirements, and that it can easily be applied by average modelers without training in formal methods.

Validating pre- and postconditions. In the following, we will focus on support for validating pre- and postconditions. This new feature was not available in the version of the tool presented in [24] but has been added recently. The input for the USE tool is a textual specification of a UML model. As an example we use the model introduced in Figure 1. The corresponding USE specification is given in Appendix A. It describes the model found in the class diagram and the OCL constraints.

Figure 4 shows a screenshot of the USE tool visualizing various aspects of the example model. The left side of the window shows static information about the model whereas the right side contains several views each showing a different aspect of the dynamic system.

A user produces different system states by (1) adding or deleting objects, (2) inserting and removing links between them, (3) setting attribute values, and (4) simulating operation calls. The screenshot shows a system state after the commands listed in Appendix B have been executed. The view at the bottom right also partially shows the sequence of commands that led to the current state. These commands can be issued directly although most of them can more conveniently be triggered by intuitive interactions with the graphical user interface. For example, objects can be created by selecting a class and dragging it onto the object diagram.

The view at the top shows an object diagram with several objects, their attribute values and links between these objects. The small view labelled "Class Invariants" indicates that the two invariants we have defined in Section 2 are satisfied by the current snapshot.

The automatically generated sequence diagram shows the message flow between objects. In this example, the operation raiseSalary with a parameter value 200 has been called for the employee Frank who previously had a salary of 4500. An interactive command window (not shown in the figure) reports the success of both the pre- and the postconditions. In case of a failing precondition the operation could not have been entered at all. A failing postcondition would be visualized with a red return arrow in the sequence diagram. In both cases, a detailed report on the evaluation of expressions gives hints to the user why the conditions failed.

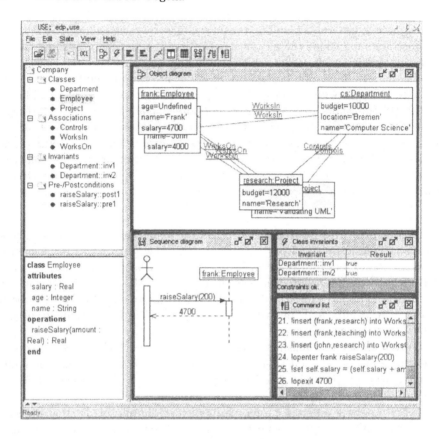

Fig. 4. Screenshot of USE tool

The commands simulating an operation call are the following.

```
-- call operation raiseSalary
!openter frank raiseSalary(200)
!set self.salary = self.salary + amount
!opexit 4700
```

An operation call is simulated by first issuing an `openter` command with a source expression, the name of the operation, and an argument list. The `openter` command has the following effect.

1. The source expression is evaluated to determine the receiver object.
2. The argument expressions are evaluated.
3. The OCL variable `self` is bound to the receiver object and the argument values are bound to the formal parameters of the operation. These bindings determine the local scope of the operation.
4. All preconditions specified for the operation are evaluated.
5. If all preconditions are satisfied, the current system state and the operation call is saved on a call stack. Otherwise, the operation call is rejected.

The side effects of an operation are specified with the usual USE commands for changing a system state. In the example, the set command assigns a new value to the salary attribute of the employee. After generating all side effects of an operation, the operation can be exited and its postconditions can be checked. The command opexit simulates a return from the currently active operation. The result expression given with this command is only required for operations that specify a result value. The opexit command has the following effect.

1. The currently active operation is popped from the call stack.
2. If an optional result value is given, it is bound to the special OCL variable result.
3. All postconditions specified for the operation are evaluated in context of the current system state and the pre-state saved at operation entry time.
4. All variable bindings local to the operation are removed.

In our example, the postcondition is satisfied and the operation has been removed from the call stack. We give another example that shows how operation calls may be nested in the simulation. It also shows that postconditions may be specified on operations without side effects. An OCL expression is given to describe the computation of a side effect free operation. In the example, we use a recursive definition of the factorial function.

```
model NestedOperationCalls

class Rec
operations
  fac(n : Integer) : Integer =
    if n <= 1 then 1 else n * self.fac(n - 1) endif
end

constraints

context Rec::fac(n : Integer) : Integer
  pre:  n > 0
  post: result = n * fac(n - 1)
```

The postcondition of the operation Rec::fac reflects the inductive case of the definition of the factorial function. The following commands show the computation of 3!.

```
!create r : Rec
!openter r fac(3)
!openter r fac(2)
!openter r fac(1)
!opexit 1
!opexit 2
!opexit 6
```

The operation calls are exited in reverse order and provide result values that satisfy the postcondition. Figure 5 shows the sequence diagram generated from this call sequence. The stacked activation frames in the diagram emphasize the recursion.

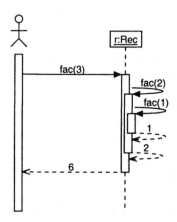

Fig. 5. Sequence diagram for recursive operation call

7   Conclusion

OCL is an important part of UML. Many constraints that cannot be expressed in the UML diagram notation can be elegantly stated with OCL expressions. We argued that a formal language like OCL also should have a formal semantics and presented our approach to developing a precise semantics of OCL. This semantics covers expressions, invariants, contexts, and pre- and postconditions. The concepts and results presented here are implemented in an UML/OCL CASE tool for rapid prototyping and validation of UML designs including OCL expressions.

References

1. T. Baar and R. Hähnle. An integrated metamodel for OCL types. In R. France, B. Rumpe, J.-M. Bruel, A. Moreira, J. Whittle, and I. Ober, editors, *Proc. OOP-SLA 2000, Workshop Refactoring the UML: In Search of the Core, Minneapolis, Minnesota, USA, 2000.*, 2000.
2. T. Baar, R. Hähnle, T. Sattler, and P. H. Schmitt. Entwurfsmustergesteuerte Erzeugung von OCL-Constraints In K. Mehlhorn and G. Snelting, editors, *Informatik 2000, 30. Jahrestagung der Gesellschaft für Informatik*, pages 389–404, Sept. 2000.
3. BoldSoft. Modelrun, 2000. Internet: http://www.boldsoft.com/products/modelrun/index.html.
4. G. Booch, J. Rumbaugh, and I. Jacobson. *The Unified Modeling Language User Guide*. Addison-Wesley, 1998.

5. P. Bottoni, M. Koch, F. Parisi-Presicce, and G. Taentzer. Consistency checking and visualization of OCL constraints. In A. Evans, S. Kent, and B. Selic, editors, *UML 2000 - The Unified Modeling Language. Advancing the Standard. Third International Conference, York, UK, October 2000, Proceedings*, volume 1939 of *LNCS*, pages 294–308. Springer, 2000.

6. T. Clark. Type checking UML static diagrams. In R. France and B. Rumpe, editors, *UML'99 - The Unified Modeling Language. Beyond the Standard. Second International Conference, Fort Collins, CO, USA, October 28-30. 1999, Proceedings*, volume 1723 of *LNCS*, pages 503–517. Springer, 1999.

7. S. Cook, A. Kleppe, R. Mitchell, B. Rumpe, J. Warmer, and A. Wills. The Amsterdam manifesto on OCL. Technical Report TUM-I9925, Technische Universität München, Dec. 1999.

8. S. Cook, A. Kleppe, R. Mitchell, J. Warmer, and A. Wills. Defining the context of OCL expressions. In R. France and B. Rumpe, editors, *UML'99 - The Unified Modeling Language. Beyond the Standard. Second International Conference, Fort Collins, CO, USA, October 28-30. 1999, Proceedings*, volume 1723 of *LNCS*, pages 372–383. Springer, 1999.

9. D. Distefano, J.-P. Katoen, and A. Rensink. On a temporal logic for object-based systems. In S. F. Smith and C. L. Talcott, editors, *Formal Methods for Open Object-Based Distributed Systems IV - Proc. FMOODS'2000, September, 2000, Stanford, California, USA*. Kluwer Academic Publishers, 2000.

10. F. Finger. Design and implementation of a modular OCL compiler. Diplomarbeit, Dresden University of Technology, Department of Computer Science, Software Engineering Group, Germany, Mar. 2000.

11. M. Gogolla and M. Richters. On constraints and queries in UML. In M. Schader and A. Korthaus, editors, *The Unified Modeling Language – Technical Aspects and Applications*, pages 109–121. Physica-Verlag, Heidelberg, 1998.

12. A. Hamie, F. Civello, J. Howse, S. Kent, and R. Mitchell. Reflections on the Object Constraint Language. In J. Bézivin and P.-A. Muller, editors, *The Unified Modeling Language, UML'98 - Beyond the Notation. First International Workshop, Mulhouse, France, June 1998*, pages 137–145, 1998.

13. C. A. R. Hoare. An Axiomatic Basis of Computer Programming. *Communications of the ACM*, 12:576–580, 1969.

14. H. Hussmann, B. Demuth, and F. Finger. Modular architecture for a toolset supporting OCL. In A. Evans, S. Kent, and B. Selic, editors, *UML 2000 - The Unified Modeling Language. Advancing the Standard. Third International Conference, York, UK, October 2000, Proceedings*, volume 1939 of *LNCS*, pages 278–293. Springer, 2000.

15. A. Kleppe and J. Warmer. Extending OCL to include actions. In A. Evans, S. Kent, and B. Selic, editors, *UML 2000 - The Unified Modeling Language. Advancing the Standard. Third International Conference, York, UK, October 2000, Proceedings*, volume 1939 of *LNCS*, pages 440–450. Springer, 2000.

16. L. Mandel and M. V. Cengarle. On the expressive power of OCL. In *FM'99 - Formal Methods. World Congress on Formal Methods in the Development of Computing Systems, Toulouse, France, September 1999. Proceedings, Volume I*, volume 1708 of *LNCS*, pages 854–874. Springer, 1999.

17. B. Meyer. *Object-Oriented Software Construction*. Prentice Hall, second edition, 1997.

18. OMG. Object Constraint Language Specification. In *OMG Unified Modeling Language Specification, Version 1.3, June 1999* [19], chapter 7.

19. OMG, editor. *OMG Unified Modeling Language Specification, Version 1.3, June 1999.* Object Management Group, Inc., Framingham, Mass., Internet: http://www.omg.org, 1999.
20. S. Ramakrishnan and J. McGregor. Extending OCL to support temporal operators. In *Proceedings of the 21st International Conference on Software Engineering (ICSE99) Workshop on Testing Distributed Component-Based Systems, LA, May 16 - 22, 1999*, 1999.
21. M. Richters. The USE tool: A UML-based specification environment, 2001. http://www.db.informatik.uni-bremen.de/projects/USE/.
22. M. Richters and M. Gogolla. On formalizing the UML Object Constraint Language OCL. In T. W. Ling, S. Ram, and M. L. Lee, editors, *Proc. 17th Int. Conf. Conceptual Modeling (ER'98)*, volume 1507 of *LNCS*, pages 449–464. Springer, 1998.
23. M. Richters and M. Gogolla. A metamodel for OCL. In R. France and B. Rumpe, editors, *UML'99 - The Unified Modeling Language. Beyond the Standard. Second International Conference, Fort Collins, CO, USA, October 28-30. 1999, Proceedings*, volume 1723 of *LNCS*, pages 156–171. Springer, 1999.
24. M. Richters and M. Gogolla. Validating UML models and OCL constraints. In A. Evans, S. Kent, and B. Selic, editors, *UML 2000 - The Unified Modeling Language. Advancing the Standard. Third International Conference, York, UK, October 2000, Proceedings*, volume 1939 of *LNCS*, pages 265–277. Springer, 2000.
25. J. Robbins et al. Argo/UML CASE tool, 2001. http://www.argouml.org.
26. J. Rumbaugh, I. Jacobson, and G. Booch. *The Unified Modeling Language Reference Manual.* Addison-Wesley, 1998.
27. S. Sendall and A. Strohmeier. From use cases to system operation specifications. In A. Evans, S. Kent, and B. Selic, editors, *UML 2000 - The Unified Modeling Language. Advancing the Standard. Third International Conference, York, UK, October 2000, Proceedings*, volume 1939 of *LNCS*, pages 1–15. Springer, 2000.
28. J. Warmer and A. Kleppe. *The Object Constraint Language: Precise Modeling with UML.* Addison-Wesley, 1998.
29. M. Wittmann. Ein Interpreter für OCL. Master's thesis, Ludwig-Maximilians-Universität München, 2000.

Appendix

A   USE Specification of the Example Model

```
-- model

model Company

class Employee
attributes
  name : String
  age : Integer
  salary : Real
operations
  raiseSalary(amount : Real) : Real
end
```

```
class Department
attributes
  name : String
  location : String
  budget : Integer
end

class Project
attributes
  name : String
  budget : Integer
end

association WorksIn between
  Employee[*]
  Department[1..*]
end

association WorksOn between
  Employee[*]
  Project[*]
end

association Controls between
  Department[1]
  Project[*]
end

-- OCL constraints

constraints

context Department inv:
  self.budget >= 0

-- Employees working on more projects than other
-- employees of the same department get a higher salary.
context Department inv:
  self.employee->forAll(e1, e2 |
    e1.project->size > e2.project->size
      implies e1.salary > e2.salary)

-- If the amount is positive, raise
-- the salary by the given amount
context Employee::raiseSalary(amount : Real) : Real
  pre:  amount > 0
  post: self.salary = self.salary@pre + amount
    and result = self.salary
```

B   Commands for Animating a Model

```
-- create department
!create cs:Department
!set cs.name = 'Computer Science'
!set cs.location = 'Bremen'
!set cs.budget = 10000

-- create employee john
!create john : Employee
!set john.name = 'John'
!set john.salary = 4000

-- create employee frank
!create frank : Employee
!set frank.name = 'Frank'
!set frank.salary = 4500

-- establish WorksIn links
!insert (john,cs) into WorksIn
!insert (frank,cs) into WorksIn

-- create project research
!create research : Project
!set research.name = 'Research'
!set research.budget = 12000

-- create project teaching
!create teaching : Project
!set teaching.name = 'Validating UML'
!set teaching.budget = 3000

-- establish Controls links
!insert (cs,research) into Controls
!insert (cs,teaching) into Controls

-- establish WorksOn links
!insert (frank,research) into WorksOn
!insert (frank,teaching) into WorksOn
!insert (john,research) into WorksOn

-- call operation raiseSalary
!openter frank raiseSalary(200)
!set self.salary = self.salary + amount
!opexit 4700
```

On the Precise Meaning of OCL Constraints

Rolf Hennicker[1], Heinrich Hussmann[2], and Michel Bidoit[3]

[1] Institut für Informatik, Ludwig-Maximilians-Universität München, Germany
hennicke@informatik.uni-muenchen.de
[2] Fakultät Informatik, Technische Universität Dresden, Germany
hussmann@inf.tu-dresden.de
[3] Laboratoire Spécification et Vérification, CNRS & ENS de Cachan, France

Abstract. When OCL is applied in concrete examples, many questions arise about the precise meaning of OCL constraints. The same kind of difficulties appears when automatic support tools for OCL are designed. These questions are due to the lack of a precise semantics of OCL constraints in the context of a UML model. The aim of this paper is to contribute to a clarification of several issues, like interpretation of invariants and pre- and postconditions, treatment of undefined values, inheritance of constraints, transformation rules for OCL constraints and computation of proof obligations. Our study is based on a formal, abstract semantics of OCL.

1 Introduction

The Object Constraint Language (OCL) is a part of the UML standard that can be used for several different purposes with quite different goals. One key application is to provide precise information in the definition of standards, like the UML standard itself. The main focus of this paper is, however, on software development, where OCL can be used for precise specification of constraints on the model level. Applying OCL to software specification has a strong potential to improve software quality and software correctness. The rules expressed in OCL can be used by advanced support tools, for instance in the following ways:

- To check the validity of constraints at system runtime, for instance by generating assertion code from OCL [13] or by using the integrity checking mechanisms of database systems [5,6].
- To experiment with symbolic representations of possible object configurations, as a means to check consistency and correctness of the rule set [17].
- To statically prove that the code never violates the constraints [11].

This paper is motivated by the experiences the authors made when preparing OCL examples for teaching purposes and when designing support tools for OCL. As soon as the technical details of OCL/UML are considered seriously, a number of semantic questions arise which cannot be answered properly by referring to the existing documentation. There is a clear lack of precise semantics for OCL constraints on a UML model.

A. Clark and J. Warmer (Eds.): Object Modeling with the OCL, LNCS 2263, pp. 69–84, 2002.
© Springer-Verlag Berlin Heidelberg 2002

However, this paper neither intends to give one more semantics for UML in general, nor for the core expression language of OCL. There is already a quite satisfactory definition for the evaluation of an OCL expression on top of an object configuration (a "snapshot" of the model), see [16]. We are addressing the "grey zone" in between UML and OCL. There is not much material yet of this kind, neither in the literature nor in the standard, which explains the interpretation of a constraint in the context of a UML model.

Another observation motivating this work is that the UML standard (draft version 1.4) [18], as far as it deals with pre- and postconditions, appears to be inconsistent with most of the scientific literature on pre- and postconditions (see Section 3 below). Here is a more comprehensive list of similar issues which need to be clarified:

- At which point in the execution of the program is the validity of an invariant enforced?
- What is the meaning of a precondition attached to an operation (without a postcondition)?
- What happens if the precondition of an operation is violated?
- What is the meaning if several constraints are attached to the same operation?
- In howfar do the constraints of a superclass have an impact on the constraints of its subclasses? How is this related to the Liskov substitution principle?
- Is it possible to specify potentially non-terminating operations with OCL? What is the meaning of a constraint in the non-termination case?

In this paper, we elaborate on each of these questions, discuss the range of possible answers and try to find out a "standard" way to answer (or exclude) the questions in a way which makes the practical construction of support tools feasible. Of course, some of the material in this paper can also be understood as a suggestion for improving the UML specification.

This paper is structured as follows: In Sections 2 through 5, an informal discussion of the semantic issues from above is carried out using a simple example. Section 2 deals with invariants, and Section 3 with pre- and postconditions. Section 3 introduces a number of semantic variations for the precise meaning of pre- and postconditions. In Section 4, we develop a simple theory of splitting and combining OCL constraints, which takes into account these semantic variants. Section 5 addresses the specific questions raised by inheritance. Section 6, finally, provides an abstract semantics for UML/OCL, which serves as a mathematical justification of the definitions and decisions taken further above. With the only exception of Section 6, the use of mathematical notation is mostly avoided in this paper, in order to reach a large audience. We assume, however, some basic familarity of the reader with UML and OCL.

2   Invariants

The most prominent use of OCL constraints is for defining *invariants*. An invariant is a very declarative way to specify precise constraints for a class diagram.

It defines addititional rules which have to be obeyed in any object configuration (object diagram) which is constructed for the actual class diagram.

The following example class diagram for bank accounts is used as a running example throughout the rest of this paper.

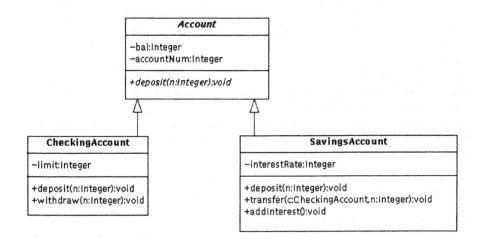

Fig. 1. Example Class Diagram for Accounts

Based on this class diagram, the following example invariant states that for any instance of a checking account, the balance of the account should never go below a given limit.

```
context CheckingAccount
inv: bal >= limit
```

2.1   Checkpoints

In the book on OCL by the main authors of the language (Jos Warmer, Anneke Kleppe), the following simple explanation for the meaning of an invariant is given:

An *invariant* is a constraint that states a condition that must always be met by all instances of the class, type or interface. [19]

In a more recent errata list for the book, a more moderate text is suggested:

Invariants must be true upon completion of the constructor and every public method but not necessarily during the execution of methods. [20]

The reason for the changed formulation is obvious: Invariants are often violated during intermediate computation steps. There should exist specific "checkpoints" during the computation at which invariants are enforced. As an example, it may be the case that during the processing of a series of money transfers the balance goes temporarily below the given limit, but comes back above the limit at the end of the overall operation. If the checkpoint is at the end of the whole series of transfers, this should not be treated as a violation of the constraint.

As suggested by Warmer and Kleppe we consider the end of the execution of each *public* operation and of each constructor as such a checkpoint. But what about private and protected operations? In general such operations may be used as auxiliary operations to compute intermediate results. Then they should not be forced to respect an invariant. For this purpose we use in this paper a property named *volatile* (with a Boolean value) such that the tagged value {*volatile* = *true*} (abbreviated by {*volatile*}) can be attached to a non-public operation. This indicates that the operation does *not* require validity of the invariants at the end of its execution.

2.2   Proposed Informal Semantics

Given these clarifications, the intuitive meaning of an invariant can be defined as follows (taking into account additionally the possibility of an undefined result):

> **Informal semantics of invariants:**
> An invariant is a predicate on object configurations (snapshots). Any constructor delivers an object configuration in which the invariant is valid. Moreover, if a public operation or a non-public operation with property *volatile* = *false* is applied to an object configuration where the invariant holds, and delivers a defined result, then the invariant also holds for the resulting object configuration.

3   Pre- and Postconditions

As soon as actual transformation of the system state is addressed, *preconditions* and *postconditions* are used. Pre- and postconditions specify operations in a descriptive, non-operational way by comparing the states before and after the execution of the operation. Before discussing the semantics of pre- and postconditions, we have to touch one important general issue.

3.1   Undefinedness

In general, the evaluation of an operation may either yield a defined or an undefined result. The "undefined" result is not a proper value but a pseudo-value indicating the non-existence of a result. In practice, there is an important distinction between two kinds of undefinedness:

- *Exception undefinedness:* In this case, the undefined result can just be considered as a special value different from all defined results. Classical examples are division by zero in integer arithmetic, or an attempt to access an object attribute through a reference which is *null*. It is relatively simple to equip programs in such a way that they can deal with this kind of non-values, e.g. by exception handling.

- *Non-termination undefinedness:* In this case, the program goes into an infinite loop and refuses to deliver a result. This kind of undefinedness is much more difficult to handle, since it cannot be easily detected, neither statically nor at runtime. Exception mechanisms are useless here.

OCL provides special treatment for undefinedness. The language was explicitly designed in such a way that the evaluation of an OCL query on a snapshot always terminates. This can be seen from the fact that recursion in explicit definition of query operations is required to always terminate (unfortunately a property which is statically undecidable). So in the interpretation of an OCL expression we have to deal only with what was called "exception undefinedness" above.

The treatment of undefinedness in OCL leads into the unpleasant situation that OCL currently uses a three-valued propositional logic for its *Boolean* sort (with values *true*, *false* and *undefined*). This makes handling of Boolean expressions counter-intuitive. For instance, the well-known law from propositional logic

$$A \Rightarrow B = \neg A \vee B$$

is no longer valid in standard OCL and has to be replaced by the rule

$$A \Rightarrow B = \neg A \vee (A \wedge B)$$

At this point, we do not follow the OCL standard in this paper. In order to enable traditional argumentation on the level of propositional logic, we assume classical two-valued logic. We strongly suggest that the standard is aligned in the same direction, for instance by regarding an undefined value in an evaluation as equivalent to *false*. Using a special logic in OCL will cause major problems in applying existing theorem proving systems, for instance.

Finally, it should be pointed out that the restriction to exception undefinedness in OCL expressions does not at all mean that all specified operations have to terminate. We require here, as OCL does, that all query operations used in OCL expressions are terminating. But other operations transforming the state may terminate or not. (Requiring also those operations to terminate would lead to a quite limited applicability range of the UML/OCL specification language.)

3.2 Semantic Variations

The discussion of undefinedness will turn out as useful for defining the semantics of pre- and postconditions. Let us start with a simple example of a precondition and a postcondition (in the context of the class diagram from above).

```
context Account::deposit(n: Integer)
pre: n >= 0
post: bal = bal@pre + n
```

The central idea of a pre/postcondition pair is a *contract* between the operation and its context. If the operation can rely on the fulfillment of its precondition, then it guarantees its postcondition. This concept is based on a solid theory of program correctness which goes back to the late Sixties ([9], [12]). There are two different classical definitions for the semantics of pre/postconditions which differ in their treatment of undefinedness.

Partial Correctness

An operation $op(x)$ is called *partially correct* with respect to a pair of a precondition PRE and a postcondition $POST$ if the following property holds: If the precondition PRE is valid for a given snapshot σ of the system and if additionally the application of op to σ leads to a defined result, then the postcondition $POST$ is valid for the resulting system state.

Total Correctness

An operation $op(x)$ is called *totally correct* with respect to a pair of a precondition PRE and a postcondition $POST$ if the following property holds: If the precondition PRE is valid for a given snapshot σ of the system, then the application of op to σ leads to a defined result and the postcondition $POST$ is valid for the resulting system state.

The difference between the two definitions is quite subtle. To put it simply, partial correctness does not impose any definedness requirements, whereas total correctness defines a contract which includes definedness of the result.

For an example, let us assume we have an object a of class *Account* with $balance = 0$. Moreover, we apply the operation $deposit(5)$ to a. The difference between the two semantic variations is as follows:

– In partial correctness semantics, it is allowed that $a.deposit(5)$ does not terminate. But when it terminates, the balance after the operation has to have the correct value 5.
– In total correctness semantics, $a.deposit(5)$ has to be defined and the balance after the operation has to have the correct value 5.

Let us now try a more elaborate case. We apply the operation $deposit(-5)$ to a. The average programmer, we are sure, would assume that the precondition $(n \geq 0)$ somehow excludes this application. But the two different definitions do *not* say anything about this application. They only cover the case when the precondition is valid, which is not the case here. So admitted implementations are, among others:

– $a.deposit(-5)$ may raise an exception.
– $a.deposit(-5)$ may go into an infinite loop.
– $a.deposit(-5)$ may just leave the balance untouched.
– $a.deposit(-5)$ may subtract 5 units from the balance.
– $a.deposit(-5)$ may subtract an arbitrary number of units from the balance.

From a practical point of view, it would be very helpful to have some definition which excludes at least the third and fourth implementation!

It is interesting to look at the UML literature for the opinions of the authors regarding the interpretation of pre- and postconditions. The UML standard [18] says that a precondition "must hold for the invocation of an operation" and that a postcondition "must hold after the invocation of the operation". This excludes all the unpleasant effects from above, but does not correspond to the classical definitions on program correctness. Secondary literature on UML is incosistent with the standard. So [3] says (p. 125): "The meaning of the precondition in UML ... is often misinterpreted. [...] The precondition is *not* the operation under which the operation is called. [...] The precondition is the condition under which the operation guarantees that the postcondition will be true." In [7], even two different styles of semantics are distinguished (p. 121), called "*pre $\implies$ post*" and "*pre&post*". The reason for using the first style of semantics is that it is easier to collect independent requirements in this style.

At this point it should be very clear that a formal framework for discussing the variants of pre/postcondition semantics in UML is helpful. The classical definitions from above, however, do not yet cover what the intention of the UML standard seems to be. But there exist other definitions in the literature. In the context of the VDM specification language [8], the support tools offer possibilities to additionally check at each operation invocation whether the precondition is fulfilled. Similarly, in the Eiffel language [15] the notion of class correctness is based on partial (or total) correctness while assertion checks can be optionally performed at runtime. An explicit statement of a clear semantics of parameter restriction is found in the results of the CIP project [4]. The idea used there for precondition semantics (called "parameter restrictions") is the following:

> If the precondition of an operation has not held at invocation time, the result of the invocation is undefined. (Or, equivalently: If the result of an operation is defined, the precondition has held at invocation time.)

Combining partial correctness with this idea gives another semantic variation. We call this semantic variation "partial exception correctness", since it somehow enforces an exception to be raised when the precondition is violated.

Partial Exception Correctness

An operation $op(x)$ is called *partially exception-correct* with respect to a pair of a precondition PRE and a postcondition $POST$ if the following two properties hold:
- The operation op is partially correct with respect to PRE and $POST$.
- If the application of op to σ leads to a defined result, then the precondition PRE has held at invocation time.

The application of this definition to the example shows a clear improvement from the practicians' point of view: The result of $a.deposit(-5)$ has to be undefined. But still, partial expection correctness does not exclude implementations where the result of "normal cases" like $a.deposit(5)$ is undefined.

A fourth semantic variation finally tries to combine total correctness with the idea of parameter restriction:

Total Exception Correctness

An operation $op(x)$ is called *totally exception-correct* with respect to a pair of a precondition PRE and a postcondition $POST$ if the following two properties hold:

- The operation op is totally correct with respect to PRE and $POST$.
- The application of op to σ leads a defined result if and only if the precondition PRE has held at invocation time.

An interesting observation is that proper semantical definitions can be given only for pairs of pre- and postconditions. However, a missing pre- or postcondition can always be given the default value *true*. So an interesting issue is how constraints can be in a correct way merged into pairs or splitted into parts.

4   Splitting of Constraints

In [19] and in the UML standard, it is suggested that complex pre- and postconditions should be splitted into smaller ones. It is obvious that splitting (and merging) of constraints is very helpful from a methodological point of view. In this section we discuss the four semantic variants under the aspect whether they are compatible with splitting (and merging) of constraints and we present transformation rules which allow us to combine constraints. The soundness of the transformation rules can be formally proven by using the semantics approach presented in Section 6.

Splitting of constraints means to specify several pre- and postcondition constraints for the *same* operation. For instance, using our example, we could require the following two constraints, in the following called *Cons1* and *Cons2*, for the operation *withdraw* of *CheckingAccount*. Please note that *Cons1* is an example of a stand-alone precondition as it is admitted in UML, extended with a trivial postcondition.

```
context CheckingAccount::withdraw(n: Integer)      -- Cons1
pre: n >= 0
post: true
```

```
context CheckingAccount::withdraw(n: Integer)      -- Cons2
pre: bal - n >= limit
post: bal = bal@pre - n
```

Intuitively, this means that both constraints should be satisfied by any realization of *withdraw*. Then it is an obvious question whether the above two constraints are equivalent to the following combined constraint, called *Cons3*.

```
context CheckingAccount::withdraw(n: Integer)      -- Cons3
pre: (n >= 0) and (bal - n >= limit)
post: bal = bal@pre - n
```

In the following, we distinguish the four different semantic variations studied in the previous section.

4.1   Splitting and Partial Correctness

If we consider partial correctness, in fact, *Cons*1 is an empty requirement. Then the question is whether *Cons*2 and *Cons*3 are equivalent. But it is obvious that *Cons*2 is indeed stronger than *Cons*3. Consider, for instance, an object *ca* of *CheckingAccount* in the state *bal* = 0, *limit* = 0 and perform *ca.withdraw*(−2). Assume that *ca.withdraw*(−2) is defined. The precondition of *Cons*2 is satisfied and hence *Cons*2 requires that in the resulting state *bal* = 2 holds. Obviously, this is not required by *Cons*3 since the precondition of *Cons*3 is violated.

However, nevertheless there exists a general transformation rule which allows us to combine OCL constraints in the following way:

Transformation Rule for Partial Correctness

```
context C::op(x: T)              context C::op(x: T)
pre: PRE1 post: POST1           pre: PRE2 post: POST2
```

The two above constraints are equivalent to

```
context C::op(x: T)
pre: true
post: (PRE1@pre implies POST1) and (PRE2@pre implies POST2)
```

Here and in the following, for an OCL expression *E* which does not contain @*pre*, *E*@*pre* denotes the OCL expression obtained from *E* by adding @*pre* to all attributes and queries occurring in *E*.

4.2   Splitting and Total Correctness

The semantics of the first OCL constraint *Cons*1 already entails that the applications *ca.withdraw*(*n*) are defined for any *CheckingAccount ca*, as soon as *n* is not negative. There is no freedom left for the implementor to leave any special case undefined which has a non-negative value of *n*. This, however, is allowed in the combined version *Cons*3 of the two OCL constraints. So, again the equivalence of the considered constraints fails.

However, also in the case of total correctness, there exists a general transformation rule which allows us to combine OCL constraints. The idea is very simple: Instead of using an *and* the two preconditions must be combined with an *or* which leads to the following rule.

Transformation Rule for Total Correctness

```
context C::op(x: T)              context C::op(x: T)
pre: PRE1 post: POST1           pre: PRE2 post: POST2
```

The two above constraints are equivalent to

```
context C::op(x: T)
pre: PRE1 or PRE2
post: (PRE1@pre implies POST1) and (PRE2@pre implies POST2)
```

4.3   Splitting and Partial Exception Correctness

In the case of partial exception correctness the good news is that indeed the transformation works as expected. Here we obtain the following general transformation rule.

Transformation Rule for Partial Exception Correctness

```
context C::op(x: T)              context C::op(x: T)
pre: PRE1 post: POST1            pre: PRE2 post: POST2
```

The two above constraints are equivalent to

```
context C::op(x: T)
pre: PRE1 and PRE2
post: POST1 and POST2
```

4.4   Splitting and Total Exception Correctness

Finally, let us consider total exception correctness. Here the bad news is that it doesn't work properly with respect to splitting of constraints. For a counterexample, assume that we want to withdraw 2 units, i.e. we are considering the application $ca.withdraw(2)$. The definition says now together with the first OCL constraint $Cons1$ (precondition $n \geq 0$) that the result of $ca.withdraw(2)$ has to be defined (since $2 \geq 0$). The second OCL constraint $Cons2$ now implies that $bal - 2 \geq limit$ (since the application $ca.withdraw(2)$ is defined). Since, this is a completely independent constraint, this holds for arbitrary object configurations, including those where e.g. $bal = 1$ and $limit = 0$. This is a contradiction, since $1 - 2 >= 0$ does not hold.

In fact, in this case, the combination of two OCL-constraints only works if the two preconditions are equivalent. In all other cases one will end up with an inconsistent specification.

5   Inheritance of Constraints

When using constraints in the presence of inheritance relations a principle goal is to respect Liskov's Substitution Principle which says:

> Wherever an instance of a class is expected, one can always substitute an instance of any of its subclasses [14].

There are two possible approaches how to deal with this requirement. One possibility is to put the responsibility on the system engineer who has to guarantee that the constraints used in his/her model satisfy the substitution principle. Several rules which achieve this goal, like strengthening of invariants in subclasses, are defined in [19]. The disadvantage of this approach is not only the risk that a system engineer may have overlooked some critical cases but also that any constraints imposed on a superclass, must either be redefined or simply be repeated for any subclass. This treatment of constraints seems also to be not consistent with the object-oriented paradigm (where attributes and operations of a superclass belong automatically to all its subclasses).

The second approach, which we find much more convenient, is to consider all constraints imposed on superclasses as implicit constraints for all of its subclasses. To illustrate this simple idea, let A be a superclass of a class B and assume that the following constraints are given:

```
context A inv: INV1              context B inv: INV2
context A::op(x: T)              context B::op(x: T)
pre: PRE1                        pre: PRE2
post: POST1                      post: POST2
```

Then the complete set of (explicit) constraints for B is computed as follows:

```
context B inv: INV1              context B inv: INV2
context B::op(x: T)              context B::op(x: T)
pre: PRE1                        pre: PRE2
post: POST1                      post: POST2
```

According to the transformation rules of the last section one may still simplify these set of constraints. For instance, if we consider partial exception correctness the completion of the constraints for B could be represented by

```
context B inv: INV1 and INV2
context B::op(x: T)
pre: PRE1 and PRE2  post: POST1 and POST2
```

In particular, when dealing with refinement relations and correctness notions for implementations it is important to know which are the complete requirements (or proof obligations) of a given class or class diagram (with constraints). For this the completion mechanism from above is appropriate which computes stepwise the complete set of requirements for each class of a given class hierarchy.

6   Abstract Semantics

The aim of this section is to provide a semantic foundation for the concepts considered in the previous sections. We do not intend to present a detailed technical approach but we rather want to provide an abstract semantics, based on set-theory, which is as simple as possible to capture our intuition about the precise meaning of OCL constraints. In contrast to other semantic approaches (cf. e.g. [2,16,1]) we do not propose a fixed interpretation but we formalize the different alternatives for the interpretation of constraints according to the various correctness notions for pre- and postconditions discussed in Section 3.

In the following we will always assume that $\mathcal{C}$ denotes a UML class diagram and if C is a class occuring in $\mathcal{C}$ we write $C \in \mathcal{C}$.

6.1   Object Configurations

For any class diagram $\mathcal{C}$ there exists a set of object configurations which represent the possible states of the system. These states are also called "snapshots". They can be graphically depicted by UML object diagrams. A detailed semantics of object configurations is given in [16]. We will use the following notations:

- $State(\mathcal{C})$ = set of possible object configurations (snapshots) of $\mathcal{C}$.
- For each $C \in \mathcal{C}$, $Id(C)$ = countably infinite set of potential object identifiers of type C.
- For each $C \in \mathcal{C}$ and $\sigma \in State(\mathcal{C})$, $Instances(C, \sigma)$ = finite subset of $Id(C)$ consisting of the existing objects of type C in the state σ.

6.2   Interpretation of Operations

The set $State(\mathcal{C})$ is solely determined by the associations and attributes occuring in the class diagram $\mathcal{C}$. To give an interpretation for the operations of the classes in $\mathcal{C}$ we use state transformation functions.

For simplicity, we will consider here only unary operations of the form $C ::$ $op(x : T)$ where T is an object type (i.e. a class name) and C is a class with an operation $op(x : T)$ [1]. We also assume that op is not a constructor which would need a special, though not difficult, treatment. Then an interpretation of op is a partial state transformation function

$$I(C :: op(x : T)) : State(\mathcal{C}) \times Id(C) \times Id(T) \to State(\mathcal{C})$$

where $State(\mathcal{C}) \times Id(C) \times Id(T) = \{(\sigma, i, j) \mid \sigma \in State(\mathcal{C}), i \in Id(C), j \in Id(T)$ such that $i \in Instances(C, \sigma)$ and $j \in Instances(T, \sigma)\}$

This means that $I(C :: op(x : T))$ can be applied to a state σ, to an existing object i of class C (representing an interpretation of $self$) and to an existing object j of class T (representing an interpretation of x). The result $I(C :: op(x : T))(\sigma, i, j)$ represents the new state after execution of op.

6.3   Semantics of Class Diagrams

To provide a semantics of a class diagram $\mathcal{C}$ we need (simultaneous) interpretations for all operations occurring in $\mathcal{C}$. For this purpose let

$$Opns(\mathcal{C}) = \text{set of all operations occuring in classes of } \mathcal{C}$$

Then we consider functions

$$I : Opns(\mathcal{C}) \to StateTransFunct$$

---

[1] The generalization of our approach to arbitrary many arguments of arbitrary types and to operations with results is straightforward.

where *StateTransFunct* denotes the set of partial state transformation functions on *StateC*) with appropriate functionality as indicated in Section 6.2 above.

Since, in the moment, we do not consider constraints, arbitrary interpretations of the operations of $\mathcal{C}$ are possible. Hence, the semantics of a class diagram $\mathcal{C}$ is given by the pair

$$Sem(\mathcal{C}) = (State(\mathcal{C}), \{I : Opns(\mathcal{C}) \to StateTransFunct\})$$

In the next step, we will attach OCL constraints to $\mathcal{C}$ which, from the semantical point of view, simply means to restrict (i.e. constrain) the set $\{I : \text{Opns(C)} \to \text{StateTransFunct}\}$ to those interpretation functions which satisfy the given OCL constraints.

6.4   Satisfaction of OCL Constraints

In this subsection we define a satisfaction relation between interpretation functions and OCL constraints. First, let us consider the satisfaction of pre- and postconditions. In fact, corresponding to the four different correctness notions discussed in Section 3, we consider four different kinds of satisfaction relations, denoted by $\models_{pc}$, $\models_{tc}$, $\models_{pec}$ and $\models_{tec}$, which reflect partial correctness, total correctness, partial exception correctness and total exception correctness respectively. As above we will, for simplicity, consider unary operations of the form $C :: op(x : T)$ which are now equipped with OCL constraints

```
context C:: op(x:T)
pre: PRE   post: POST
```

Thereby, *PRE* and *POST* are OCL expressions of type *Boolean* containing (at most) the free variables *self* and *x*. We write $PRE_{\sigma,v}$ for the interpretation of *PRE* in a state $\sigma \in State(\mathcal{C})$ w.r.t. a valuation v such that $v(self) \in Instances(C, \sigma)$ and $v(x) \in Instances(T, \sigma)$. Since POST can contain expressions which refer to an "old" state and, as well, expresions which refer to the "new" state (after execution of *op*) by using the @*pre* construct we need two states σ and σ' for its interpretation which is denoted by $POST_{\sigma,\sigma',v}$.

In general *PRE* and *POST* may also contain queries. Then, we need additionally an interpretation function I on $Opns(\mathcal{C})$ (cf. above) and we write $PRE_{\sigma,v,I}$ and $POST_{\sigma,\sigma',v,I}$ for the corresponding interpretations. We have now the necessary prerequisites to define the satisfaction relations.

Definition 1. *Let* $I : Opns(\mathcal{C}) \to StateTransFunct$ *be an interpretation function.*

1. *Satisfaction w.r.t. partial correctness*
   $I \models_{pc}$ context $C :: op(x : T)$ pre : PRE post : POST
   if for all $(\sigma, i, j) \in State(\mathcal{C}) \times Id(C) \times Id(T)$ *the following holds:*
   if $PRE_{\sigma,v,I} = true$ *and* $I(op)(\sigma, i, j)$ *is defined then* $POST_{\sigma,I(op)(\sigma,i,j),v,I} = true$ *(where* $v(self) = i, v(x) = j$*).* [2]

---

[2] $I(op)$ abbreviates $I(C :: op(x : T))$.

2. **Satisfaction w.r.t. total correctness**
   $I \models_{tc}$ context C :: op(x : T) pre : PRE post : POST
   if for all $(\sigma, i, j) \in State(\mathcal{C}) \times Id(C) \times Id(T)$ *the following holds:*
   if $PRE_{\sigma, v, I} = true$ *then* $I(op)(\sigma, i, j)$ *is defined and* $POST_{\sigma, I(op)(\sigma, i, j), v, I} =$
   true (where v is as above).
3. **Satisfaction w.r.t. partial exception correctness**
   $I \models_{pec}$ context C :: op(x : T) pre : PRE post : POST
   if for all $(\sigma, i, j) \in State(\mathcal{C}) \times Id(C) \times Id(T)$ *the following holds:*
   if $I(op)(\sigma, i, j)$ *is defined then* $PRE_{\sigma, v, I} = true$ *and* $POST_{\sigma, I(op)(\sigma, i, j), v, I} =$
   true (where v is as above).
4. **Satisfaction w.r.t. total exception correctness**
   $I \models_{tec}$ context C :: op(x : T) pre : PRE post : POST
   if for all $(\sigma, i, j) \in State(\mathcal{C}) \times Id(C) \times Id(T)$ *the following holds:*
   $I(op)(\sigma, i, j)$ *is defined if and only if* $PRE_{\sigma, v, I} = true$ *and in this case*
   $POST_{\sigma, I(op)(\sigma, i, j), v, I} = true$ *(where v is as above).*

Let us now consider invariants attached to classes $C \in \mathcal{C}$. As discussed in Section 2 an invariant

```
context C inv: INV
```

requires that all public operations and all non-public operations *op* of $\mathcal{C}$ which have the property {volatile=false} respect the invariant *INV*. More precisely, this means that if *INV* is satisfied in some state σ and if in this state *op* is defined and yields the new state σ' then *INV* holds in σ'. Obviously, this expresses just partial correctness w.r.t. *INV* as pre- and postcondition.

Definition 2. *Let* $I : Opns(C) \to StateTransFunct$ *be an interpretation function.*

1. **Satisfaction of invariants**
   $I \models$ context C inv : INV
   if $I \models_{pc}$ contextC :: op(...) pre : INV post : INV *for all public operations and all non-public operations op of the class C which have the property* {volatile = false}. [3]
2. **Satisfaction of a set of constraints**
   Let Cons be a set of OCL constraints.
   $I \models_c Cons$
   if $I \models$ inv *for each invariant constraint* inv $\in$ *Cons and* $I \models_c$
   prepost *for each pre- postcondition constraint* prepost $\in$ *Cons where*
   $c \in \{pc, tc, pec, tec\}$.

As a consequence of Definitions 1 and 2 we obtain the following result which can be proven by a straightforward propositional logic reasoning.

Theorem 1. *The transformation rules for pre- and postconditions presented in Section 4 are sound w.r.t. their corresponding satisfaction relations.*

---

[3] Note that also all inherited operations from superclasses of C are considered to be operations of C.

6.5   Semantics of Class Diagrams with Constraints

A class diagram $\mathcal{C}$ together with a set $Cons$ of constraints consisting of invariants attached to classes of $\mathcal{C}$ and pre- and postconditions attached to operations occurring in $\mathcal{C}$ can be represented by a pair $(\mathcal{C}, Cons)$. Its semantics is given by constraining the set of interpretation functions on $Opns(\mathcal{C})$ to those interpretations which satisfy the completion $Compl(Cons)$ of the given constraints (cf. Section 5 for the discussion of completions). Thereby, we distinguish again four possibilities according to the different satisfaction relations considered above.

$$Sem_c(\mathcal{C}, Cons) =$$
$$(State(\mathcal{C}), \{I : Opns(\mathcal{C}) \to StateTransFunct \mid I \models_c Compl(Cons)\})$$

where $c \in \{pc, tc, pec, tec\}$.

This definition induces in a straightforward way different kinds of correctness notions for implementations provided by object-oriented programs, written e.g. in Java. In fact, each program P intended to implement a given class diagram $\mathcal{C}$ with constraints $Cons$ can be considered as a particular interpretation function I_P. Then the program P is a correct implementation of $(\mathcal{C}, Cons)$ if $I_P \in Sem_c(\mathcal{C}, Cons)$.

7   Conclusion and Outlook

In this paper we have proposed several variants for a precise meaning to OCL constraints in the context of a UML model based on a formal abstract semantics. Moreover, we have defined a set of transformation rules to derive a single pair of pre- and postconditions from a system of independently specified constraints, taking into account inheritance as well as the semantic variants. To our knowledge, neither the comparative investigation of semantics nor the treatment of inheritance in the context of OCL constraints has been studied systematically up to now.

Which of the discussed variants is adequate for UML/OCL? Current UML documentation informally defines a semantics which is close to partial exception correctness. Nevertheless, other variants are used frequently in the literature, and with good reason. So the definitions used in the current standard may be too limited and special for all users of the language and all phases of the development process. This work is an attempt to provide the terminology and formal basis to clearly distinguish between the variants in a semantically richer variant of UML, as well as to build adequate tools including "bridges" between the variants.

References

1. Bidoit, M., Hennicker, R., Tort, F., Wirsing, M.: Correct Realizations of Interface Constraints with OCL. Proc. UML '99, The Unified Modeling Language - Beyond the Standard, Springer LNCS 1723, 399-415, 1999.
2. Brickford, M., Guaspari, D.: Lightweight Analysis of UML. Draft Technical Report, Odyssey Research Associates, 1998.

3. Cheesman, J., Daniels, J.: UML Components. Addison-Wesley, 2001
4. The CIP Language Group (F.L. Bauer et al.): The Munich Project CIP, Vol. I: The Wide Spectrum Language CIP-L. Springer LNCS 183, 1985
5. Demuth, B., Hussmann, H.: Using UML/OCL Constraints for Relational Database Design. Proc. UML '99, The Unified Modeling Language - Beyond the Standard, Springer LNCS 1723, 598-613, 1999.
6. Demuth, B., Hussmann, H., Loecher, St.: OCL as a Specification Language for Business Rules in Data Base Applications. Proc. UML '01, The Unified Modeling Language, To appear (Springer LNCS), 2001.
7. D'Souza, D.F., Wills, A.C.: Objects, Components and Frameworks with UML. The Catalysis Approach. Addison-Wesley, 1999
8. Fitzgerald, J., Larsen, P.G.: Modelling Systems. Practical Tools and Techniques in Software Development. Cambridge University Press, 1998
9. Floyd, R.W.: Assinging Meanings to Programs. *Proc. Symp. on Appl. Math.* **19**, American Mathematical Society 1967
10. Gamma, E., Helm, R., Johnson, R., Vlissides, J.: Design Patterns. Elements of Reusable Object-Oriented Software. Addison-Wesley, 1995
11. Reus, B., Wirsing, M., Hennicker, R.: A Hoare Calculus for Verifying Java Realizations of OCL-Constrained Design Models. Proc. FASE 2001 - Fundamental Aspects of Software Engineering, Springer LNCS 2029, 285-300, 2001.
12. Hoare, C.A.R.: An Axiomatic Basis of Computer Programming. *Communications of the ACM* **12**, pp. 576-583, 1969
13. Hussmann, H., Demuth, B., Finger, F.: Modular Architecture for a Toolset Supporting OCL. Proc. UML 2000, The Unified Modeling Language - Advancing the Standard, Springer LNCS 1939, 278-293, 2000.
14. Liskov, B., Wing, J.: A Behavioral Notion of Subtyping. ACM Trans. on Prog. Lang. and Systems, Vol. 16 (6), 1811–1841, 1994
15. Meyer, B.: Object-oriented Software Construction. Prentice Hall, 1988.
16. Richters, M., Gogolla, M.: On Formalizing the UML Object Constraint Language OCL. Proc. 17th Int. Conf. Conceptual Modeling (ER '98) Springer LNCS 1507, 449-464, 1998.
17. Richters, M., Gogolla, M.: Validating UML Models and OCL Constraints. Proc. UML 2000, The Unified Modeling Language - Advancing the Standard, Springer LNCS 1939, 265-277, 2000.
18. OMG Unified Modeling Language Specification, Version 1.4 draft. February 2001
19. Warmer, J., Kleppe, A.: The Object Constraint Language. Precise Modeling with UML. Addison-Wesley, 1999
20. Klasse Objecten: Errata for "The Object Constraint Language, Precise Modeling with UML". Available at http://www.klasse.nl.

Expressing UML Class Diagrams Properties with OCL

Martin Gogolla and Mark Richters

University of Bremen, FB 3, Computer Science Department
Postfach 330440, D-28334 Bremen, Germany
{gogolla|mr}@informatik.uni-bremen.de

Abstract. The Unified Modeling Language UML is a complex language offering many modeling features. Especially the description of static structures with class diagrams is supported by a rich set of primitives. This paper shows how to transfrom UML class diagrams involving cardinality constraints, qualifiers, association classes, aggregations, compositions, and generalizations into equivalent UML class diagrams employing only binary associations and OCL constraints. Thus we provide a better understanding of UML features. By reducing more complex features in terms of basic ones, we suggest an easy way users can gradually extend the set of UML elements they commonly apply in the modeling process.

1   Introduction

The Unified Modeling Language UML [OMG99c,OMG99b,OMG99a] being heavily influenced by OMT [RBP+91], Booch [Boo94], and OOSE [JCJÖ92] is a complex language with many modeling features. But up to now, no overall agreed semantic background has been developed. So naturally the question arises how to deal with the language element variety, for example, to relate the different language elements. In this paper we study UML class diagrams and compare the language elements available there. The general idea here is to explain advanced UML features by some more basic UML constructs. A similar approach [GPP98] has been taken by us for UML state diagrams concerning the UML dynamic modeling aspects.

Although UML provides a rich set of language features, many projects are forced to restrict themselves to utilizing only a small set of the language. This is partly due to a current lack of sufficiently reliable and efficient tools supporting the whole language and partly due to the fact that more time and effort is needed to learn and adapt additional features. Indeed, using only a small set of features can reduce the complexity of a design and facilitate communication. Our approach enables a smooth transition from utilizing a basic set of language features to more sophisticated ones by explaining them in terms of already known features. On the other hand, giving a definition in terms of simple features possibly helps identifying certain repeating patterns in existing designs which may better be

A. Clark and J. Warmer (Eds.): Object Modeling with the OCL, LNCS 2263, pp. 85–114, 2002.
© Springer-Verlag Berlin Heidelberg 2002

represented by more suitable special features, thus emphasizing a particular design decision.

Our work is related to recent approaches handling formal aspects of UML and other object-oriented methods. Work has been done on the basis of well-established traditional approaches to specification like Z and VDM: [SF97, FBLPS97] focuses on the UML type system, a general integration of Z with object-orientation is discussed in [Ebe97], and in [Lan96,BLM97] an object calculus enhancing the expressibility of object-oriented notations has been proposed. Other approaches treat in detail the UML predecessor OMT [BCV96,WRC97], and in particular class diagrams [BC95] in connection with Larch are discussed. [BHH+97] sketches a general scenario for most UML diagrams without going into technical details, and [Öov98] presents a general framework for relationships in UML. [WB98] integrates structure and behavior specification on the basis of transition systems. [Cla99] gives a type system for static UML diagrams. [KC99] studies class diagrams by means of using Object-Z. [RACH00] concentrates on active classes, and [TE00] discusses class diagrams in connection with sequence diagrams.

The structure of the rest of this paper is as follows. Sections 2 to 6 point out how to translate n-ary associations with cardinality restrictions, qualifiers, association classes, aggregations and compositions, and generalizations, respectively. The UML subset we use employs general binary associations with additional constraints formulated in OCL [WK98,WK99]. These sections all have the same structure. First, we motivate the handled concept by citing respective parts from the "official" UML material: the semantics document [OMG99c], the notation guide [OMG99b], and the OCL description [OMG99a]. Then, a general translation scheme is presented, which is explained afterwards by an example. The paper ends with some concluding remarks.

2   Binary Associations with Cardinalities

2.1   Statements from UML Material

- *[An] association [denotes] the semantic relationship between two or more classifiers [classes] that involves connections among their instances.* Semantics.
- *A multiplicity item specifies the range of allowable cardinalities that a set may assume.* Notation.
- *[Multiplicity:] When placed on a target end, specifies the number of target instances that may be associated with a single source instance across the given association.* Semantics.

Fig. 1. Equivalence Rule for Cardinality Notation

2.2   General Translation

Simple Cardinality Restrictions: In Fig. 1 we have indicated how to translate an association with cardinality restrictions (1 for low and h for high) into an equivalent association with an explicit constraint. Specifying role names ra and rb in the diagram implies that the role name identifiers can be used as operations ra: B -> Set(A) and rb: A -> Set(B). For example, ra returns for an A object the set of B objects related to the argument. The constraint requires that, for a single A object, the size of the set of related B objects is restricted by the lower bound lb and by the upper bound hb (analogously, for the other side of the association).

```
A.allInstances->forAll( a | a.rb->size>=lb and a.rb->size<=hb )
and
B.allInstances->forAll( b | b.ra->size>=la and b.ra->size<=ha )
```

Factoring Out Common Subexpressions: This little example already shows a minor deficiency of OCL: Common subexpressions have to be repeated as often as they are needed. For example, the term a.rb->size appears (and must appear) twice in the example. In OCL there is no structuring mechanisms for expressions. An alternative would be to provide a "let" construct in order to factor out common subexpressions. This would make expressions easier to understand especially complex ones with nested quantifiers and queries. Then, the first part of the above constraint could be shortened to the following, more readable expression.

```
let s=a.rb->size in
   A.allInstances->forAll( a | s>=lb and s<=hb )
```

However, in order to be in full accordance with all versions of OCL (OCL 1.1 does not include let) we refrain from taking advantage of such abbreviations.

Simplifying Resulting Formulas for Special Cases: If the lower bound in a cardinality specification is 0, then a comparison like a.rb.size>=0 is always true. In this case the comparison may be left out in the defining formula. If the upper bound specification is * (which means that no finite upper bound is given), then there is no need to include an upper bound restriction in the formula. Thus the UML default cardinality specification 0..* would be translated into the "empty" restricting constraint.
If lower and upper bounds of the cardinality specification coincide, say the left cardinality specification in Fig. 1 is h..h or equivalently only h, then the resulting formula can be simplified as follows.

```
B.allInstances->forAll( b | b.ra->size=h )
```

Avoiding Explicit Reference to All Instances: In order to make the OCL
expression shorter and more readable, we omit in the following OCL formulas the explicit reference to all instances of a class, if this construction is clear
from the context. Thus, for a class C the term C->forAll(...) is short for
C.allInstances->forAll(...). Analogously we define C->exists(...),
C->select(...) and C->includes(...). Therefore, the above OCL expression is abbreviated to the following formula.

```
A->forAll( a | a.rb->size>=la and a.rb->size<=ha )
and
B->forAll( b | b.ra->size>=lb and b.ra->size<=hb )
```

Ordered Associations: Marking an association end as ordered, for example
the left end with the role name ra, would change the signature of the operation induced by the role name from set to list, for example from ra:
B -> Set(A) to ra: B -> Sequence(A), but the constraint would be the
same (because size is defined for all collection types).

Sequence of Integer Intervals: In general, cardinalities are given as a sequence of integer intervals, not just as a single interval. This extension can
be captured by the corresponding constraint, as well. For example, if we had
the cardinality specifications la..ha, la'..ha' and lb..hb, lb'..hb' instead of la..ha and lb..hb, the constraint would look like:

```
A->forAll( a | a.rb->size>=lb and a.rb->size<=hb
               or
               a.rb->size>=lb' and a.rb->size<=hb' )
and
B->forAll( b | b.ra->size>=la and b.ra->size<=ha
               or
               b.ra->size>=la' and b.ra->size<=ha' )
```

2.3 Example

The class diagram in Fig. 2 refers to the design of a chess game application. A
rook protects at least 2 and at most 14 squares. On the other hand, a square
can be protected either by no rook or one rook or two rooks. The formula below
is a direct translation of the general scheme into the example context.

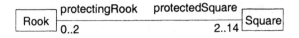

Fig. 2. Example for Cardinality Notation

```
Rook->forAll( r |
  r.protectedSquare->size>=2 and r.protectedSquare->size<=14 )
and
Square->forAll( s |
  s.protectingRook->size>=0 and s.protectingRook->size<=2 )
```

3   N-ary Associations with Cardinalities

3.1   Statements from UML Material

- *An n-ary association is an association among three or more classes (a single class may appear more than once). Notation.*
- *Multiplicity for n-ary associations may be specified but is less obvious than binary multiplicity. The multiplicity of a role represents the potential number of instance tuples in the association when the other N-1 values are fixed. Notation.*

3.2   General Translation

Ternary Associations: As indicated in the original UML statements, the translation of n-ary associations with cardinality restrictions is a bit more involved in comparison to the binary case. The diagram in Fig. 3 keeps on the right hand side the starting situation except the cardinality requirement. Please note that throughout this paper we assume a multiplicity of *
if no explicit specification is given an a class diagram. The formula for the translation fixes the pair of objects on the opposite side of the cardinality specification and requires, analogously to the case with binary associations, that the size of the set of related objects is restricted by the given lower and upper bounds. The formula expresses the connection between three participating objects as R(a,b,c).

```
A->forAll( a |
  B->forAll( b |
    C->select( c | R(a,b,c) )->size>=1
    and
    C->select( c | R(a,b,c) )->size<=h )
  )
)
```

Ternary Associations in OCL: The above constraint does not obey the exact OCL syntax, because the name of an association with appropriate parameters is not allowed as a boolean expression in OCL. It is however necessary to express this, but it cannot be done by using only role names. For example, if we have R(A,B,C) and we want to require that R(a,b,c) holds for objects a,b,c, we cannot express this as

```
a.rb->includes(b) and b.rc->includes(c) and c.ra->includes(a)
```

or

```
a.rb->select( b | b.rc->select(c)->size>0 )->size>0
```

or something similar because

R	A	B	C
	a	b	c'
	a'	b	c
	a	b'	c

fulfills the `includes` and the `select` expression without having an appropriate tuple in R.

Fig. 3. Equivalence Rule for Ternary Association

N-ary Associations: Above, we have shown only the translation for a ternary association. The formula can be generalized to the arbitrary case in Fig. 4 with n participating classes by introducing a universally quantified variable for each of the $n - 1$ classes on the opposite side of the cardinality specification.

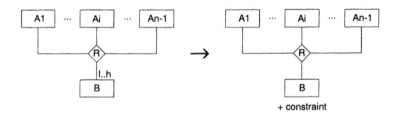

Fig. 4. Equivalence Rule for N-ary Association

```
A1->forAll( a1 |
    ...
    Ai->forAll( ai |
```

```
. . .
An-1->forAll( an-1 |
  B->select( b | R(a1,...,ai,...,an-1,b) )->size>=l
  and
  B->select( b | R(a1,...,ai,...,an-1,b) )->size<=h )
)
. . .
)
. . .
)
```

3.3 Example

The example in Fig. 5 shows a ternary association where students can be examined by teachers on certain subjects. The cardinality restriction requires that a student can be examined on a single subject at most three times (each time by a different teacher).

```
Student->forAll( st |
  Subject->forAll( su |
    Teacher->select( t | Examine(st,su,t) )->size>=0
    and
    Teacher->select( t | Examine(st,su,t) )->size<=3
  )
)
```

4   From N-ary to Binary Relationships

4.1   Statements from UML Material

– *An n-ary association is an association among three or more classes (a single class may appear more than once).* Notation.
– *Each instance of the association is an n-tuple of values from the respective classes.* Notation.

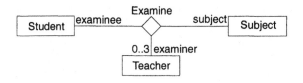

Fig. 5. Example for Cardinality Notation in N-ary Association

4.2   General Translation

Translating N-ary Associations: N-ary associations can be translated
strictly to binary associations. Thus, all static structure constructions discussed here could finally be reduced to a set of binary associations. As depicted in Fig. 6, a ternary association with unrestricted cardinality translates
into three classes plus an additional class representing the association. The
cardinalities in the diagram assure that an R object, which represents a link,
is connected to exactly one A, one B object, and one C object. For representing unique association links we need the following constraint. It states that
two different R objects are equal, whenever they are connected to the same
set of A, B, and C objects. In other words, two links are identical, if they refer
to the same source objects.

```
R->forAll( r, r' |
  ( r.ra=r'.ra and r.rb=r'.rb and r.rc=r'.rc ) implies r=r'
)
```

Translating Cardinalities of N-ary Associations: A   given   cardinality
specification 1..h for the association end (for example) at class C can be
expressed by the following constraint. The constraint requires that, for a
given pair (a,b) consisting of an A and a B object, the set of related R
objects, i.e. links, is restricted by the given lower and upper bound. The
constraint uses operations ra: R -> A and rb: R -> B which are induced
by the role names and the cardinality restrictions.

```
A->forAll( a |
  B->forAll( b |
    R->select( r | r.ra=a and r.rb=b )->size>=1
    and
    R->select( r | r.ra=a and r.rb=b )->size<=h
  )
)
```

Translating Induced Operations of N-ary Associations: It is also possible to give derivations for operations which are induced in the original class
diagram by role names. For example, in the original class diagram we have
the operation ra: C -> Set(A). For a given C object c we could form in the

Fig. 6. Translation of Ternary Association

original class diagram the term `c.ra` yielding a set of `A` objects connected to object `c`. This term can be expressed in the resulting class diagram as:

```
A->select( a | R->exists( r | r.rc=c and r.ra=a ) )
```

Uniformity versus Semantic Adequacy: Translating complex associations to binary associations has the advantage that the resulting models have a uniform look in that only a small set of features is used and possess equivalent state spaces. This translation has however the drawback that "semantic" information is lost. The notion of semantics here does not refer to formal semantics but to "application" semantics in the following sense: the left class diagram in Fig. 6 clearly states through the explicit association symbol that there are three classes and that there is one association between them; in the right class diagram the information that class `R` is not a "plain" class but really a relationship is only represented implicitly. The translation is in a way analogous to the translation of semantic data model schemata to relational data model schemata. Indeed, the realm of "Semantic Data Models" provides adequate modeling techniques in order to represent different real world phenomena also in different forms in class diagrams (or semantic data model schemata as class diagrams are called there).

4.3   Example

In Fig. 7 we show how the Examine example of Fig. 5 is translated. The association translates into a new class, and each "arm" of the old association is transformed into a connection from the new class to one of the original classes. The constraint requires that if two examine objects have the same set of examinees, subjects, and examiners, then the two examine objects coincide.

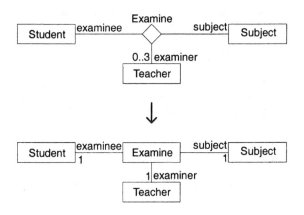

Fig. 7. Example for Translation of Ternary Association

```
Examine->forAll( e, e' |
  ( e.examinee=e'.examinee and
    e.subject=e'.subject and
    e.examiner=e'.examiner ) implies e=e'
)
```

5   Qualifier

5.1   Statements from UML Material

- *A qualifier is an attribute or list of attributes whose values serve to partition the set of objects associated with an object across an association. The qualifiers are attributes of the association.* Notation.
- *The multiplicity attached to the target role denotes the possible cardinalities of the set of target objects selected by the pairing of a source object and a qualifier value.* Notation.
- *[A] qualifier [is] an association attribute or tuple of attributes whose values partition the set of objects related to an object across an association.* Semantics.

5.2   General Translation

Figure 8 shows that a qualifier is translated into an association class (if the association class is already present, the qualifier translates into an additional attribute of the association class). The respective constraint requires that the size of the set of B objects determined by a combination of an A object and a q attribute value is restricted by the given lower and upper bound. Regarding the operations used in the defining formula, the role name rb implies we have an operation rb: A -> Set(B). Due to the additional association class AC, we have further operations ra: AC -> A, rb: AC -> B, ac: A -> Set(AC), and ac: B -> Set(AC).

```
A->forAll( a |
  a.ac->forAll( ac |
    a.rb->select( b |
      b.ac->exists( ac' | ac'.q=ac.q and ac'.ra=a ) )->size>=l
    and
    a.rb->select( b |
      b.ac->exists( ac' | ac'.q=ac.q and ac'.ra=a ) )->size<=h
  )
)
```

In the next section we show how to further reduce association classes to n-ary associations.

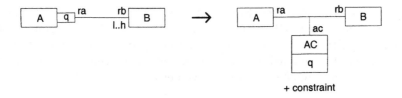

Fig. 8. Equivalence Rule for Qualifier

5.3   Example

The example in Fig. 9 taken from the UML notatation guide expresses that an account number at a given bank either uniquely determines a person or the account number is not connected to a person at all. The defining formula makes use of implicit role names and induced operations as follows: `person: Bank -> Set(Person)`, `bank: Account -> Bank`, `person: Account -> Person`, `account: Bank -> Set(Account)`, and `account: Person -> Set(Account)`.

The formula expresses the following: (1) For all banks b and all accounts a at this bank, we select from all persons p connected with the bank b those who possess an account a' at bank b having the same account number as account a. (2) The size of this set of selected persons is either 0 or 1.

```
Bank->forAll( b |
  b.account->forAll( a |
    b.person->select( p |
      p.account->exists( a' |
        a'.account#=a.account# and a'.bank=b ) )->size>=0
    and
    b.person->select( p |
      p.account->exists( a' |
        a'.account#=a.account# and a'.bank=b ) )->size<=1
  )
)
```

Fig. 9. Example for Qualifier

In this context, the OCL term b.person[123456] denotes a person having the account with number 123456 at bank b. Therefore, if we denote argument types of a function with underscores _, the notation _.person[_] : Bank account# -> Person can be regarded as a partial operation returning for a given bank and a given account number the respective person.

6 Association Classes

6.1 Statements from UML Material

- *An association class is an association that also has class properties (or a class that has association properties).* Notation.
- *An association class is an association that is also a class. It not only connects a set of classifiers [classes] but also defines a set of features that belong to the relationship itself and not any of the classifiers.* Semantics.
- *Navigation from an association class to one of the objects on the association will always deliver exactly one object.* OCL.

6.2 General Translation

In Fig. 10 the translation of association classes into ternary associations is shown. The specified role names induce the operations ra: C -> Set(A) and rb: C -> Set(B) (and, of course, ra: B -> Set(A) and rb: A -> Set(B), but these are not needed in the formula below). The induced formula expresses the idea that each C object "points" to a unique pair of A and B objects. In other words, R constitutes an injective function from the class C into the product of A and B.

```
C->forAll( c |
  c.ra->size=1 and c.rb->size=1 and
  C->forAll( c' | (c.ra=c'.ra and c.rb=c'.rb) implies c=c' )
)
```

Alternatively, we can require that (1) each (A,B)-pair is connected to exactly one C object (the formula below states that for each (A,B)-pair the size of the

Fig. 10. Equivalence Rule for Association Class

set of connected C objects is equal to one) and (2) a pair of (A,B) objects is connected to a unique C object (the formula below states that if two C objects have links to the same pair of (A,B) objects, then the two C objects coincide).

```
A->forAll( a |
  B->forAll( b |
    ( C->select( c | R(a,b,c) )->size=1 or
      C->select( c | R(a,b,c) )->size=0 )
    and
    C->forAll( c, c' | ( R(a,b,c) and R(a,b,c') ) implies c=c' )
  )
)
```

6.3   Example

In Fig. 11 the bank example introduced in Fig. 9 is carried out further by paraphrasing it as a ternary association called Connection between Bank, Account, and Person. The constraint demands that (1) an account is related to exactly one bank and to exactly one person, and (2) there cannot be a different account with the same links.

```
Account->forAll( a |
  a.bank->size=1 and a.person->size=1
  and
  Account->forAll( a' |
    ( a.bank=a'.bank and a.person=a'.person ) implies a=a'
  )
)
```

Fig. 11. Example for Association Class

The alternative formula would be the following one. This constraint employs the name of the association Connection as a predicate symbol.

```
Bank->forAll( b |
  Person->forAll( p |
```

```
( Account->select( a | Connection(b,p,a) )->size=1 or
  Account->select( a | Connection(b,p,a) )->size=0 )
and
Account->forAll( a, a' |
  ( Connection(b,p,a) and Connection(b,p,a') ) implies a=a'
)
)
)
```

7   Aggregation and Composition

7.1   Statements from UML Material

- *[A filled diamond] signifies the strong form of aggregation known as composition.* Notation.
- *Composition is a form of aggregation with strong ownership and coincident lifetimes of part with the whole. The multiplicity of the aggregate may not exceed one (it is unshared).* Notation, line -7.
- *[AggregationKind= "aggregate"] The part may be contained in other aggregates.* Semantics.
- *[AggregationKind= "composite"] The part is strongly owned by the composite and may not be part of any other composite.* Semantics.
- *Aggregation [is] a special form of association that specifies a whole-part relationship between the aggregate (whole) and a component part.* Semantics.
- *Composition [is] a form of aggregation with strong ownership and coincident lifetime as part of the whole. Parts with non-fixed multiplicity may be created after the composite itself, but once created they live and die with it (i.e. they share lifetimes). Such parts can also be explicitly removed before the death of the composite.* Semantics.
- *Both kinds of aggregations define a transitive, antisymmetric relationship, i.e. the instances form a directed, non-cyclic graph. Composition instances form a strict tree (or rather a forest).* Semantics.

7.2   General Translation

Aggregate-part (or whole-part) relationships touch three areas to be discussed: Existential dependency, sharing, and instance reflexivity. (1) In principle, existential dependency comes in two facets: The part can existentially depend on the aggregate (a part can only exist inside an aggregate), or, the other way round, the aggregate can existentially depend on the part (an aggregate can only exist if its parts exist). (2) Forbidding sharing means that two aggregates cannot have a part in common. With respect to sharing, one can further distinguish the situation where the two aggregates are objects of the same class from the situation where it is possible that the two aggregates belong to different classes. (3) Forbidding instance reflexivity means that a part cannot directly or indirectly be part of itself.

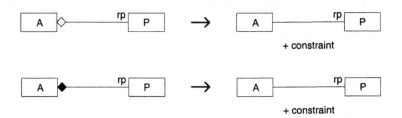

Fig. 12. Equivalence Rule for Aggregation and Composition

As indicated in Fig. 12, both UML versions of aggregate-part relationships, namely aggregations and compositions, are translated into binary associations. General associations differ from aggregate-part relationships in that instance reflexivity is forbidden for aggregations and compositions. For compositions we require in addition the part to be existentially dependent from the aggregate and a strong form of forbidding sharing. Below, we define the facets of aggregate-part relationships independent from these UML requirements as OCL constraints.

Existential Dependency for the Part: The part is existentially dependent from the aggregate. In technical terms, this means that a P object can only exist if it is connected to an A object.

```
P->forAll( p |
  A->exists( a | a.rp->includes(p) ) )
```

Existential Dependency for the Aggregate: The aggregate is existentially dependent from the part. In technical terms, this means that an A object can only exist if it is related to a P object.

```
A->forAll( a |
  P->exists( p | a.rp->includes(p) ) )
```

Both forms of existential dependency can be expressed alternatively as a cardinality constraint with a lower bound of one.

Combining Both Forms of Existential Dependency: Both forms of existential dependency can be combined into one notion: Part and aggregate can be existentially coincident. In technical terms, A and P objects are existentially coincident.

```
P->forAll( p |
  A->exists( a | a.rp->includes(p) ) )
```

and
```
P->forAll( p |
  A->exists( a | a.rp->includes(p) ) )
```

Weak Form of Forbidding Sharing: A P object cannot be shared by two different A objects. In technical terms, if two aggregates comprise one common part, then the aggregates coincide.

```
P->forAll( p |
  A->exists( a, a' |
    ( a.rp->includes(p) and a'.rp->includes(p) )
    implies
    a=a' ) )
```

Strong Form of Forbidding Sharing: A P object cannot be shared by two different objects belonging to (potentially) different classes A1 and A2. As shown in Fig. 13, this constraint has to be given for any two classes A1 and A2 being potential aggregates for class P.

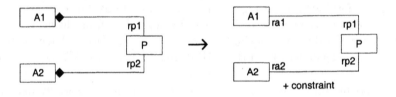

Fig. 13. Equivalence Rule for Composition with Strong Form of Forbidding Sharing

```
P->forAll( p |
  A1->exists( a1 |
    A2->exists( a2 |
      ( a1.rp1->includes(p) and a2.rp2->includes(p) )
      implies
      a1=a2 ) ) )
```

Although in the above formula a1 and a2 may be objects of different classes, the comparison a1=a2 is syntactically well-formed, because in OCL we have A1<Any and A2<Any, and =: Any x Any -> Bool.

As an alternative, but equivalent formulation we can set up a constraint requiring that a part p cannot have connections to both an A1 object and an A2 object.

```
P->forAll( p | p.ra1->isEmpty or p.ra2->isEmpty )
```

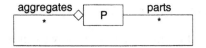

Fig. 14. Reflexive Aggregation

Forbidding Instance Reflexivity for Aggregation: A P object cannot be part of itself. In Fig. 14 we have a reflexive aggregation (one class participates twice) where the role names define operations `parts: P -> Set(P)` and `aggregates: P -> Set(P)`. Without any further restriction, a P object p can be a *direct* part of itself, i.e. `p.parts->includes(p)` is possible. The formula below disallows this. It goes even further by forbidding that p is an *indirect* part of itself by using the transitive closure of the operation `parts`, here called `partsClosure: P -> Set(P)`. The term `partsClosure(p)` yields the parts of p, the parts of parts of p and so on. This intuition is reflected by the following "informal" definition.

```
partsClosure(p) =
  parts(p) +
  [ parts(p') | p.parts->includes(p') ] +
  [ parts(p'') | p.parts->includes(p') and
                 p'.parts->includes(p'') ] +
  ...
```

If we want to define the transitive closure formally as in the defintion below, we have to use the iterate function of OCL. The operation `partsClosure` has one parameter, the part whose (sub-)parts we want to calculate, and it returns a set of parts. First, we consider all direct parts of the given part and initiate an iteration over this set with the variable p. In the variable `acc` (which is able to hold a set of parts) we accumulate the result step by step beginning with the direct parts of the given part. If the considered part in the "iteration" variable p is already present in the accumulator `acc`, the accumulator does not change. If the value of p is not already in `acc`, we build the union of the accumulator and the result of the recursive application of `partsClosure` to the value of p.

```
partsClosure(start : P) : Set(P) =
  start.parts->iterate(
    p : P;
    acc : Set(P) = start.parts;
    if acc.includes(p)
      then acc else acc.union(p.partsClosure) endif
  )
```

After having defined the transitive closure of `parts` formally, we can now simply state the requirement that a part cannot contain itself as a part by forbiddding that a part lies in `partsClosure` applied to the part.

```
P->forAll( p | not( p.partsClosure->includes(p) ) )
```

The situation in Fig. 14 is more or less the easy to understand situation where it is syntactically possible that a part can be a part of itself. The situation can be more involved if the reflexivity on the class diagram level is established with some intermediate steps as shown in Fig. 15. But nevertheless, the corresponding definition can be generalized to this case.

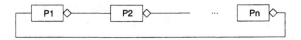

Fig. 15. General Case for Reflexive Association

Fig. 16. Combination of Aggregation and Generalization

Another complication comes into the picture because aggregation and generalization (see below) can interact with each other. As the left side of Fig. 16 shows even if there is no direct reflexive aggregation, due to the syntactic specialities of generalizations, a part could be a part of itself in this context. As indicated in the right side of Fig. 16, if the generalization goes into the "other" direction, this complication does not occur. Through examples following the schema sketched in Fig. 17 we will see that the left side of Fig. 16 is a common situation when one models with both aggregation and generalization.

7.3   Example

The "Paper" Example. The example in Fig. 18 shows one ordinary association, one aggregation, and two compositions. As an example for an ordinary association, we see that a paper can be connected to a conference (for instance, submitted to a conference). The components of a paper are described by aggregation and composition. Thus a paper consists of (1) one or more authors,

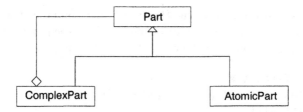

Fig. 17. General Example for Combination of Aggregation and Generalization

(2) exactly one abstract, and (3) one or more sections. The association between a paper and an author is classified as an aggregation, the ones connecting a paper with abstracts and sections as compositions. This means two different papers can share an author, but an abstract and the paper's sections exclusively belong to one paper, thus sharing is not possible. However, a paper has coincident lifetime with its components (authors, abstract, and sections), but a paper can exist without any connection to a conference (and conferences can exist without being connected to a paper). Please note, instance reflexivity is not applicable in this example.

Existential Dependency for the Aggregate: A paper is existentially dependent from its components, i.e. a paper cannot exist without authors, abstract, and sections.

```
Paper->forAll( p |
  Author->exists( au | p.author->includes(au) ) )
Paper->forAll( p |
  Abstract->exists( ab | p.abstract->includes(ab) ) )
Paper->forAll( p |
  Section->exists( s | p.section->includes(s) ) )
```

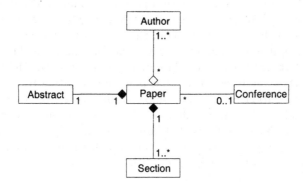

Fig. 18. Example for Ordinary Association, Aggregation, and Composition

Existential Dependency for the Part: A paper component which is classified by composition is existentially dependent from the paper, i.e. an abstract
or a section cannot exist without a corresponding paper.

```
Abstract->forAll( a |
  Paper->exists( p | p.abstract->includes(a) ) )
Section->forAll( s |
  Paper->exists( p | p.section->includes(s) ) )
```

We have taken the same restricting formula inside the existentially quantified
formula for the whole-dependent-from-part and the part-dependent-from-
whole cases because, for example, p.author->includes(au) is equivalent
to au.paper->includes(p).

Forbidding Sharing for Composition: An abstract and a section cannot be
shared by two different papers. In this example the weak and the strong
form of forbidding sharing coincide because neither Abstract nor Section
participate as parts in other compositions.

```
Abstract->forAll( a |
  Paper->exists( p, p' |
    ( p.abstract->includes(a) and p'.abstract->includes(a) )
    implies
    p=p' ) )
Section->forAll( s |
  Paper->exists( p, p' |
    ( p.section->includes(s) and p'.section->includes(s) )
    implies
    p=p' ) )
```

The "Brain" Example. The class diagram in Fig. 19 attempts to show in a
single domain three kinds of relationships: plain association, aggregation, and
composition. Please try to take it with a portion of humor. The diagram shows
the classes Human and Brain. The association KnowsByName reflects that humans
know other humans by name. In general, this association has no special properties. For example, it is not reflexive, symmetric, or transitive. The aggregation
involved is the Fatherhood relationship. In a mental sense, the child can be considered as a part of the father. But what is more interesting from the technical
point of view, the fatherhood relationship (and its transitive closure) is not reflexive, i.e. nobody is the father of himself. The composition Possession shown
between Human and Brain reflects that humans exclusively possess brains: sharing of brains is not possible. We discuss the formalities of the induced formulas
and some object states for the diagram below.

Existential Dependency for Composition: All brains are possessed by humans.

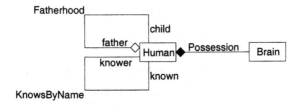

Fig. 19. Brain Example - Class Diagram

```
Brain->forAll( b |
  Human->exists( h | h.brain->includes(b) ) )
```

Forbidding Sharing for Composition: A brain is possessed by only one human.

```
Brain->forAll( b |
  Human->exists( h, h' |
  ( h.brain->includes(b) and h'.brain->includes(b) )
  implies
  h=h' ) )
```

Forbidding Instance Reflexivity for Aggregation: A human cannot be a descendant of herself or himself. For the formalization of this constraint we need the transitive closure of the operation `child: Human -> Set(Human)`. The operation `child` yields all children of a given father, and, in consequence, the operation `childClosure: Human -> Set(Human)` returns for a given father his children plus his children's children and so on. This operation is a derived operation for the class **Human**.

```
Human->forAll( h | not( h.childClosure->includes(h) ) )
```

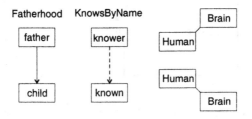

Fig. 20. Brain Example - Object Diagram Conventions

The object diagrams hereafter follow the layout conventions sketched in Fig. 20:
`Fatherhood` links are denoted by solid arrows, `KnowsByName` links by dotted

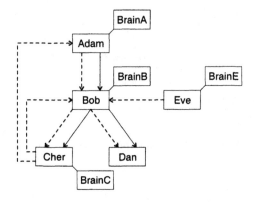

Fig. 21. Brain Example - Valid Object Diagram

arrows, and `Possession` links are visualized by showing the brain object in the upper or lower right diagonal of the corresponding human.

In Fig. 21 we have depicted a *valid* object diagram for the class diagram in Fig. 19. As we see there, if a human has a brain, then it has its own brain, i.e. brain sharing is not possible. However, there are humans without brains, but there are no brains without humans. Two different humans can have the same father, i.e. sharing is possible for `Fatherhood` links. For `KnowsByName` links, arbitrary (even cyclic) connections are allowed.

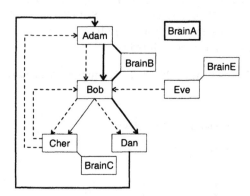

Fig. 22. Brain Example - Invalid Object Diagram

In Fig. 22 we have depicted an *invalid* object diagram for the class diagram in Fig. 19. There are three reasons for this invalidity (in the diagram we have shown the respective parts with thick lines). (1) There is a brain which is not possessed by a human. (2) There is a brain (`brainB`) shared by two humans. (3) There is a cycle (`Adam -> Bob -> Dan -> Adam`) in the `Fatherhood` links. These three items correspond to violations against the three above given constraints (in that order). To yield a valid object diagram, all three violations must be removed.

8 Generalization

8.1 Statements from UML Material

- *Generalization is the taxonomic relationship between a more general element and a more specific element that is fully consistent with the first element and that adds information.* Notation; Semantics.
- *An instance of the more specific element may be used where the more general element is allowed.* Semantics.
- *The following constraints are predefined. Overlapping: A descendent may be descended from more than one of the subclasses. Disjoint: A descendent may not be descendent from more than one of the subclasses. Complete: All subclasses have been specified (...); no additional subclasses are expected. Incomplete: Some subclasses have been specified but the list is known to be incomplete.* Notation.

8.2 General Translation

Simple Generalizations: As shown in Fig. 23, UML generalizations are transformed to special binary associations. The cardinalities make sure that each specialized object is related with exactly one general object, although not necessarily every general object has a link to a special object. In other words, we have a total mapping from special to general objects. An additional constraint assures the injectivity of the mapping, or, in other words, a special object is associated with a unique general object (no two special objects are associated with the same general object). The defining formula employs `rg` as the role name with an induced operation `rg: S -> G`.

```
S->forAll( s, s' | s<>s' implies s.rg<>s'.rg )
```

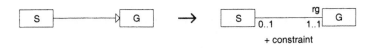

Fig. 23. Equivalence Rule for Generalization

This simple translation for generalizations does even handle type substitutability in the context of subtype polymorphism: Wherever an object of the general class G is expected (for example as an argument of an operation), we can substitute a specialized object of class S after applying the "type cast" rg. For example, if op: boolean is an operation in class G, the expression s.rg.op would be allowed for the S object s.

Disjoint Generalizations: Generalization relationships can further be classified as disjoint or complete. We explain these classifications for the case with two subclasses. The cases with more subclasses can be developed analogously. A disjoint generalization has to partition specialized classes into disjoint sets. We can realize this requirement by demanding that any two special objects from different classes map into different objects in the general class.

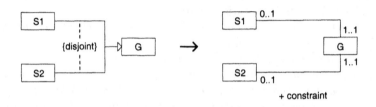

Fig. 24. Equivalence Rule for Disjoint Generalization

```
S1->forAll( s1 | S2->forAll( s2 | s1.g<>s2.g ) )
```

Complete Generalizations: Complete generalizations serve to describe the case that a general class completely covers its subclasses. It is forbidden that there is a general object which is not represented as a special object in one of the special classes.

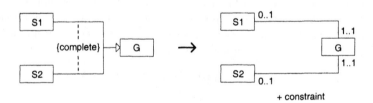

Fig. 25. Equivalence Rule for Complete Generalization

```
G->forAll( g |
  S1->exists( s1 | s1.g=g )
  or
  S2->exists( s2 | s2.g=g )
)
```

Overlapping and Incomplete Generalizations: The other syntactic possibilities, namely overlapping and incomplete generalizations, can be regarded as the default cases which hold when no further classification about the nature of the generalization is made. No constraints have to be given under these circumstances. Overlapping corresponds to "not disjoint" and incomplete (of course) to "not complete". Thus, overlapping does not mean that the respective sets actually must overlap but that they are allowed to do so.

8.3   Example

First, we explain a simple example where vehicles are specialized to cars. Afterwards, we give class diagrams for the four different combinations of disjoint and complete generalizations:

Disjoint	Complete	Example
+	+	Female, Male → Person
+	−	Oak, Elm, Birch → Tree
−	+	LandVehicle, WaterVehicle, AirVehicle → Vehicle
−	−	I-Citizen, F-Citizen → Person

Fig. 26. Example for Generalization

The "Car" Example. The example in Fig. 26 shows a specialization of vehicles to cars. The constraint requires, that two given distinct cars are mapped to distinct vehicles by the "type cast" `vehicle` (the operation induced by the association).

```
Car->forAll( c, c' | c<>c' implies c.vehicle<>c'.vehicle )
```

The "Female/Male" Example. The class diagram in Fig. 27 represents a disjoint and complete classification, i.e. a partitioning, of persons by their sex into female and male persons. First we give the constraint for the disjointness condition and afterwards the formula for the completeness requirement.

```
Female->forAll( f |
  Male->forAll( m | f.person<>m.person ) )

Person->forAll( p |
  Female->exists( f | f.person=p ) or
  Male->exists( m | m.person=p ) )
```

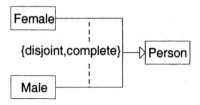

Fig. 27. Example for Disjoint and Complete Generalization

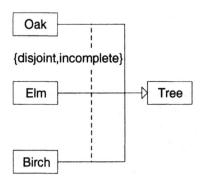

Fig. 28. Example for Disjoint and Incomplete Generalization

The "Oak/Elm/Birch" Example. This example taken from the UML notation guide specializes trees to oaks, elms, and birches. It is a disjoint but incomplete generalization because, for instance, palms are trees but they are not covered by any of the special classes. The constraint formulates the disjointness condition pairwise for each two classes.

```
Oak->forAll( o |
  Elm->forAll( e |
    Birch->forAll( b |
      o.tree<>e.tree and
      o.tree<>b.tree and
      e.tree<>b.tree ) ) )
```

The "Amphibian Vehicle" Example. The example in Fig. 29 is the inevitable amphibian vehicle example. It represents an overlapping and complete generalization. It is overlapping due to the existence of, say, planes who are able to land or water. It is complete because land, air, and water are the only "media" where transportation can take place on earth. The formula requires that each vehicle is also represented as a land, water, or air vehicle.

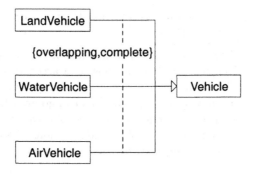

Fig. 29. Example for Overlapping and Complete Generalization

```
Vehicle->forAll( v |
  LandVehicle->exists( l | l.vehicle=v ) or
  WaterVehicle->exists( w | w.vehicle=v ) or
  AirVehicle->exists( a | a.vehicle=v ) )
```

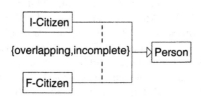

Fig. 30. Example for Overlapping and Incomplete Generalization

The "Citizenship" Example. The example in Fig. 30 describes specializations of class **Person** to Italian and French citizens. No restricting constraint has to be given in this case. The class diagram is overlapping because people are allowed to have both the Italian and the French citizenship. Assuming a "European" context, it is incomplete because, for example, Spanish people are not covered.

9   Conclusion

We have achieved guiding rules for UML designers in order to cope with the UML diagram variety. Our approach can be seen as a way to give semantics to an advanced UML language layer. What remains to be done is to give semantics to the "low-level" UML layer by stating a translation into an abstract model.

Such a model together with a semantics for the UML constraint language OCL has already been worked out [RG98].

We have translated all discussed UML features into n-ary associations with additional constraints. Due to the modeling power of associations and OCL this seems natural, especially because the association concept is a very general one which is able to model many situations. But one can go even further and transform all n-ary associations into an additional class (plus the classes given before) resolving the n-ary association into n binary associations. Thus we have translated all considered class diagram features into binary associations.

References

[BC95]   R. Bourdeau and B. Cheng. A Formal Semantics for Object Model Diagrams. *IEEE Transactions on Software Engineering*, 21(10):799–821, 1995.

[BCV96]   E. Bertino, D. Castelli, and F. Vitale. A Formal Representation for State Diagrams in the OMT Methodology. In K.G. Jeffery, J. Kral, and M. Bartosek, editors, *Proc. Seminar Theory and Practice of Informatics (SOFSEM'96)*, pages 327–341. Springer, Berlin, LNCS 1175, 1996.

[BHH+97]   Ruth Breu, Ursula Hinkel, Christoph Hofmann, Cornel Klein, Barbara Paech, Bernhard Rumpe, and Veronika Thurner. Towards a Formalization of the Unified Modeling Language. In Mehmet Aksit and Satoshi Matsuoka, editors, *Proc. 11th European Conf. Object-Oriented Programming (ECOOP'97)*, pages 344–366. Springer, Berlin, LNCS 1241, 1997.

[BLM97]   J.C. Bicarregui, Kevin Lano, and T.S.E. Maibaum. Objects, Associations and Subsystems: A Hierarchical Approach to Encapsulation. In Mehmet Aksit and Satoshi Matsuoka, editors, *Proc. 11th European Conf. Object-Oriented Programming (ECOOP'97)*, pages 324–343. Springer, Berlin, LNCS 1241, 1997.

[Boo94]   Grady Booch. *Object-Oriented Analysis and Design with Applications*. Benjamin Cummings, Redwood City, 1994.

[Cla99]   Tony Clark. Type checking UML static diagrams. In Robert France and Bernhard Rumpe, editors, *UML'99 - The Unified Modeling Language. Beyond the Standard. Second International Conference, Fort Collins, CO, USA, October 28-30. 1999, Proceedings*, volume 1723 of *LNCS*, pages 503–517. Springer, 1999.

[Ebe97]   Jürgen Ebert. Integration of Z-Based Semantics of OO-Notations. In Haim Kilov and Bernhard Rumpe, editors, *Proc. ECOOP'97 Workshop on Precise Semantics for Object-Oriented Modeling Techniques*. Technische Universität München, Informatik-Bericht TUM-I9725, 1997.

[FBLPS97] R. France, J.M. Bruel, M. Larrondo-Petrie, and M. Shroff. Exploring the Semantics of UML type structures with Z. In H. Bowman and J. Derrick, editors, *Proc. 2nd IFIP Conf. Formal Methods for Open Object-Based Distributed Systems (FMOODS'97)*, pages 247–260. Chapman and Hall, London, 1997.

[GPP98]   Martin Gogolla and Francesco Parisi-Presicee.   State Diagrams in
             UML: A Formal Semantics using Graph Transformations. In Bernhard
             Rumpe, Manfred Broy, Derek Coleman, and Tom S.E. Maibaum, edi-
             tors, *Proc. ICSE'98 Workshop on Precise Semantics of Modeling Tech-
             niques (PSMT'98)*, 1998.
             http://www4.informatik.tu-muenchen.de/~rumpe/icse98-ws/.
[JCJÖ92]   Ivar Jacobsen, Magnus Christerson, Patrik Jonsson, and G.G. Övergaard.
             Object-Oriented Software Engineering. Addison-Wesley, 1992.
[KC99]   Soon-Kyeong Kim and David Carrington.   Formalizing the UML class
             diagram using object-z. In Robert France and Bernhard Rumpe, editors,
             *UML'99 - The Unified Modeling Language. Beyond the Standard. Second
             International Conference, Fort Collins, CO, USA, October 28-30. 1999,
             Proceedings*, volume 1723 of *LNCS*, pages 83–98. Springer, 1999.
[Lan96]   Kevin Lano. Enhancing Object-Oriented Methods with Formal Notations.
             Theory and Practice of Object Systems, 2(4):247–268, 1996.
[OMG99a]   OMG, editor. *Object Constraint Language (Version 1.3)*. OMG, 1999.
             http://www.omg.org.
[OMG99b]   OMG, editor. *UML Notation Guide (Version 1.3)*. OMG, 1999.
             http://www.omg.org.
[OMG99c]   OMG, editor. *UML Semantics (Version 1.3)*. OMG, 1999.
             http://www.omg.org.
[Öov98]   Gunnar Öovergaard. A Formal Approach to Relationships in The Unified
             Modeling Language. In Bernhard Rumpe, Manfred Broy, Derek Coleman,
             and Tom S.E. Maibaum, editors, *Proc. ICSE'98 Workshop on Precise
             Semantics of Modeling Techniques (PSMT'98)*, 1998.
             http://www4.informatik.tu-muenchen.de/~rumpe/icse98-ws/.
[RACH00]   Gianna Reggio, Egidio Astesiano, Christine Choppy, and Heinrich Huss-
             mann. Analysing UML active classes and associated state machines – A
             lightweight formal approach. In Tom Maibaum, editor, *Proc. Fundamen-
             tal Approaches to Software Engineering (FASE 2000), Berlin, Germany*,
             volume 1783 of *LNCS*. Springer, 2000.
[RBP⁺91]   J. Rumbaugh, M. Blaha, W. Premerlani, F. Eddy, and W. Lorensen.
             Object-Oriented Modeling and Design. Prentice Hall, Englewood Cliffs,
             1991.
[RG98]   Mark Richters and Martin Gogolla. On Formalizing the UML Object
             Constraint Language OCL. In Tok-Wang Ling, Sudha Ram, and Mong Li
             Lee, editors, *Proc. 17th Int. Conf. Conceptual Modeling (ER'98)*, pages
             449–464. Springer, Berlin, LNCS 1507, 1998.
[SF97]   M. Shro and R. B. France. Towards a Formalization of UML Class Struc-
             tures in Z. In *Proc. 21st Annual Int. Computer Software and Applications
             Conference (COMPSAC'97)*, pages 646–651. IEEE, 1997.
[TE00]   A. Tsiolakis and H. Ehrig. Consistency analysis of UML class and se-
             quence diagrams using attributed graph grammars. In H. Ehrig and
             G. Taentzer, editors, *Proc. of Joint APPLIGRAPH/GETGRATS Work-
             shop on Graph Transformation Systems, Berlin, March 2000*, 2000. Tech-
             nical Report no. 2000/2, Technical University of Berlin.
[WB98]   Roel Wieringa and Jan Broersen. A minimal transition system semantics
             for lightweight class- and behavior diagrams. In Manfred Broy, Derek
             Coleman, Tom S. E. Maibaum, and Bernhard Rumpe, editors, *Proceed-
             ings PSMT'98 Workshop on Precise Semantics for Modeling Techniques*.
             Technische Universität München, TUM-I9803, 1998.

[WK98]   Jos Warmer and Anneke Kleppe. *The Object Constraint Language: Precise Modeling with UML*. Addison-Wesley, 1998.

[WK99]   Jos Warmer and Anneke Kleppe. OCL: The constraint language of the UML. *Journal of Object-Oriented Programming*, May 1999.

[WRC97]   Enoch Y. Wang, Heather A. Richter, and Betty H. C. Cheng. Formalizing and Integrating the Dynamic Model within OMT. In *Proc. 19th Int. Conf. on Software Engineering (ICSE'97)*, pages 45–55. ACM Press, 1997.

The Amsterdam Manifesto on OCL

Steve Cook[1], Anneke Kleppe[2], Richard Mitchell[3], Bernhard Rumpe[4],
Jos Warmer[5], and Alan Wills[6]

[1] IBM European Object Technology Practice, UK,
http://www.ibm.com/
sj_cook@uk.ibm.com

[2] Klasse Objecten, NL-3762CT Soest, Netherlands,
http://www.klasse.nl/
A.Kleppe@klasse.nl

[3] University of Brighton, Brighton BN2 4GJ, UK,
http://www.it.brighton.ac.uk/staff/rjm4/
Richard.Mitchell@brighton.ac.uk

[4] Technische Universität München, Institut für Informatik, 80290 München,
http://www.in.tum.de/~rumpe/
Bernhard.Rumpe@in.tum.de

[5] Klasse Objecten, NL-3762CT Soest, Netherlands,
http://www.klasse.nl/
J.Warmer@klasse.nl

[6] TriReme International, Manchester, UK,
http://www.trireme.com/
alan@trireme.com

Abstract. In November 1998 the authors participated in a two-day workshop on the Object Constraint Language (OCL) in Amsterdam. The focus was to clarify issues about the semantics and the use of OCL, and to discuss useful and necessary extensions of OCL. Various topics have been raised and clarified. This manifesto contains the results of that workshop and the following work on these topics. Overview of OCL.

1 Overview of OCL

The Object Constraint Language (OCL) is a textual specification language, designed especially for the use in the context of diagrammatic specification languages such as the UML [Booch98]. The UML offers several kinds of diagrams, dedicated to describe different aspects of a system, such as structure, interaction, state based

A. Clark and J. Warmer (Eds.): Object Modeling with the OCL, LNCS 2263, pp. 115-149, 2002.
© Springer-Verlag Berlin Heidelberg 2002

behaviour or deployment. However, when regarding the UML diagrams as a language, it turns out that the diagram-based UML is limited in its expressiveness. Although the UML is powerful and covers many important situations, it is often not sufficient to describe certain important constraints. Using natural language on the one hand introduces freedom of misinterpretations and on the other hand gives tools no chance to cope with it.

Therefore the Object Constraint Language was introduced as a textual add-on to the UML diagrams. OCL is deeply connected to UML diagrams, as it is used as textual addendum within the diagrams, e.g. to define pre- and postconditions, invariants, or transition guards, but also uses the elements defined in the UML diagrams, such as classes, methods and attributes. The following example taken from the Journal of Object-Oriented Programming [Warmer99b] shows some important features of the OCL and how to apply them in class diagrams.

1.1   Example of the Use of Constraints

In this article we will use the example class diagram from Figure 1. It shows a model of a hotel. The hotel has a number of rooms that can be rented by guests. There are also a number of bathrooms, which are either connected to a specific room, or are used to service multiple rooms on the floor. The modelled hotel has a number of business rules that are very common to hotels:

- The number of guests in each room doesn't exceed the number of beds in the room.

- The hotel allows one extra bed for a child of up to 4 years old per room.

- All guests in each room need are officially registered in the hotel.

- The bathroom connected to a room may only be used by guests of that room.

- Bathrooms not connected to a room may only be used by guests of rooms on the same floor.

Examining the example class diagram, we find that many of the common business rules for hotels can not or at least not easily be expressed in the diagram. We will show in the following how to express these business rules as OCL constraints on the class diagram. This will keep the diagram simple and easy to understand while adding details to the model under construction.

Using the size property on a collection also allow us to describe the first business rule as an invariant constraint on the association from Room to Guest. There can be no more guests in a room than there are beds (business rule number 1).

```
context Room invariant:
guests->size <= numberOfBeds
```

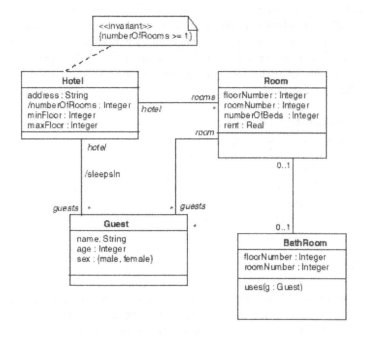

Fig. 1. Example class diagram

This kind of constraint on the multiplicity of an association occurs quite often in practice. The UML class model specifies multiplicity 'zero to many' in cases where the actual upper (or lower) bound of the multiplicity is not known beforehand, but depends on the value of an attribute of an object at runtime.

The *exists* operation evaluates to true if the argument expression evaluates to true for at least one element in the collection. Using this we can rewrite the constraint stated above about the number of guests allowed in a room. The hotel in the example allows for an extra bed for a child of four years at most (business rule number 2). Therefore the constraint given above must be adjusted to:

```
context Room invariant:
guests->size <= numberOfBeds or
( guests->size = numberOfBeds + 1 and
   guests->exists(g : Guest | g.age <= 4)
)
```

The *collect* operation results in a new collection. The elements of the resulting collection are the values of the argument expression for each element in the original collection. An example of an invariant using *collect* is shown for Hotel. This constraint expresses our business rule number 3:

```
context Hotel invariant:
guests = rooms->collect(guests)->asSet
```

For the hotel in the example the business rules have been established that a guest can only use a bathroom when it is either attached to his/her room, or when it is not attached to a room and located on the same floor as his/her room (number 4 and 5). These business rules are specified in the precondition of the operation *uses* of Bathroom. The number of uses is counted in attribute *usage* (that we deliberately omitted in the class diagram):

```
context Bathroom::uses(g : Guest)
pre: if room->notEmpty then
          room.guests->includes(g)
     else
          g.room.floorNumber = self.floorNumber
     endif
post: usage = usage@pre + 1
```

1.2   Status of OCL

OCL has syntactic similarities to Smalltalk (amongst others [Lalonde90]). OCL could also be given a Java/C++-like syntactic flavour without affecting the usefulness of OCL. Syntactic flavour is to a large extent a matter of taste. However, more important are the concepts within the language. Here we name the most important features of OCL. Please, be reminded that this manifesto is not an introduction to OCL, this can be found e.g. in [Warmer99a]:

- Tight integration with the UML notation
- Pure specification language without operational elements
- Basic types like Boolean, Integer, Float
- Container types Collection, Bag, Sequence, and Sets with appropriate operators
- The full typesystem also includes the types induced by class definitions within UML
- Navigation expressions to navigate along associations with various multiplicities
- Boolean operators to allow full propositional logic
- Existential and universal quantifiers over existing sets of objects
- Specifications are (to a large extent) executable and can therefore be used as assertions when animating the UML diagrams or generating code

OCL is a specification language that tries to mediate between the practical users needs and the theoretical work that has been done in that area. In particular much of the theoretical work was done in the areas of algebraic specification languages, such as Spectrum [Broy93-1, Broy93-2], CIP [Bauer85], ACT ONE [Ehrig85], ACT TWO

[Ehrig90], TROLL [Conrad92, Hartmann94, Jungclaus91], logic systems such as HOL [Gordon93, Paulson94], LCF [Gordon79, Regensburger94]. Other theoretical work worth mentioning is on model based specification techniques such as Z [Spivey88, Spivey89] and VDM [Jones90], functional programming languages such as Gofer [Jones93], Haskell [Hudak92] and ML [Paulson91], object-oriented methods such as Syntropy [Cook94], and also the data base query languages such as SQL [Date87].

The best ideas from these areas, such as navigation expressions or container types as abstract data types, have been taken and combined into a language that is dedicated to software engineers. OCL does not only have a syntax similar to Smalltalk, but also provides expressive operator names to increase readability of OCL constraints.

The current status of OCL is as follows:

The official OCL specification in version 1.3 has been published by the OMG together with the UML specification in version 1.3.

Parsers for OCL specifications, written in Java are available at:

http://www.software.ibm.com/ad/ocl
http://www.db.informatik.uni-bremen.de/umlbib/
http://www-st.inf.tu-dresden.de/UMLToolset/

A comprehensive list of publications can also be found at http://www.uni-bremen.de/umlbib/.

In [Rumpe98] we have discussed that there exist several degrees of formality of a notation. If the syntactic shape of a notation is precisely defined, e.g. for OCL a grammar is given, then the syntax is formalised. However, based on the syntax the meaning of the notation has still to be defined.

OCL does currently not have a formally defined meaning and can therefore only be regarded as semi-formal. Due to the tight connection of OCL with the UML diagrams, the definition of a formal semantics for OCL must be based on a formal semantics for the UML. This is a difficult task.

1.3   Contents of This Paper

The manifesto documents the results of a two-day workshop held in Amsterdam discussing various topics and issues of the OCL. The results have been classified roughly in four groups: bug fixes; clarifications; extensions; applications. Some of the issues discussed below do not fall clearly into one of these categories, but belong to several groups. E.g. it is sometimes necessary to propose an extension in order to fix a bug in the language. The following four chapters are structured along this four groups. Each discussed topic corresponds to one section.

2   Bug Fixes of the Language

2.1   Remove Direct Type

In UML 1.1 the standard operation "oclType" would result in the type of an object. Because objects can have multiple types, this operation was ill defined. In UML 1.3 this operation has been removed. The operations "oclIsTypeOf" and "oclIsKindOf" can be used instead.

2.2   Adaptation of OclAny

OCL provides a special type, called "OclAny". This type is meant to be a common supertype of all types. The specification of OclAny in the UML 1.1 and 1.2 definitions was inconsistent. It includes the basic types, such as Boolean, types defined in UML diagrams, like Flight, and collection types, like Set(Flight). In particular Set(OclAny) is again a type included in OclAny. Although, there are type systems dealing with such a situation, these type systems are rather complex. Also for practical purposes this complication is not necessary.

To remedy this situation, the type OclAny was adapted in UML 1.3 to include only the basic types of OCL and the types defined within the UML diagrams. In particular, none of the collection types, e.g. Set(Flight) or Sequence(Boolean), are subtypes of OclAny. It is still possible to build and work with Set(OclAny), but this type is not included in OclAny. Please note, that there is also no inclusion in the other direction, although elements of OclAny could be regarded as one element sets, bags, or sequences as in OBJ [Goguen92].

The adaptation of OclAny leads to an improved and simplified type system. Using this fix of the type system and ignoring the two meta-types OclExpression and OclType, we get a strong type system in the sense, that type checking can be done within the parser.

2.3   "allInstances" Considered Dangerous

The definition of "allInstances" is problematic. It is unclear in what context all instances should be taken. It is much better style and much clearer to make sure that any collection of objects is only reached by navigation.

The following paragraph has been added to the UML 1.3 OCL specification to warn users of the potential pitfalls of using allInstances. The future use of OCL will show, whether this is sufficient or a more relased use e.g. of Integer. allInstances will be needed.

From theory we know that only the use of the existential and universal quantifier over infinte sets, like Integers, make a logic language first order, otherwise it is a propositional logic only.

NB: The use of `allInstances` has some problems and its use is discouraged in most cases. The first problem is best explained by looking at the types like Integer, Real and String. For these types the meaning of `allInstances` is undefined. What does it mean for an Integer to exist? The evaluation of the expression `Integer.allInstances` results in an infinite set and is therefore undefined within OCL. The second problem with `allInstances` is that the existence of objects must be considered within some overall context, like a system or a model. This overall context must be defined, which is not done within OCL. A recommended style is to model the overall contextual system explicitly as an object within the system and navigate from that object to its associated instances without using `allInstances`.

3   Clarifications of the Syntax and Semantics of OCL

3.1   Introduction to the Boolean Operators and Undefined Expressions in OCL

OCL provides the following operators with Boolean arguments and/or results:
=, not, and, or, xor, implies, if-expression.
This section presents informal definitions of the operators, aimed at users of OCL. The definitions are intended for incorporation into the next release of the definition of OCL. It in fact turns out that also the given definitions are intended to give an intuitive explanation, the characterisation of an operation through truth-tables and through reduction to known operations, as used below, is a fully precise definition.
The definitions are presented in two parts. First, the meanings of the operators are given using truth tables and equations. Then there is a short discussion of the use of Boolean operators within OCL constraints.
In UML, and hence in OCL, the type Boolean is an enumeration whose values are "false" and "true", and a Boolean expression is one that evaluates to a Boolean value. In what follows, b, b1 and b2 are expressions of type Boolean.

3.1.1   The = Operator

Two Boolean expressions are equal if they have the same value. The following table defines the equality operator. Thus equality can be used, for instance, to denote the equivalence of two properties.

b1	b2	b1 = b2
false	false	true
false	true	false
true	false	false
true	true	true

3.1.2   The NOT Operator

The not operator is defined by

b	not b
true	false
false	true

the following table.

3.1.3   The AND Operator

The and operator is commutative, so that

(b1 and b2) = (b2 and b1)

It is defined by the following two equations.

(false and b) = false
(true and b) = b

Applying the above commutativity rule to the equations, we get:

(b and false) = false
(b and true) = b

and therefore the following table holds:

b1	b2	b1 and b2
false	false	false
false	true	false
true	false	false
true	true	true

3.1.4.   The OR Operator

The or operator is also commutative, so that

(b1 or b2) = (b2 or b1)

It is defined by the following two equations.

(false or b) = b
(true or b) = true

Once again, it is possible to apply the commutativity rule to the defining equations to produce two more equations:

(b or false) = b
(b or true) = true

and a truth table:

b1	b2	b1 or b2
false	false	false
false	true	true
true	false	true
true	true	true

3.1.5   The XOR Operator

The xor operator ("exclusive or") holds if exactly one of its arguments holds. It is therefore similar to the or operator, but excludes the case that both arguments are true. The xor operator is commutative, so that

(b1 xor b2) = (b2 xor b1)

It is defined in terms of the and, or and not operators.

(b1 xor b2) = ((b1 or b2) and not (b1 and b2))

3.1.6   The IMPLIES Operator

The implies operator allows us to formalise statements of the following kind:
"if b1 is true then b2 must also be true (but if b1 is false we don't say anything about b2)".
Such a statement can be formalised by the OCL expression

b1 implies b2

which constrains b2 to be true whenever b1 is true. The implies operator is defined by the following equations:

(false implies b) = true
(true implies b) = b

It follows that the expression "b1 implies b2" can be false exactly if b1 is true and b2 is false.

3.1.7   The IF-Expression

An if-expression takes the form

if b then e1 else e2 endif

in which b is a Boolean expression and e1 and e2 are OCL expressions of compatible types. If b is true, the value of the whole expression is e1. If b is false, the value of the whole expression is e2.

In contrast to an if statement in procedural languages, an if expression has a value. Therefore the else clause is always necessary. The resulting type of the if-expression is the least type T such that the types of both argument expressions e1 and e2 conform to that type. (See also the type conformance rules of OCL). However, if multiple inheritance is allowed, there need not be one least type T (but more such types). In this case a typechecker needs help through explicit type information for the arguments or the result.

Here is a small example. Assume that count is an integer variable and x is a real variable. The literals 100 and 0 are Integers. The if-expression

> if (count <= 100) then x/2 else 0 endif

has type real (because e1 and e2 are of type real and integer, respectively, and integer conforms to real). The value of the whole expression is (x/2) if (count<=100). The value of the whole expression is the real number 0 if (count>100).

3.1.8   Boolean Operators and Undefined Expressions

The meanings of the Boolean operators have been presented in the preceding subsections. The meanings have been chosen to support the intuitions of those who write and read OCL constraints. Sometimes it is necessary to write expressions of the form

> "if b1 is true, b2 should also be true"

even though we know that "b2" has no meaning when "b1" is false.

Here is an example, based on a fragment of a model of a library system, which has two associations between class Title and class Reservation.

Title	1	*	Reservation
		allReservations	
			madeOn : Timestamp
	0..1	0..1	pending : Boolean
		oldestPending	

To reserve a title means to put in a request to borrow any copy with that title. A reservation object is created as part of the act of reserving a title. If one or more of the reservations for a particular title is pending then there must be an "oldestPending", which is the reservation that is next in line to be satisfied when a copy with the right title becomes available. (If there are no pending reservations, there is no "oldestPending" reservation, and "allReservations" captures only historical information.)

There is also a Timestamp class, and we are interested in one of its methods.

Timestamp
notAfter(other : Timestamp) : Boolean

The "notAfter" query returns true if the receiver is a timestamp that is at the same time as, or earlier than, the "other" timestamp.

Here is an invariant to define the intended meaning of the "oldestPending" association. The OCL definition includes a comment to explain the formal part.

```
context t: Title invariant:
  t.allReservations->select(pending)->isEmpty implies
      t.oldestPending->isEmpty
and
  t.allReservations->select(pending)->notEmpty implies
      ( t.oldestPending->notEmpty and
          t.allReservations->select(pending)->forall(   r
|
              t.oldestPending.madeOn.notAfter(r) ) )
-- In the context of a title t
--    if there are no pending reservations for t (check
by selecting
--    the pending ones and seeing if the resulting set
is empty) then
--        there is no oldest pending reservation
-- and
--    if there are some pending reservations for t then
--        there must be an oldest pending and
--            for all reservations, r, that are pending
for t,
--                the timestamp showing when the oldest
pending
--                reservation was made is NOT after the
timestamp of r
```

More loosely, the invariant says that, if there are some pending reservations, there must be an oldest one, and this oldest one has the property that there is not an even older one. The specification intentionally doesn't say which is the oldest pending reservation out of two with equal time stamps.

The example was chosen to illustrate how the definitions of the Boolean operators avoid a problem with expressions that have no defined meaning.

In the very last line of the formal version of the invariant, what does the subexpression "t.oldestPending" mean when there are no pending reservations? The intuition behind the formal specification is that, when there are no pending reservations, there is no "oldest pending" reservation, so the question is irrelevant. To support this intuition, the "implies" operator is defined so that "a implies b" is true whenever "a" is false - we do not need to examine "b".

However, the formal logic underpinning OCL does assign a "virtual value" to "b". This value is neither true nor false, but represents "undefined". As a consequence the Boolean type does have three values, "true", "false", and "undefined" and the Boolean operations need to be defined on "undefined" as well. Fortunately, we can use this special value to describe the desired behaviour of our operations. We e.g. can define that "false implies undefined" is true (the formal logic is known as Kleene logic). Please note, that the value "undefined" was an invention of semantics modellers (formalists) to get their understanding of the semantics of a logic like OCL right. The technique of introducing virtual values was very successful, and is nowadays often used to model certain situations, like "nil" models the absence of an object to navigate to.

As the example concerning reservations illustrates, modellers usually do not need to consider "undefined" values explicitly. They model them out by carefully exploiting definitions such as "false implies b is true, for any expression b that has type Boolean". As a result, most of the time, modellers can choose freely to work with any one of these three informal pictures of what Boolean expressions mean when they have subexpressions that cannot be given a value.

One interpretation of this situation is operational: operators such as "and" and "implies" are evaluated by a process that stops as soon as the answer is knowable (for example, when either of b1 or b2 in "b1 and b2" is found to be false).

Boolean expressions can have the values false, true or undefined, and the rules for evaluating the operators take care of undefined values by including such rules as "false and undefined = false"

In another yet consistent interpretation all Boolean expressions are either true or false, but, because the modeller has (deliberately) under-specified an expression, it might not be possible to determine which. However, rules such as "false and b = false" mean that, even if "b" is underspecified, so that its value is not known, the value of "false and b" is still known (its value is false).

When a modeller does need full, formal definitions of the Boolean operators, for example, to construct formal proofs, such definitions are available.

3.2   Precise Definition of the Boolean Operators on the Undefined Value

Based on the introduction to the Boolean operators in OCL, we in this section present the plain, precise facts. We describe the effect of the operators

=, not, and, or, xor, implies, if-expression

through truth tables and present some of the laws that still hold. The presented logic is called 3-valued logic in [Kleene52], and therefore often also called Kleene Logic.

3.2.1   The = Operator

First of all, it should be clarified, what equality on undefined values means. There are basically two version of equality. The so called "strong equality" and the "weak equality". Strong equality is capable of comparing undefined values. In particular the last line of the table allows us to check in the specification whether a value is undefined.

b1	b2	b1 = b2
false	false	true
false	true	false
true	false	false
true	true	true
undefined	true	false
undefined	false	false
true	undefined	false
false	undefined	false
undefined	undefined	true

Unfortunately the strong equality cannot be implemented. In an implementation instead a weak or strict equality must be used. This is why specification languages normally in addition introduce a weak equality (e.g. named as "==") with the following properties:

b1	b2	b1 == b2
false	false	true
false	true	false
true	false	false
true	true	true
undefined	true	undefined
undefined	false	undefined
true	undefined	undefined
false	undefined	undefined
undefined	undefined	undefined

Fortunately both versions fulfil the equality law:

b1 = b2   is equal to   b2 = b1

b1 == b2   is equal to   b2 == b1

Please note that the strong equality is defined for the undefined values in all other types as well. Eg. "1/0 = sqr(-1)" yields "true" as both sides are equal to the undefined value of type Real.

Currently OCL does not have both versions of equality. The strong equality is important to deal with undefined values (e.g. to describe that a certain value is not undefined). In contrast, weak equality can be defined like a normal function. So we choose "=" to be the strong equality.

3.2.2   The NOT Operator

b	not b
true	false
false	true
undefined	undefined

It remains valid that:

not not b=b

3.2.3   The AND Operator

b1	b2	b1 and b2
false	false	false
false	true	false
false	undefined	false
true	false	false
true	true	true
true	undefined	undefined
undefined	false	false
undefined	true	undefined
undefined	undefined	undefined

Some basic laws for the and operator:

commutative:	(b1 and b2)	=	(b2 and b1)
associative:	((b1 and b2) and b3)	=	(b1 and (b2 and b3))
false is dominant:	(b and false)	= false	=(false and b)
true is neutral:	(b and true)	= b =	(true and b)
idempotence:	(b and b)	=	b

Note that although the and operator sometimes returns undefined values on undefined arguments, this operator can be implemented. However, both arguments need to be evaluated in parallel until the first return the value false.

3.2.4   The OR Operator

b1	b2	b1 or b2
false	false	false
false	true	true
false	undefined	undefined
true	false	true
true	true	true
true	undefined	true
undefined	false	undefined
undefined	true	true
undefined	undefined	undefined

Some basic laws for the or operator:

commutative: (b1 or b2)		=		(b2 or b1)
associative: ((b1 or b2) or b3)		=		(b1 or (b2 or b3))
true is dominant:	(b or true)	= true	=	(true or b)
false is neutral:	(b or false)	= b =		(false or b)
idempotence: (b or b)		=		b

3.2.5   The XOR Operator

The xor operator ("exclusive or") holds if exactly one of its arguments holds. It is therefore similar to the or operator, but excludes the case that both arguments are true. Therefore the xor operator relies more on the values of its arguments:

The xor operator is defined in terms of the and, or and not operators.

(b1 xor b2)   =   ((b1 or b2) and not (b1 and b2))

From this definition, we derive the following truth table:

b1	b2	b1 xor b2
false	false	false
false	true	true
false	undefined	undefined
true	false	true
true	true	false
true	undefined	undefined
undefined	false	undefined
undefined	true	undefined
undefined	undefined	undefined

Some basic laws for the xor operator:

commutative:	(b1 xor b2)	=	(b2 xor b1)
associative:	((b1 xor b2) xor b3)	=	(b1 xor (b2 xor b3))

3.2.6   The IMPLIES Operator

The implies operator is defined in terms of the and, or and not operators.
   (b1 implies b2)   =   ((not b1) or b2)

b1	b2	b1 implies b2
false	false	true
false	true	true
false	undefined	true
true	false	false
true	true	true
true	undefined	undefined
undefined	false	undefined
undefined	true	true
undefined	undefined	undefined

Some basic laws for the implies operator:

   (b1 implies (b2 implies b3))   =   ((b1 and b2) implies b3)

The implies operation has a lot of uses. E.g. the actual postcondition of a method is given by "pre implies post", provided that "pre" and "post" are the explicitly given conditions. Unfortunately the standard rule (b implies b) = true does not hold for b = undefined.

Please note that there exists no symmetric equivalent "<=>" or "bi-implies" in OCL. Instead the strong equality "=" must be used to describe that two Boolean expressions are equal. This is a bit awkward because "=" has a higher precedence than "<=>" would have. Therefore in the above laws we needed to set a number of extra brackets.

3.2.7   The IF-Expression

The if expression can be charactericed by the following three equations:

if true then x else y endif	=	x
if false then x else y endif	=	y
if undefined then x else y endif	=	undefined

resembling exactly the standard if-then-else-semantics. A law for the if then else:

if b1 then x else y endif	=	if (not b) then y else x endif

3.3   Clarify the Meaning of Recursive Definitions

Recursion always occurs if an element refers to its own definition while being defined. Functions and methods can be recursive. Famous examples are the factorial function:

fac(n) = if (n==1) then return(1) else return(n* **fac**(n-1));

Or list traversals as e.g. used in container classes:

list.**length**() = if (list.elem==NIL) then return(0) else return 1 + **length**(list.next);
But structures may also be recursive, for example by including an attribute in a class that refers to the class itself (used in list implementations) or to a superclass (used in part-whole-structures). Also OCL constraints may use recursive definitions, like the following:

```
context Person invariant:
ancestors = parents->union(parents.ancestors)
```

Which is defined in the context of the following class:

Person
parents: Set(Person) ancestors: Set(Person)

In the above constraint ancestors is meant to be the transitive closure of the relation defined by parents. Reading the constraint as a functional program, then we actually have defined what we wanted to.

When dealing with recursive specifications instead of programs, then there are typically more than one solutions. This can be easily seen regarding the OCL constraint

$$a = a*a - 4*a + 6$$

This is not a valid mathematical definition for a, but a binomial equation with two solutions (a=2 or a=3). Both are valid and none is preferable. The same situation arises with the ancestors. Let's look at the following object structure, where Joe is Mary's dad and Pete's grandpa:

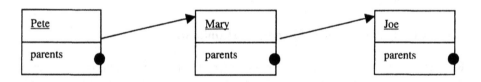

The desired solution is covered by the following object structure (disregarding the parents attribute):

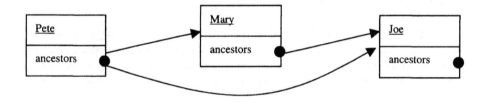

But there are more solutions to the ancestor constraint as shown in the following object structure:

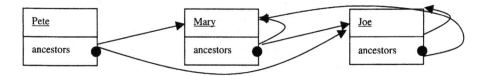

It demands that Mary and Joe are both ancestors of each other and themselves. Through checking the constraint on the ancestors attribute, we find that both shown object diagrams are valid structures. And there are a lot more.

Fortunately, there is a unique characterisation of all possible object structures that furthermore distinguishes one solution from all others. The first object structure shown, is contained in all others, in the sense that each solution must contain at least the link from Pete to Mary, from Pete to Joe and from Mary to Joe. This solution is "minimal" and therefore corresponds to the "minimal fixpoint" and is identical to what we get, if "executing" the ancestor definition as if it would be a program.

Unfortunately, such a minimal solution does not always exist, sometimes there are several ones, sometimes none at all. Even worse, it may be difficult to find out, whether a recursive definition has a unique solution. For example the equation about "a" from above does have two solutions, but none of it can be preferred in the domain-theoretic sense. This is also reflected, if you try to "execute" the equation, by iterative application. The sequence

$$a_{n+1} = a_n * a_n - 4 * a_n + 6$$

starting with, say $a_n = 0$, leads to a limit of $+\infty$ and therefore no solution at all.

It may, furthermore, happen that the modeller does not want to get the minimal solution. Consider a specification, where Person stands for computer nodes, "parents" is replaced by "TCP-connection" and "ancestors" is the transitive closure of all "connections", describing to whom a connection can be made. Then the constraint tells us, that connection includes all TCP-connection, but other kinds of connections may exist, that want to add connections later.

By the way, these considerations have been explored fully with the fixpoint theory. Fixpoint techniques, like the one provided by Kleene [Kleene52] and Tarski [Tarsky55] give an unambiguously defined semantics for recursive definitions. If fixpoint theory is familiar, then you know about the results discussed above. If not, then just accept the results presented here, as you probably don't want to bother with the technical issues here. From first order logic languages, we know how to deal with that situation. There are two approaches possible, both have their merits and problems.

One approach is to use "loose semantics": Only the constraints are valid that are explicitly given or can be derived from given constraints. No implicit "minimal solution" semantics is used, when recursive equations occur. If a minimal solution is desired, a special keyword or stereotype is to be added to the constraint. The keyword could be "executable" or "operational" to give a hint to the operational semantics of recursive definition.

Another approach is to use the minimal solution as default and provide a keyword, like "loose" to indicate that any solution is possible.

Although the first approach is somewhat cleaner, as it does not add implicit constraints, the second one is probably more practical. A solution can be to include both kinds of keywords to allow to explicitly mark which kind of semantics is to be used.

Some technical remarks on recursion. Recursion can be more complicated through involvement of several elements, like in

```
context Person invariant:
grandancestors = parents.ancestors;
ancestors = parents->union(grandancestors)
```

where the recursion is mutually dependent between ancestors and grandancestors, but not direct. But the standard keywords can be extended to such cases.

The nature of first order logic languages does not allow to uniquely characterise a minimal solution. This is only possible by adding second order principles, such as induction or term generation of the specified elements. Usually introducing special keywords (like the ones proposed above) provides such principles. Although we recommend not to use the technique (see Sec. 2.3) we can use the built in OCL Integers and their induction principle built in and therefore provides the necessary techniques. It is a bit awkward, but the minimal solution can be specified through using natural numbers and explicitly mimicking induction over natural number n:

```
Person
parents: Set(Person)
_____
ancestors: Set(Person)
ancestors-up-to(n:Nat): Set(Person)
```

```
context Person invariant:
ancestors-up-to(n) =
    if (n==1) then parents else
        parents->union(parents.ancestors-up-to(n-1))
Integer->forall(n | ancestors-up-to(n) = ancestors-up-
to(n+1) and n>=1
    implies ancestors = ancestors-up-to(n) )
```

The use of an appropriate keyword is absolutely preferred.

From our experience using OCL for specification, we found that recursive situations frequently occur. Particular sources are recursive data structures (lists, containers, part-wholes, directory structures, hierarchical, and graph-containing structures). Usually recursion of OCL constraints is accompanied with the existence of an association circle in the class diagrams. When one or several associations form a circle, building paths through them can lead to recursive structures.

3.4   Use Path Concept Only for Packages

The UML and OCL specification uses a double colon "::" to denote pathnames. This is used e.g. for denoting Classes in other packages as with "Packagename:: Classname". The same construct has been used in OCL to denote the use of a redefined feature. Because this uses the same notation for something else than a pathname, it was considered to make the specification less consistent.

In UML 1.3 the use of "::" to access redefined features has been removed. Instead, one has to use the "oclAsType" operation to cast an object to its supertype and then access the redefined feature.

3.5   Other Subjects That Should Be Clarified

During our meeting we discussed other subjects in the OCL standard that needed clarification. However, up to September 1999 we did not have the opportunity to discuss them further and include a clarification in this manifesto. The subjects were:

- Explain navigation paths like "a.b.c" without flattening
- Precisely define the scope of invariants
- Type expressions in OCL
- Extensions to OCL to make it more useful

3.6   New Operator "oclIsNew" for Postconditions

3.6.1   Rationale:

One of the most common ways to denote the existence of new objects was the use of "allInstances". Because this operation is not well-defined (see section 2.3) there should be another way to denote that an instance has been created. The operation "oclIsNew" has been added to the OclAny type for this purpose.

3.6.2   Syntax:

The syntax of "oclIsNew" in UML 1.3 is as follows:

```
object.oclIsNew : Boolean
```

3.6.3   Semantics:

In UML 1.3 the operation "oclIsNew" can only be used in a post condition. It evaluates to true if the *object* is created during performing the operation. I.e. it didn't exist at precondition time.

3.7   New Operator "isUnique"

3.7.1   Rationale:

In practice one often wants to ensure that the value of an attribute of an object is unique within a collection of objects. The isUnique operation gives the modeller the means to state this fact. This operator is now part of the OCL 1.3.

3.7.2   Syntax:

```
collection->isUnique(expr : OclExpression) : Boolean
```

3.7.3   Semantics:

The isUnique operation returns true if "expr" evaluates to a different value for each element in the collection, otherwise the result is false.
More formally:

```
collection->isUnique(expr : OclExpression)
```

is identical to

```
collection->forAll(e1, e2| if e1 <>e2 then e1.expr <>
e2.expr)
```

3.7.4   Example Usage:

```
context LoyaltyProgram invariant:
serviceLevel->isUnique(name)
```

3.8   Add a "let" Statement to Define Local Variables and Functions

3.8.1   Rationale:

For larger constraints it is cumbersome and error prone to repeat identical sub expressions. The possibility to define a local variable within a constraint solves this problem.
Sometimes a sub-expression is used more than once in a constraint. The `let` expression allows one to define a variable, which can be used in the constraint.

3.8.2   Syntax:

The syntax of a Let expression is exemplified as follows:

```
context Person invariant:
let income : Integer = self.job.salary->sum in
if isUnemployed then
    income < 100
else
    income >= 100
endif
```

3.8.3   Semantics:

The variable defined in a let statement can be used within the OCL expression. The value of the expression is substituted for the variable. Because semantically nothing can change during evaluation of a constraint, it is not necessary to define whether the expression at the left hand side is evaluated once at the start, or at each occurrence in the OCL expression.

3.9   Introduce a Read-Only Modifier for Attributes[1]

3.9.1   Rationale

In current UML, attributes are either public, protected, or private. These modifiers constrain visibility of attributes to foreign classes, subclasses and to other methods of the same class. Whenever an attribute is visible, it can be both read and changed. Sometimes, it is useful to constrain the visibility to be readable, but not changeable. For example, current time, a counter, or a reference to certain objects could be read-

---

[1] Note, that this is actually a proposal for extending UML.

only to the environment, but writable to the own methods. Currently such values must be private and used through (rather expensive) method access. We therefore introduce the concept of a read-only-modifier in combination with private and protected.

3.9.2   Syntax

public read attributename
public read   protected write attributename
protected read attributename

3.9.3   Semantics

In addition to the existing three modifiers, we introduce the above given modifier combinations with the following meaning:

public read	read access is public, write is private (!)
public read protected write	read access is public, write is protected
protected read	read access is protected, write is private

Write access is always at least as constrained as read access. The three variants, where the write access is more constrained than the read access, are covered above. Shortcuts, like "pubread", "protread" and "protwrite" are possible, but not very elegant.

3.9.4   Example Usage:

Person
public read parents: Set(Person)
protected read ancestors: Set(Person)

3.10   Constant Declarations for Object Properties

3.10.1   Rationale

Some properties of objects never change. Marking them to show this allows for some additional checking, e.g. such properties can never be mentioned as changing in a postcondition, and also allows for more reasoning to be done over the object model.

3.10.2   Syntax

```
context object invariant:
constant <attribute>
constant <query()>
constant <rolename>
```

3.10.3   Semantics

Where an attribute or query has been declared as constant, no postcondition can be specified which implies any change to the value of that attribute or query, unless the postcondition also states that the object to which that attribute or query is applied is new.

Where an association end (role name) has been declared as constant, no postcondition can be specified which implies any change to the collection of objects denoted by that role name, unless the postcondition also states that the object to which that role name is applied is new.

Note that this declaration relates to the attribute 'changeability' of StructuralFeature (superclass of Attribute), where one of the values is *frozen*. The class AssociationEnd (rolename) has the same attribute in the UML metamodel, but Operation (query) is lacking this attribute.

3.10.4   Example Usage

```
context Customer invariant:
constant dateOfBirth
```

3.11   Enhance the Abilities to Define Context of OCL Specifications

Expressions written in Object Constraint Language (OCL) within a UML model assume a context, depending upon where they are written. In UML 1.3 the exact nature of this context is not fully defined. Furthermore there is no mechanism for defining the context for OCL expressions in extensions to UML. In a separate paper [Cook99a] the context of OCL expressions is defined and a precise and flexible mechanisms for how to specify this context is proposed.

3.12   Other Extensions That Were Discussed

During our meeting other extensions and improvements were discussed:
- Useful syntactic abbreviations for existing constructs
- Add "effect" definitions (from Catalysis) for postconditions

4 Application of OCL

The following issues demonstrate different uses and extensions of OCL towards increasing its expressiveness. These are just suggestions whose value needs to be carefully examined and the proposed concepts improved accordingly.

4.1   Using OCL to Define Events, Operations, and Actions

4.1.1   Background and Rationale

UML/OCL allows us to specify operations using preconditions and postconditions. Catalysis introduces the idea of joint actions. A key difference between operations and joint actions is that operations are *localised* on a single type, whereas joint actions are joint over two or more types. UML/OCL should explicitly embrace joint actions, and to go even further, allow *events,* which are not localised on any types at all.
Note that there's nothing original here. The ideas presented here come from Syntropy [Cook94] and Catalysis [D'Souza99].

4.1.2   Operations

Users of object technology are familiar with the idea of what Smalltalk and Java call a method, C++ calls a member function, Eiffel calls a routine, and UML calls an operation. Those familiar with Syntropy, Fusion, OCL, Eiffel, etc. will know about using preconditions and postconditions to specify the behaviour of an operation.
The general form of an operation specification in OCL is this:

```
context  Typename::operationName(parameter1  :  Type1,
... ): ReturnType
  pre :  parameter1 ...
  post:  result = ...
```

Within the assertions labelled *pre:* and *post:* the term *self* refers to an object of type *Typename.* Note that if the return type is void, it can be omitted.
Example
In a model of a library, there could be an operation *borrow* on type *Library,* specified along these lines (assume that every library object has a clock object):

```
operations Libary::borrow( m : Member, c : Copy, d :
Date )
  -- Member m borrows copy c to be returned on date d
```

```
pre:
   -- The date is in the future
   d > self.clock.today
      . . .
```

post:

```
      -- There's a new loan object recording that m has
borrowed c
         Loans.allInstances -> exists( n | n.isNew and ... )
```

The operation is localised on the library. It is natural to think of the operation *borrow* being called on a library object, or of a library object "receiving" a call to its *borrow* operation. The term *self* in the precondition refers to the library that "receives" the call.

4.1.3   Joint Actions

In Catalysis, we can have joint actions. They are joint in the sense that they are localised on two or more types.
Example
The borrow action can be seen as a joint action between a member and a library system.

```
action (m : Member, lb : Libary)::borrow( c : Copy, d :
Date )
         -- A joint  action  in  which  a  member  and  a
library system
         -- collaborate in the borrowing of a copy c by
the member
         -- from the library, to be returned on date d
```

pre:

```
      -- The date is in the future
      d > lb.clock.today
         . . .
```

post:

```
      -- There's a new loan object recording that m has
borrowed c
         Loans.allInstances -> exists( n | n.isNew and ... )
```

Note that the library is now identified by name. The term *self* is no longer unambiguous.

4.1.4   Events

An operation is localised on a single type. A joint action is less localised. We don't need to think of borrowing as an operation on a library. We can think of it as a piece of behaviour that a member and a library collaborate in performing.

We can go further, and have no localisation at all. We call a fully de-localised operation an *event*, following Syntropy.

Example

The borrowing of a copy by a member from a library, with a certain return date, can be seen as an event that involves a number of objects. The event has a before state and an after state, but is not done *to* any particular object. Rather, it can affect any of the objects identified in the event's signature, and any object that can be reached from them.

```
event borrow( lb : Library, m : Member, c : Copy, d :
Date )
            -- An event in which member m borrows copy c
from library l,
            -- to be returned on date d
pre:
        -- The date is in the future
        d > lb.clock.today
        ...
post:
        ...
```

There is no receiving object, and nothing for the term *self* to refer to.

More strictly, what is specified above is an event type. Any event occurrence will identify instances of types Library, Member, etc.

4.2   Adding Dynamics to OCL

4.2.1   Rationale

Currently OCL expressions state only static requirements. Class invariants are static by nature and even guard conditions, pre- and postconditions express static information. They only constrain changes in the object's state. Although this is very useful, one would often like to express more dynamic constraints.

What can not currently be expressed using OCL is, for instance, what should happen at the exact moment that a condition becomes true. Another example is, the case where one would like to express that although the state of the object is not changed, events must have occurred due to the invocation of the current operation.

4.2.2   Proposed Features

Special features need to be introduced in OCL to be able to specify these dynamic constraints. We propose to add two stereotypes for constraints to UML and their syntax to OCL that will support dynamic constraints:
the **action** stereotype, which indicates a constraint on the triggering of messages, and
the **called** stereotype, which indicates a constraint that ensures certain messages are send.
To explain these new features the example UML model shown in Figure 2 will be used.

4.2.3   The Action Stereotype for Constraint

An action constraint states that when a Boolean expression becomes true, a list of messages must be send. The constraint can be used to guarantee the sending of the messages, but not the completion of the invoked operations. The messages in the messagelist can only be sent to the contextual object or objects navigable from the contextual object.

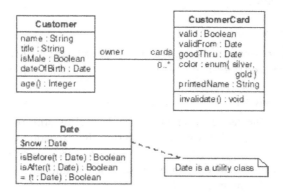

Fig. 2. Another example class diagram

4.2.3.1   Syntax:

```
context class action:
    on booleanExpression do messagelist
```

Where booleanExpression is an OCL expression of the boolean type and messagelist is defined as featureCall ("," featureCall)* (featureCall as defined in the formal grammar of OCL).

4.2.3.2   Semantics:

To define the semantics of an action constraint we propose that an action constraint has the same semantics as an automatic, conditional transition in a statechart. Figure 3 shows a statechart with the same meaning as the example below.

4.2.3.3   Example Usage:

```
context CustomerCard action:
on self.goodThru.isAfter(Date.now) do
self.invalidate()
```

Fig. 3. Statechart that resembles the action constraint

4.2.4   The Called Stereotype for Constraint

A called constraint can only be used in the context of an operation. A called constraint states that every time the contextual operation is executed a message or a list of messages is being sent. Again, there is no guarantee that the invoked operations are completed. The messagelist may be included in ordinary OCL-expressions, allowing e.g. if-then-else-clauses. The else branch may be empty, in which case the keyword 'else' may be omitted.

4.2.4.1   Syntax:

```
context class.operation(paramlist): resultType
called: messagelist
```

4.2.4.2   Semantics:

The semantics of the called constraint can be defined in terms of sequence diagrams. Stating that a message Y has been send during the execution of an operation X is equal to requiring that in every sequence diagram where operation X is called, this call is followed by message Y. In the case of a conditional message, the call X is followed by a guard and message Y.

4.2.4.3   Example Usage:

```
context CustomerCard::invalidate(): void
pre:    -- none
post:   valid = false
called: if valid@pre = true then
            if customer.special then
customer.sendPoliteInvalidLetter()
            else customer.sendInvalidLetter()
            endif
        endif
```

4.2.5   Consequences of Introducing Dynamics

What is described above is a proposal of which the consequences need to be examined. Some of these are:

As in pre and postconditions we do need some formalisation of the concept 'time'. Perhaps we only need to specify 'moment', 'before' and 'after'.

There surely will be a relation to the proposed UML action language specification, which needs to be investigated further.

4.3   Mapping STD to Object States Using OCL

4.3.1   Rationale

A state machine for a Classifier defines the states in which an instance of the classifier can be. It is common to use the state of an object in preconditions, postconditions and invariants. Therefore, it is useful to enhance OCL to be able to refer to those states.

4.3.2   Syntax

The standard operation "oclInState" has been added to OclAny.

```
        object.oclInState(state : OclState) : Boolean
```

4.3.3   Semantics

Results in true if *object* is in the state *state*, otherwise results in false. The argument is a name of a state in the state machine corresponding with the class of *object*.

The type OclState is used as a parameter got the operation "oclInState". There are no properties defined on OclState. One can only specify an OclState by using the name of the state, as it appears in a state machine. These names can be fully qualified by the nested states and the state machine that contain them.

4.4   Using Prefaces to Customise UML

The UML is extensible, and so can be regarded as a family of languages. Implicitly or explicitly, any particular UML model should be accompanied by a definition of the particular UML family member for the model. The definition should cover syntactic and semantics issues. A preface is a mechanism for associating models with such definitions.

This topic was further elaborated on in an article to be published in the proceedings of the Tools Pacific 1999 conference. Readers are referred to [Cook99b].

4.5   Explicit Import of UML and OCL Metamodels Used to Customise UML

Often we generate OCL expressions as strings. For a thorough treatment, this is not a satisfying approach. Although OCL is not a graphic language, it has an abstract syntax and can therefore be included in the meta-model approach in quite the same way as other UML diagrams are. Figure 4 contains a subset of an OCL preface, a similar, but much more detailed approach has been used in [Richters99].

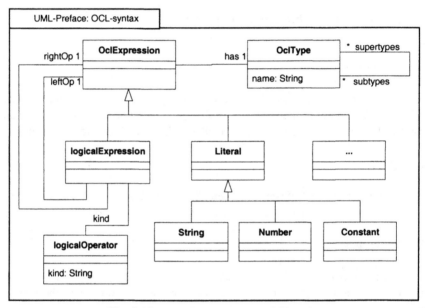

Fig. 4. UML-Preface package for OCL (subset)

Using the OCL preface allows manipulating OCL expressions in the same way as ordinary class structures. OCL on the meta-level can be used to constrain OCL expressions on the modelling level, without the usual conflicts, which arise when two levels are mixed. In particular, OCL has a strong type system, both on the meta-level and the level below. However, through manipulating OCL expressions on the meta-level, we can easily construct OCL expressions on the modelling level that are not well formed. It is not as easy as it was when using strings, but still e.g. variables may be used that do not exist or are of a wrong type.

To deal with that issue, the class "OclExpression" can offer an appropriate query, e.g. "correctExpr()" that discovers well-formedness errors of OCL expressions on the modelling level. The type "OclExpression" as part of OCL's own type system is not necessary anymore.

4.6   Other Subjects Discussed

- Expression placeholders
- Define a basic inference calculus
- How to deal with exceptions in OCL

Acknowledgements. We would like to thank Mark Richters for his comments on an earlier version of the paper.

References

[Bauer85]   F. L Bauer, R. Berghammer, M. Broy, W. Dosch, F. Geiselbrechtinger, R. Gnatz, E. Hangel, W. Hesse, B. Krieg-Brückner, A. Laut, T. Matzner, B. Möller, F. Nickl, H. Partsch, P. Pepper, K. Samelson, M. Wirsing, H. Wössner. The Munich Project CIP, Vol 1: The Wide Spectrum Language CIP-L. Springer Verlag, LNCS 183, 1985

[Booch98]   G. Booch, J. Rumbaugh, and I. Jacobson. The Unified Modelling Language User Guide. Addison Wesley Longman, Reading, Massachusetts, 1998

[Broy93-1]   M. Broy, C. Facchi, R. Grosu, R. Hettler, H. Hussmann, D. Nazareth, F. Regens-burger, O. Slotosch, K. Stoelen. The Requirement Design Specification Language. An Informal Introduction, Part 1. Spectrum. TUM-I9312. TU Munich. 1993

[Broy93-2]   M. Broy, C. Facchi, R. Grosu, R. Hettler, H. Hussmann, D. Nazareth, F. Regens-burger, O. Slotosch, K. Stoelen. The Requirement Design Specification Language. An Informal Introduction, Part 2. Spectrum, TUM-I9312, TU Munich, 1993

[Cook94]   S. Cook and J. Daniels, Designing Object Systems, object-oriented modelling with Syntropy, Prentice Hall, 1994

[Cook99a]   S. Cook, A. Kleppe, R. Mitchell, J. Warmer, A. Wills, Defining the Context of OCL Expressions. In: <<UML>>'99 The Unified Modelling Language. Eds.: R. France, B. Rumpe. Springer Verlag, LNCS 1723, 1999.

[Cook99b]   Steve Cook , Anneke Kleppe, Richard Mitchell, Bernhard Rumpe, Jos Warmer, Alan Wills, Defining UML Family Members with Prefaces, Proceedings of Tools Pacific '99, 1999

[Conrad92]   S. Conrad, M. Gogolla, R. Herzig. TROLL light: A Core Language for Specifying Objects. Technical Report 92-06. TU Braunschweig. 1992

[Date87]   J. C. Date. A Guide to SQL Standard. Addison Wesley. 1987

[D'Souza98]   D'Souza D. and Wills A. Objects, Components and Frameworks with UML: The Catalysis Approach. Addison Wesley, 1998

[Ehrig85]   H. Ehrig, B. Mahr, Fundamentals of Algebraic Specification 1, Springer Verlag, 1985

[Ehrig90]   H. Ehrig, B. Mahr, Fundamentals of Algebraic Specification 2, Module Specifications Constraints, Springer Verlag, 1990

[Goguen92]   J. Goguen, T. Winkler, J. Meseguer, K. Futatsugi, J.-P. Jouannaud. Introducing OBJ. Technical Report CSL-92-03. Computer Science Laboratory, SRI. 1992

[Gordon93]   M. Gordon, T. Melham. Introduction to HOL: A Theorem Proving Environment for Higher Order Logic. Cambridge University Press. 1993

[Gordon79]   M. Gordon, R. Milner, C. Wadsworth. Edinburgh LCF: A Mechanised Logic of Computation. Springer Verlag, LNCS 78. 1979

[Hartmann94]   T. Hartmann, G. Saake, R. Jungclaus, P. Hartel, J. Kusch. Revised Version of the Modelling Language TROLL. Technical Report 94-03. TU Braunschweig. 1994

[Hudak92]   P. Hudak, S. P. Jones, P. Wadler. Report on the Programming Language Haskell. A Non-strict Purely Functional Language. Sigplan Notices. Vol. 27. ACM Press. 1992

[Jones90]   C. B. Jones. Systematic Software Development Using VDM. Prentice Hall. 2nd Edition. 1990

[Jones93]   M. P. Jones. An Introduction to Gofer. 1993

[Jungclaus91]   R. Jungclaus, G. Saake, T. Hartmann, C. Sernadas. Object-oriented Specification of Information Systems: The TROLL Language. TU Braunschweig. Technical Report 91-04. 1991

[Lalonde90]   W. Lalonde and J. Pugh, Inside Smalltalk, vol 1, Prentice Hall, 1990

[Kleene52]   S. Kleene. Introduction to Metamathematics. Van Nostrand. 1952

[OCL1.3]   OMG Unified Modeling Language Specification Version 1.3 beta R7, June 1999

[OCL1.4]   OMG Unified Modeling Language Specification Version 1.4, to appear 1999/2000.

[Paulson91]   L. Paulson. ML for the Working Programmer. Cambridge University Press. 1991

[Paulson94]   L. Paulson. Isabelle: A Generic Theorem Prover. Springer Verlag, LNCS 929. 1994

[Regensburger94] F. Regensburger. Phd Thesis. HOLCF: Eine konservative Erweiterung von HOL um LCF. TU Munich. 1994

[Richters99]   M. Richters, M. Gogolla: A Metamodel for OCL. In: <<UML>>'99 The Unified Modelling Language. Eds.: R. France, B. Rumpe. Springer Verlag, LNCS 1723, 1999.

[Rumpe98]   B. Rumpe: A Note on Semantics (with an Emphasis on UML). In: Second ECOOP Workshop on Precise Behavioral Semantics. Technical Report TUM-I9813. Technische Universität München. Juni, 1998

[Spivey88]   J. Spivey. Understanding Z. Cambridge University Press. 1988

[Spivey89]   J. Michael Spivey. An Introduction to Z and Formal Specifications. IEE/BCS Software Engineering Journal, vol. 4, no. 1, pp 40-50. 1989

[Tarski55]   A. Tarski. A lattice-theoretical fixpoint theorem and its application. Pacific Journal of Mathematics, vol. 5, pp. 285-309. 1955

[Warmer99a]   Warmer J. and Kleppe A. The object constraint language. Precise modelling with UML. Addison Wesley Longman, 1999

[Warmer99b]   Warmer J. and Kleppe A. OCL: the constraint language of the UML. In the Journal of Object-Oriented Programming, May 1999.

An OCL Extension for Real-Time Constraints

Stephan Flake and Wolfgang Mueller

C-LAB, Paderborn University, Fürstenallee 11
33102 Paderborn, Germany
{flake, wolfgang}@c-lab.de

Abstract. The Object Constraint Language (OCL) was introduced to support the specification of constraints for UML diagrams and is mainly used to formulate invariants and operation pre- and postconditions. Though OCL is also applied in behavioral diagrams, e.g., as guards for state transitions, it is currently not possible to specify constraints concerning the dynamic behavior and timing properties of such diagrams.
This article discusses OCL's application for the dynamic behavior of UML Statechart diagrams and presents an OCL extension for specification of state-oriented time-bounded constraints. We introduce operations to extract state configurations from diagrams and define additional predicates over states and state configurations. The semantics of our OCL extension is given by employing time-bounded Computational Tree Logic (CTL) formulae. An example of a flexible manufacturing system with automated guided vehicles demonstrates the application of our extension.

1 Introduction

Currently, the Unified Modeling Language (UML) is well accepted in research and industry for a wide spectrum of applications. With the broad acceptance of UML, the Object Constraint Language (OCL) also has received a considerable visibility. OCL provides means for the specification of constraints in the context of UML diagrams, focusing on class diagrams and on guards in behavioral diagrams. However, OCL presently lacks sufficient specification means to cover constraints about the dynamic behavior of such diagrams, i.e., state configurations and evolution of states as well as state transitions over time cannot be expressed, so that OCL is currently not applicable for real-time specifications.

On the other hand, formal verification methods like equivalence and model checking have been well accepted through past years for some application domains. In particular, model checking has received a wide industrial acceptance for electronic system and protocol verification. Similar to the complementary means of UML and OCL, model checking needs a system description and a property specification as input, where properties are typically specified by formulae in temporal logics, mostly in Computational Tree Logic (CTL). Though already frequently applied, it often turns out that the specification of properties is regarded as a task too cumbersome for modelers and programmers who are not familiar with formal methods. With our OCL-based approach for model checking specification, it is possible to replace cryptic CTL specifications by more meaningful

A. Clark and J. Warmer (Eds.): Object Modeling with the OCL, LNCS 2263, pp. 150–171, 2002.
© Springer-Verlag Berlin Heidelberg 2002

(extended) OCL specifications which are better tailored to the mental model of programmers.

In order to make OCL applicable for real-time specification in general and for model checking specification in particular, we introduce OCL extensions by concepts from temporal logics based upon a time-bounded variant of CTL. As we introduce our extensions on the basis of an OCL metamodel, they are seamlessly integrated into the existing OCL syntax and semantics (OCL Version 1.4). We enhance OCL by the notion of future-oriented state configurations as well as state transitions over time. All extensions come with a well defined semantics which is given by a translation of OCL statements to time-bounded CTL formulae. Though we present our approach as a constraint specification over the state space of UML Statechart diagrams by addressing future-oriented behavior, it is applicable without further modification for other state-oriented means like Activity Diagrams and also easily adaptable to past-oriented temporal logics.

The remainder of this article is structured as follows. In the next section, we give a brief overview of related works w.r.t. OCL extensions for formal verification. Section 3 gives an introduction to model checking and property specification by means of time-bounded CTL. In Section 4, we introduce our OCL extensions by collections of states and their operations and provide a semantics of the temporal operations by their relation to temporal logic formulae. Section 5 illustrates an application example before Section 6 briefly outlines our implementation. Finally, Section 7 summarizes and concludes this article.

2   Related Work

There currently exist very few approaches to apply OCL in the context of formal verification frameworks, though UML Statechart diagrams already apply well as a graphical front-end for model checking [3].

The KeY project aims to facilitate the use of formal verification for software specifications [1]. As OCL currently has no formal semantics, this approach translates OCL constraint specifications to dynamic logic (DL), an extension of Hoare logic. DL is used as input for formal verification. In that approach, OCL is applied to specify constraints on design patterns without modifying OCL.

Two other approaches consider temporal extensions for OCL. Distefano et al. define BOTL (Object-Based Temporal Logic) in order to facilitate the specification of static and dynamic properties [5]. BOTL is based on a combination of CTL and an OCL subset. Syntactically, BOTL is very similar to temporal formulae in CTL. Another temporal extension of OCL is defined by Ramakrishnan et al. [9,10]. They extend OCL by additional rules with unary and binary temporal operators, e.g., always and never. Unfortunately, the resulting syntax does not combine well with current OCL concepts. Again, temporal expressions appear to be similar to temporal logics formulae.

In contrast to previous approaches we introduce extensions to static OCL concepts towards dynamic concepts with only minor modifications to existing OCL syntax and semantics. In order to seamlessly integrate to existing OCL, our work is based on an OCL metamodel [2]. We have selected that model since it clearly separates metalevel and instance level for OclType. However, we think that an adaptation to another OCL metamodel such as [11] is possible without significant problems. Though our extensions are kept compliant with OCL syntax and existing types and operations, they also have direct correspondence to temporal tree logic formulae for easy code generation in a formal verification framework. Moreover, our work also covers the specification of real-time constraints, as the underlying concepts covers Clocked CTL (CCTL), a time-bounded variant of CTL [12].

3 Model Checking

Symbolic model checking is mainly due to pioneering work of two groups: Clarke/ Emerson and Quielle/Sifakis [4]. Temporal logic based model checking is well established in hardware-oriented systems design for electronic circuits and protocol verification and receives growing interest in software design. Though the general problem is PSPACE-complete, symbolic representations like Binary Decision Diagrams allow verifications with up to 10^{120} states.

For model checking, given a parallel finite state machine (the model) and a temporal logic formula (the property specification), a model checker outputs either 'yes' if the model satisfies the formula or 'no' if the formula does not hold. In the latter case, usually a counter example can automatically be generated to show a particular model execution sequence which leads to a situation that contradicts the formula.

In the context of model checking, model representation is mostly based on Kripke structures (i.e., unit-delay temporal structures) which are derived from finite state machines. A Kripke structure $M = (P, S, s_0, T, L)$ is a tuple with a set of atomic propositions P, a set of states S, an initial state $s_0 \in S$, a transition relation between the states $T \subseteq S \times S$ such that every state has a successor state, and a state labeling function $L : S \rightarrow 2^P$.

For property specification, most model checkers are based on branching-time temporal tree logic specification. Temporal tree logic (TL) expresses information about states and future state transition paths. An execution path defines one possible future execution path starting from the current state as root. All possible execution paths establish an infinite tree with the current state as its root. One of the most frequently applied TLs is the Computational TL (CTL).

In CTL, temporal operators are always preceded by a path quantifier. Starting from the current state, the path quantifier either specifies to consider all possible execution paths (**A**) or it specifies that at least one execution path must exist (**E**) that satisfies the following formula part. Temporal operators specify the ordering of events along future-oriented execution paths. Table 1 gives an overview of the CTL operators.

In general, a CTL formula f can be built by applying the following recursive grammar:

$$f := \begin{array}{l} a \mid f \vee f \mid f \mathbin{/} f \mid f \wedge f \mid f \oplus f \\ \mid \mathbf{EX}\ f \mid \mathbf{EF}\ f \mid \mathbf{EG}\ f \mid \mathbf{E}(f\ \mathbf{U}\ f) \\ \mid \mathbf{AX}\ f \mid \mathbf{AF}\ f \mid \mathbf{AG}\ f \mid \mathbf{A}(f\ \mathbf{U}\ f) \end{array}$$

where a is an atomic proposition.

Table 1. Temporal Operators

Name	Operator	Description
next-time	$\mathbf{X}\,f$	next state on the path has to satisfy f
eventually	$\mathbf{F}\,f$	some arbitrary state on the path has to satisfy f
always	$\mathbf{G}\,f$	every state on the path has to satisfy f
until	$f\,\underline{\mathbf{U}}\,g$	some state s on the path has to satisfy g
		and all states on the path up to s have to satisfy f

There are extensions to basic model checking for the verification of real-time systems. One variation is defined by Kropf and Ruf in [12] in the context of the RAVEN model checker. They extend Kripke structures to I/O-Interval structures and CTL to time-bounded Clocked CTL. The major difference with respect to Kripke structures is the introduction of a transition labeling function $I : T \rightarrow 2^{\mathbb{N}}$ with [min,max]-delay times. A state may be basically left at min-time and must be left after max-time.

Clocked CTL is a time-bounded variant of CTL with $\mathrm{X}_{[x]}, \mathrm{F}_{[x,y]}, \mathrm{G}_{[x,y]}, \underline{\mathrm{U}}_{[x,y]}$, where $x \in \mathbb{N}_0, y \in \mathbb{N}_0 \cup \{\infty\}$ are time bounds. The symbol ∞ is defined through: $\forall i \in \mathbb{N}_0 :$ $i < \infty$. In the case of only one parameter the lower bound is set to zero by default. If no interval is specified, the lower bound is implicitly set to zero and the upper bound is set to infinity. If the X-operator has no time bound, it is implicitly set to one.

In order to integrate more general concepts for specification of real-time systems, the extensions introduced in the next section refer to Clocked CTL concepts.

4   Real-Time OCL Extensions

In the domain of database systems, different types of *semantic integrity constraints* are distinguished [6]. *Static constraints* define required properties on nontransient system states, i.e., static properties within one system state. *Transition constraints* deal with system changes between two subsequent states. In real-time systems design, we additionally identify *temporal constraints* that consider sequences of state transitions in combination with time bounds. While static and transition constraints can already be expressed with OCL, it currently lacks means to express temporal constraints.

To overcome this, we introduce temporal OCL operations that enable modelers to specify state-oriented behavior. The OCL extensions presented in this article reason about possible future object states since we define the semantics based on a future oriented tree temporal logic without loss of generality. Accordingly, OCL can also be easily extended for specification of past-oriented constraints.

In the following, we first outline the concepts of our extensions based on an OCL metamodel. Thereafter, we describe the new types and their operations as well as necessary extensions to the predefined OCL type `OclAny`. The final paragraph of this section gives the semantics of the new operations by their translation to Clocked CTL expressions.

4.1   OCL Metamodel

At present, there are two metamodel proposals for OCL [11,2]. We have selected the
metamodel proposed by Baar and Hähnle [2] since it seems to be considerably stable
and sufficiently generic for our purpose. That metamodel covers the complete OCL type
system and aims to overcome difficulties in specifying metalevel constraints. Figure 1
gives an overview of that metamodel in form of a UML class diagram. In that figure, we
have marked our extensions as bold, and it can be easily seen that our modifications are
only marginal. We only require the additional metaclass `GenericParameter` and two
new basic OCL types: `OclPath` and `OclConfiguration`.[1]

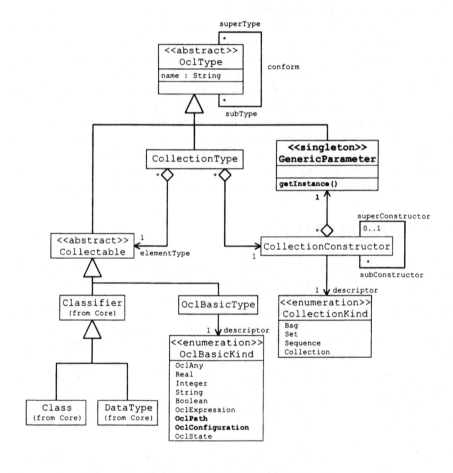

Fig. 1. Extented OCL Metamodel

---

[1] Note here that compared to [2] we have removed the literal `Enumeration` from `OclBasic-`
`Kind`, due to issue 3143 in [14] (`Enumeration` instances are now retrieved from model classes
by their path name).

The main idea of this metamodel is to consider the type OclType purely as a metatype, while all other predefined types are instances of (a subtype of) OclType, i.e., there is no subtype relationship between OclType and the predefined types like Integer, String, or Boolean. Instead, subtype relationships between OCL types are explicitly modeled by the association conform. The operations attributes(), operations(), and associationEnds() of OclType are in this metamodel only available for instances of the metaclass Classifier by inheritance from the UML core metamodel which does not affect OCL in its usage at the application level. Collection types are aggregations of a collection kind and an element type. An additional class CollectionConstructor is used to model the conformance between collection kinds, e.g., type Set conforms to Collection. The metamodel comes with OCL well-formedness rules to ensure that only predefined type names can be instantiated and that the conformance relationships are composed along the lines of standard specifications. Based on this metamodel, we introduce the following modifications.

- A unique generic parameter is defined in a singleton class GenericParameter. A generic parameter is required in declarations for instances of CollectionConstructor as a placeholder for a concrete basic OCL type. In OCL standard documents, this generic parameter is usually denoted as T, e.g., Collection(T). As OclType has no operations in this metamodel, it is possible to regard GenericParameter as a subtype of OclType, and we add well-formedness rules to ensure the correct instance name:

```
context GenericParameter
inv: self.name = 'T'

context OclType
inv: self.allInstances->isUnique(name)
```

- Two new basic type names OclConfiguration and OclPath are added as literals to the enumeration OclBasicKind; detailed descriptions can be found in the next section.

4.2 States and Configurations

Current OCL already supports the retrieval of states from Statechart diagrams. States are regarded to be of type OclState. However, this type is only marginally outlined in the OCL standard and thus needs to be elaborated with respect to its combined usage with UML Statechart diagrams and the underlying formal model of state machines[2] which is a part of the UML metamodel[3]. In that metamodel, state machines may have several kinds of states which are given as subtypes of the metaclass StateVertex. For our work, we are only interested in the states that represent a specific behavior, namely composite and simple states, and we do not consider pseudo, synch, stub, final, and submachine

---

[2] see [7], Section 3.75
[3] see [7], Section 2.12

states here. The following code illustrates our extension of OclState that introduces new attributes and operations compliant to the UML state machine metamodel.[4]

```
DataType <<enumeration>> StateType {
  composite,
  simple
}


OclBasicType OclState <supertype> OclAny {
  stateType      : StateType;
  isConcurrent   : Boolean;
  isRegion       : Boolean;
  parentState()  : OclState;
  subStates()    : Set(OclState);
  isActive()     : Boolean;
  notActive()    : Boolean;
  anySubState()  : OclState;
}
```

We outline and informally describe the properties of OclState using the terms and identifiers of the UML state machine metamodel. Let s be an instance of type OclState. The enumeration attribute stateType points out whether s is a composite or a simple state. The boolean attribute isConcurrent indicates whether s contains concurrent substates (denoted as *regions*), and the boolean attribute isRegion checks whether s is a substate of a concurrent state. The state machine metamodel defines an association connecting states and their direct substates, and the corresponding association ends are subvertex and container. For s, we define the operations subStates() and parentState() which return the states accessible via this association. In the case of a top level state, s.parentState() returns undefined. Correspondingly, s.subStates() returns an empty set, if s is a simple state. isActive() evaluates to true if s is currently active. Its dual notActive() becomes true if s is not active. We also need the operation anySubState() which returns one non-deterministically chosen substate. When no substates are defined, the operation returns undefined.

Compliant with common OCL practice[5], we take some implicit presumptions for the remainder of this article. We assume that there is at most one Statechart diagram (resp. one state machine) for each classifier. In order to be directly accessible from OCL, all simple and composite states of a state machine have to be available as instances of OclState. Their properties are set according to their state machine specification.

Configurations. Currently, the only possibility to retrieve information about states in OCL is given by the boolean operation oclInState() of type OclAny. This is not sufficient since in concurrent Statechart diagrams an overall state can only be uniquely

---

[4] A grammar of the language we are using for declarations of basic and generic OCL types can be found in Appendix A.

[5] see [7], Section 7.5.10: States are already directly accessible in OCL expressions.

described by tuples of substates and thus needs additional operations on them. We refer to such a tuple as a *configuration*. More precisely, we consider a configuration as a set of simple states that uniquely and completely describe an overall state of a given Statechart diagram.

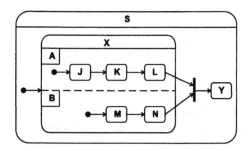

Fig. 2. Concurrent Statechart Diagram

Figure 2 gives an example of a concurrent Statechart diagram. That example has the top level state S which also denotes the classifier this Statechart diagram belongs to. Here, the initial configuration can be described by Set{X::A::J,X::B::M}. For this Statechart, S.oclInState(X::A::J) returns true in current OCL, although X::A::J is not a complete configuration of S. When investigating complete configurations on the level of simple states, we currently have to write

S.oclInState(X::A::J) and S.oclInState(X::B::M)

since only the operation oclInState() is available. It is easy to see that such specifications are not easily manageable for complex Statecharts. To overcome this, we introduce the new basic type OclConfiguration and add the operation config():
Set(OclConfiguration) to OclAny. This operation returns the set of all valid configurations, i.e., all sets of *simple* states that are required to uniquely cover complete configurations. Table 2 gives some usage examples of config() when applied to the Statechart of Fig. 2. The notion of configuration also applies to substates, e.g., X::A and X::A::J. Note here that in the resulting sets all configurations are given by their complete path names and that the name of the topmost state is not included in the path of a configuration.

The operation config() returns a set of configurations, or more precisely, a set of sets of simple states, which is not flattened like other OCL operations on collections are. Note here that not necessarily all configurations have the same number of states, e.g., {Y} and {X::A::J,X::B::M} are both valid configurations for S. The operation config() checks configurations for their validity. For instance,

```
context S
inv: self.config->includes(c:OclConfiguration |
                      c = Set {X::A::J,X::B::M} )
```

checks if Set{X::A::J,X::B::M} is a valid configuration for S. This also includes a check for the newly introduced OCL type OclConfiguration.

Table 2. Sample Usages of the Operation config()

Expression	Result
S.config	{X::A::J, X::A::K, X::A::L} × {X::B::M, X::B::N} ∪ {Y}
S.config→size	$3 * 2 + 1 = 7$
X::A.config	{X::A::J, X::A::K, X::A::L}
X::A.config→size	3
X::A::J.config	{X::A::J}
X::A::J.config→size	1

The next section presents basic operations for instances of that type, while Section 4.3 investigates on dynamic issues of configurations with respect to the runtime execution of state machines.

Operations of OclConfiguration. As we interpret OclConfiguration as a new built-in type for a representation of specific sets of OclStates, most operations of Ocl type Set can be reused. We only have to elaborate on operations that return collections, since the result might be an arbitrary set of OclStates rather than a valid configuration. Therefore, we cannot directly adopt operations like union(), intersection(), including(), excluding(), symmetricDifference(), select(), reject(), collect() for OclConfigurations without modification. Nevertheless, access to those set operations is still possible via type cast operations, e.g., asSet().

Again, we use the grammar given in Appendix A to present the operations defined for OclConfiguration.

```
OclBasicType OclConfiguration <supertype> OclAny {
    --
    -- operations adopted from generic type Set
    --
    =          (c:OclConfiguration)  : Boolean;
    <>         (c:OclConfiguration)  : Boolean;
    size       ()                    : Integer;
    count      (s:OclState)          : Integer;
    isEmpty    ()                    : Boolean;
    notEmpty   ()                    : Boolean;
    exists     (e:OclExpression)     : Boolean;
    forAll     (e:OclExpression)     : Boolean;
    includes   (s:OclState)          : Boolean;
    includesAll (t:Set(OclState))    : Boolean;
    excludes   (s:OclState)          : Boolean;
    excludesAll (t:Set(OclState))    : Boolean;
    --
    -- new operations
    --
```

```
isActive     ()                          : Boolean;
notActive    ()                          : Boolean;
--
-- type cast operations
--
asSet        ()                          : Set(OclState);
asBag        ()                          : Bag(OclState);
asSequence   ()                          : Sequence(OclState);
}
```

Except the two newly introduced operations isActive() and notActive() all other operations of OclConfiguration can be immediately adopted from the generic types Collection and Set[6]. The semantics of isActive() and notActive() is described in the style of the official OCL specification as follows, where cfg denotes an instance of OclConfiguration in the context of a classifier C.

```
-------------------------------------------------------------------
cfg->isActive() : Boolean

    True if all states of cfg are active.

pre:  C.config->includes(cfg)
post: result = cfg->forAll(s : OclState | s.isActive)
-------------------------------------------------------------------
cfg->notActive() : Boolean

    True if at least one of the states of cfg is not active.

pre:  C.config->includes(cfg)
post: result = not cfg->isActive
-------------------------------------------------------------------
```

To access OclConfiguration properties, we make use of the arrow-operator. This solution is chosen to keep the compliance with existing OCL and its syntax for collection operations, although OclConfiguration is defined as a basic type.

OclPath. In order to reason over execution sequences of state machines, we require means to represent sequences of configurations. Note here that our notion of *sequence* assumes strong successorship, i.e., no other configuration may occur between two subsequent elements of a specified sequence. Additionally, a configuration in a sequence may hold for a certain time or a time interval. In that case, a time specification is appended to the expression as an additional qualifier.

Instances of a new basic type OclPath – representing sequences of OclConfigurations – are declared by the following grammar:

---

[6] see [7] Section 7.8.2

```
cfgSequence        := "Sequence" "{" cfgExprList "}"
cfgExprList        := cfgExpr (qualifiers)?
                        ( "," cfgExpr (qualifiers)? )*
cfgExpr            := ("not")?
                       ( configuration
                         | "(" configurationList ")"
                       )
configuration      := stateName
                     | "Set" "{" stateName ("," stateName)* "}"
configurationList  :=  configuration ("or" configuration)*
stateName          := pathName
qualifiers         := "[" actualParameterList "]"
```

where the non-terminals `pathName`, `qualifiers`, and `actualParameterList` are defined according to the official OCL Grammar. Note here that OCL already covers sequence declarations through `literalCollection`, so that there is no need to add or modify rules with that respect.

In the above grammar, `qualifiers` refers to a [min,max]-time interval specification corresponding to the Clocked CTL time intervals introduced in Section 3. Thus, this expression has one or two comma seperated subexpressions. The latter is of type $Integer \times (Integer \cup \{'inf'\})$, specifying discrete [min,max]-time intervals with an optional infinite upper bound. In the case of only one subexpression, that expression has to evaluate to type `Integer` and specifies both lower and upper bound. Configuration expressions without qualifiers implicitly have the interval [1,'inf'] as a default.

For an `OclPath` example, we take the Statechart diagram in Fig. 2 and define in the context of S:

```
let V = X::A
let W = X::B
```

The following `let`-expression specifies a sequence for state `S::X` which changes from the initial configuration $\{V::J,W::M\}$ to $\{V::K,W::M\}$ after some time, is staying in this configuration between 5 and 50 time units, then changes to $\{V::L,W::M\}$ or $\{V::K,W::N\}$, remaining in this configuration for exactly 10 time units, and finally changes to configuration $\{V::L,W::N\}$.

```
let p = Sequence {  Set {V::J,W::M},
                    Set {V::K,W::M} [5,50],
                  ( Set {V::L,W::M} or Set {W::K,W::N} ) [10]
                    Set {V::L,W::N}
                 }
```

OclPath Operations. An instance of `OclPath` is interpreted as a possible execution sequence composed of OclConfigurations for a given Statechart diagram, resp. state machine. Similar to `OclConfiguration`, the existing OCL sequence operations can be immediately applied to `OclPath`. Nevertheless, we do not define all common sequence operations for `OclPath`, as many of them would result in arbitrary collections of OclConfigurations which are not valid OclPaths. Note here that access to all common sequence operations is still available through type casting.

The typeOclPath is defined as follows where the semantics of all operations can be directly derived from the generic OCL types `Collection` and `Sequence`[7].

```
OclBasicType OclPath <supertype> OclAny {
    --
    -- basic operations derived from OclCollection
    --
    =           (p:OclPath)                  : Boolean;
    <>          (p:OclPath)                  : Boolean;
    size        ()                           : Integer;
    isEmpty     ()                           : Boolean;
    notEmpty    ()                           : Boolean;
    count       (t:OclConfiguration)         : Integer;
    exists      (e:OclExpression)            : Boolean;
    forAll      (e:OclExpression)            : Boolean;
    includes    (t:OclConfiguration)         : Boolean;
    includesAll (s:Set(OclConfiguration))    : Boolean;
    excludes    (t:OclConfiguration)         : Boolean;
    excludesAll (s:Set(OclConfiguration))    : Boolean;
    --
    -- basic operations derived from OclSequence
    --
    at          (i:Integer)                  : OclConfiguration;
    first       ()                           : OclConfiguration;
    last        ()                           : OclConfiguration;
    append      (t:OclConfiguration)         : OclPath;
    prepend     (t:OclConfiguration)         : OclPath;
    subSequence (l:Integer,u:Integer)        : OclPath;
    --
    -- type cast operations
    --
    asSet       ()              : Set(OclConfiguration);
    asBag       ()              : Bag(OclConfiguration);
    asSequence  ()              : Sequence(OclConfiguration);
}
```

4.3   Temporal Operations

Temporal operations have to be introduced to obtain object values with respect to certain points in time. Since our application domain is future-oriented branching time logic, we focus our definition only on future-oriented operations. However, same concepts also apply to past operators and can be introduced correspondingly.

---

[7] see [7] Section 7.8.2

For our extension we first consider the @pre operator which is already available in OCL. This operator is only allowed in operation postconditions and used to recall the value of an object when the operation was called. Correspondingly, we define @post that regards future points in time. For a seamless integration of that operator, we interpret the symbol @ as an individual operator, such as the dot- and arrow-operators. This means to take pre and post as *operations* of OclAny and restrict the @-operator to be used only for those temporal operations. Under these assumptions we only need very few minor changes w.r.t. the OCL grammar, so that main syntax and semantics of OCL can be kept. For a complete summary of all OCL grammar changes, the reader is referred to Appendix B.

Extensions to OclAny. The OCL basic type OclAny is the abstract superclass of all OCL basic types and all other model classes (i.e., instances of the metatypes Class or DataType w.r.t. a given UML class diagram). In order to introduce temporal operations to OCL we extend OclAny with the operations pre(), post(), and next(). For the sake of completeness, the operation config() (cf. Section 4.2) is also listed in the following code fragment.

```
OclBasicType OclAny {
  -- keep standard OclAny operations
  ....
  -- new operations
  config () : Set(OclConfiguraion);
  pre    () : OclAny;
  post   () : Set(OclPath);
  next   () : Set(OclConfiguration);
}
```

As the return type of operation pre() can here only be declared as OclAny, we have to ensure type consistency by an additional postcondition. We define post() as an operation that returns a set of OclPaths, i.e., a *set* of possible future execution sequences. It is to be defined as a set since there can be various possible orders of executions in a Statechart diagram. Operation next() returns a set of all possible configurations after one time unit. Furthermore, we allow the declaration of a [min,max]-time interval in combination with post(), as already introduced for OclPath.

The informal semantics is given as follows, where obj denotes an instance of OclAny.

```
obj@pre() : OclAny
  This operation may be used in operation postconditions only. It
  returns the value of obj at the time of entering the respective
  operation.
post: result.oclIsTypeOf(obj)
```

```
obj@post()[a,b]  : Set(OclPath)
  Returns a set of possible future execution sequences in the
  interval [a,b]. The configurations of time points a and b are
  included.
```

```
obj@post()[b]  : Set(OclPath)
  Same as obj@post[b,b]. b must be of type Integer.
```

```
obj@post()  : Set(OclPath)
  Same as obj@post[1,'inf'].
```

```
obj@next()  : Set(OclConfiguration)
  Similar to obj@post[1,1], but @next returns a set of
  OclConfigurations that are valid after the next time step.
```

Until-Operator. For our temporal OCL extension, we have to introduce a logical until operator to be able to express causal dependencies between subsequent configurations. To define the semantics, we first have to define a validation relation $\models$ over OCL expressions that result in OclConfigurations:

Definition 1. *Given a time step t, a classifier S, its configuration c at time step t, and an OclExpression* expr. *Let* res *be the result from evaluating* expr *at time step t, then*

$$(c,t) \models \text{expr} \quad :\Leftrightarrow \quad \begin{cases} \text{expr.evaluationType} = \text{OclConfiguration} \\ \text{and S.config} \rightarrow \text{includes(expr)} \\ \text{and c} = \text{res} \end{cases}$$

We say that expr *is satisfied by* c *at time step t, if and only if* expr *evaluates to a valid instance* res *of* OclConfiguration *in the context of* S *and* c *equals* res.

The binary logical operator until is defined for pairs of OclExpressions that both evaluate to instances of type OclConfiguration. Optionally, until can be supplied with an interval declaration according to the grammar rules introduced for [min,max]-time intervals in Section 4.2. Implicitly, the interval is set to [1,'inf'] by default.

The logical operator until is defined as follows.

Definition 2. *Given a time step t, a classifier S, and its configuration c at time step t. Let p be an instance of* OclPath *whose configurations are all valid in* S. *Let* expr1, expr2 *be two OCL expressions.*

$$(c,t) \models (\text{p}:\text{OclPath} \mid \text{expr1 until}[a,b]\,\text{expr2})$$

$$:\Leftrightarrow$$

there exists an i, $a \le i \le min(\text{p.size},b)$, *such that* $(\text{p.at}(i), t+i) \models$ expr2
and for all $j, 1 \le j < i$, *holds:* $(\text{p.at}(j), t+j) \models$ expr1

Translating Temporal OCL Expressions to CCTL. We can now formally define our temporal OCL extensions by their translation to Computational CTL formulae as they were introduced in Section 3. We focus on OCL invariants, so that all corresponding CCTL formulae start with the AG operator, i.e., with 'always globally'. Table 3 lists temporal OCL operations that directly match to CCTL expressions. In that table, expr is of type OclExpression and configuration of type OclConfiguration. The table gives a translation by templates and it should be easy to see how it is applied to nested expressions. Due to space limitations we additionally use a compact form for the OCL expressions in that table, e.g., we use

```
obj@post[a,b]->exists(forAll(expr))
```

instead of explicitly declaring the iterators:

```
obj@post[a,b]->exists(p:OclPath |
                      p->forAll(c:OclConfiguration | expr))
```

Table 3. Temporal OCL Expressions and Equivalent CCTL Formulae

Temporal OCL Expression	Respective CCTL Formula
inv: obj@post[a,b]→exists(forAll(expr))	AG EG$_{[a,b]}$(expr)
inv: obj@post[a,b]→exists(exists(expr))	AG EF$_{[a,b]}$(expr)
inv: obj@post[a,b]→exists(includes(configuration))	AG EF$_{[a,b]}$(configuration)
inv: obj@post[a,b]→exists(expr1 until[c,d] expr2)	AG EG$_{[a,b]}$ E(expr1 $\underline{U}_{[c,d]}$ expr2)
inv: obj@post[a,b]→forAll(forAll(expr))	AG AG$_{[a,b]}$(expr)
inv: obj@post[a,b]→forAll(exists(expr))	AG AF$_{[a,b]}$(expr)
inv: obj@post[a,b]→forAll(includes(configuration))	AG AF$_{[a,b]}$(configuration)
inv: obj@post[a,b]→forAll(expr1 until[c,d] expr2)	AG AG$_{[a,b]}$ A(expr1 $\underline{U}_{[c,d]}$ expr2)

Configuration sequences translate to CCTL formulae as follows. Let $e_1, e_2, ..., e_n$ be elements of a sequence declaration, where e_i can be either simple OclConfigurations or complex expressions, specified with time intervals $[a_i, b_i]$. The temporal OCL expression

```
obj@post[a,b] →includes(Sequence{e1[a1,b1], e2[a2,b2], ..., en})
```

translates to the CCTL formula

$$AG_{[a,b]} \text{ EF}(\text{ E}(e_1 \underline{U}_{[a_1,b_1]} \text{ E}(e_2 \underline{U}_{[a_2,b_2]} \text{ E}(...\text{E}(e_{n-1} \underline{U}_{[a_{n-1},b_{n-1}]} e_n)...)))).$$

Note here that the path quantifier, which is applied to each sequence element, depends on the preceding operations.

5   Example

The following section outlines the previously described concepts by the example of a Holonic Manufacturing System (HMS) case study. The HMS case study was introduced by the IMS Initiative TC 5. It is composed of a set of different manufacturing stations and a transport system as shown by the virtual 3D model in Fig. 3. The different manufacturing stations transform workpieces, e.g., by milling, drilling, or washing. Additional input and output storages are for primary system input and output. The transport system consists of a set of AGVs (Automated Guided Vehicles), i.e., autonomous vehicles that carry workpieces between stations. We assume that stations have an input buffer for incoming workpieces and that each AGV can take only one workpiece at a time.

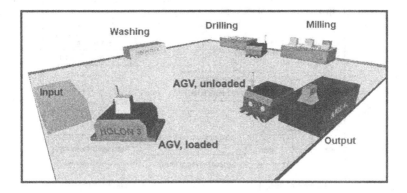

Fig. 3. 3D Model of the Manufacturing Scenario.

The whole system is basically characterized by the following application flow.

- An AGV v_i is idle until it receives a request for delivery from a station s_k. Then, it
  1. sends the distance d_i from its current position to s_k,
  2. moves to s_k on notification of acceptance from s_k,
  3. takes the workpiece from s_k and moves it to the next destination,
  4. moves to a parking position and returns to Step 1.
- Once having located a completed workpiece at its output, a station s_k
  1. sends a request for delivery to the next destination station s_{dest},
  2. is waiting for a notification from s_{dest} for a specific time period,
  3. returns to Step 1 if s_{dest} does not reply or answers with a reject to the request,
  4. broadcasts a request for delivery to all AGVs,
  5. is collecting messages with distances d_i from idle AGVs v_i for a specific time period,
  6. returns to Step 4 if no AGV replies,
  7. selects one AGV v_i from all received distances d_i, notifies AGV v_i for its acceptance and notifies the other AGVs for their rejection.

5.1 UML Statechart Diagrams

We assume that AGVs, stations, and the input and output storages are all modeled by class diagrams and that their behavior is given by Statechart diagrams. We focus here on the subaspects of the specification of a station input buffer that is in charge of delivery request management. The corresponding Statechart diagram (see Fig. 4) is separated into two parallel substates, one for handling messages from other stations which request an notification acceptance for delivery (Acceptor). The second one processes the loading after the acceptance of a delivery (Loader).

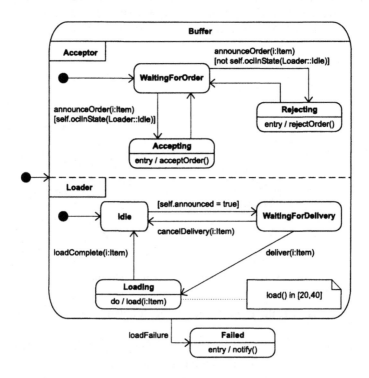

Fig. 4. Statechart Diagram of the Input Buffer

To model behavior over time, we are using text annotations. In our example, there is a time interval assigned to state Loading: "load in [20,40]" means that Loading takes between 20 and 40 time units. If the buffer fails for some reason, e.g., a sensor is sending a failure signal, the buffer enters a failure state, notifies the AGVs and other stations, and gives an error report.

5.2 OCL Constraints

We now specify some example constraints for the buffer of the previously described Statechart diagram, applying our OCL extension with temporal operations.

We first request that new workpieces have to periodically arrive at the input buffer within time intervals of at most 100 time units. In other words, state Loading can always be reached again within 100 time units. The corresponding OCL expression is

```
context Buffer
inv: Loader@post[1,100]->forAll(p:OclPath|p->includes(Loading))
```

Note that Buffer::Loader is a composite sequential state and that its configurations can be expressed by single states. The next invariant defines that a buffer must not accept a new order when still waiting for a delivery:

```
context Buffer
inv: self@post->forAll(p:OclPath | p->excludes(
            Set{Acceptor::Accepting, Loader::WaitingForDelivery}))
```

Finally, we present an example for an application of a configuration sequence and the usefulness of let-expressions in complex constraints. We request that immediately after an order is accepted, Buffer::Acceptor returns to state WaitingForOrder and Buffer::Loader changes to WaitingForDelivery. Thereafter, the order should arrive within 100 time units at the buffer, and state Loading is entered, while Acceptor must not be in state Accepting.

```
context Buffer
def: let waitForOrder   = Acceptor::WaitingForOrder
     let waitForDeliver = Loader::WaitingForDelivery
inv: let acceptPath =
         Sequence {
            Set{Acceptor::Accepting,Loader::Idle}[1],
            Set{waitForOrder,waitForDelivery}[1,100],
            Set{not Acceptor::Accepting,Loader::Loading}
         } in
      self@post->includes(acceptPath)
```

6   Implementation

The temporal extensions as presented here are integrated into our OCL parser and type checker (see Fig. 5). The checker is implemented in Java 1.3 using Swing components. The visual capture loads and edits OCL types, model descriptions, and OCL constraints in parallel. The parsers are implemented with JavaCC (www.webgain.com) based on an early implementation of OCL Version 1.1 [8]. Correctly parsed types are integrated into type tree structures. Class models and Statecharts are currently modeled by textual means. For this, we have implemented a system to parse textual descriptions of class models and Statecharts. Constraints with temporal operations are automatically translated to CCTL formulae for model checking.

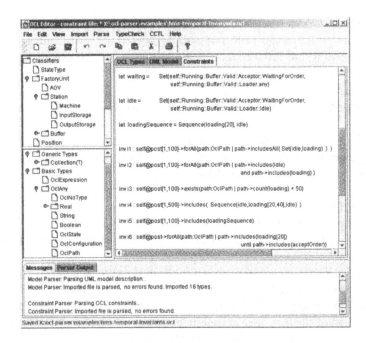

Fig. 5. OCL Parser and Type Checker

7 Summary and Conclusion

We have presented an OCL extension for the specification of real-time constraints in state-oriented UML diagrams. Our extensions were outlined on the basis of an OCL metamodel. The presented approach has demonstrated that an OCL extension for real-time specification is possible with only little changes to syntax and semantics of current OCL. It has been demonstrated that extensions into that direction are not in conflict with general OCL concepts. Due to the increasing importance of real-time systems we think that enhancements for real-time systems specification are worth to be considered in future official OCL versions.

The semantics of our extensions are given by their translation to Clocked CTL formulae which also provides a sound basis for a combined UML and OCL application for formal verification by model checking. The presented extensions are based on a future-oriented temporal logic. However, the general concepts can be easily extended to past-oriented constraints and to a generalization to capture various additional logics.

Acknowledgements. This work has been supported by the DFG project GRASP within the DFG Priority Programme "Integration von Techniken der Softwarespezifikation für ingenieurwissenschaftliche Anwendungen". We appreciate the help of Prof. P.H.P. Bhatt for valuable discussions and proof reading.

References

[1] W. Ahrendt, T. Baar, B. Beckert, M. Giese, E. Habermalz, R. Hähnle, W. Menzel, and P. H. Schmitt. The KeY Approach: Integrating Object Oriented Design and Formal Verification. In M. Ojeda-Aciego, I. P. de Guzmán, G. Brewka, and L. M. Pereira, editors, *8th European Workshop on Logics in AI (JELIA), Malaga, Spain*, volume 1919 of *Lecture Notes in Computer Science*, pages 21–36. Springer-Verlag, Oct. 2000.

[2] T. Baar and R. Hähnle. An Integrated Metamodel for OCL Types. In R. France, B. Rumpe, J.-M. Bruel, A. Moreira, J. Whittle, and I. Ober, editors, *Proc. of OOPSLA 2000, Workshop Refactoring the UML: In Search of the Core*, Minneapolis, Minnesota, USA, 2000.

[3] U. Brockmeyer and G. Wittich. Tamagotchis Need Not Die – Verification of STATEMATE Designs. In B. Steffen, editor, *Tools and Algorithms for the Construction and Analysis of Systems*, volume 1384 of *Lecture Notes in Computer Science*, pages 217–231. Springer-Verlag, 1998.

[4] E. Clarke, O. Grumberg, and D. Peled. *Model Checking*. MIT PRESS, 1999.

[5] D. Distefano, J.-P. Katoen, and A. Rensink. On a Temporal Logic for Object-Based Systems. In S. F. Smith and C. L. Talcott, editors, *Proc. of FMOODS'2000 – Formal Methods for Open Object-Based Distributed Systems IV*, Stanford, CA, USA, September 2000.

[6] R. Elmasri and S. B. Navathe. *Fundamentals of Database Systems*. Addison-Wesley World Student Series, 3rd edition, 2000.

[7] Object Management Group (OMG). UML Unified Modeling Language Specification, Version 1.3, March 2000. URL: http://www.omg.org/technology/documents/formal/uml.htm (last visited on July 11th, 2001).

[8] OCL Parser, Version 0.3, 1997. URL: http://www-4.ibm.com/software/ad/library/standards/ocl-download.html (last visited on July 11th, 2001).

[9] S. Ramakrishnan and J. McGregor. Extending OCL to Support Temporal Operators. In *Proc. of the 21st International Conference on Software Engineering (ICSE99), Workshop on Testing Distributed Component-Based Systems*, Los Angeles, May 1999.

[10] S. Ramakrishnan and J. McGregor. Modelling and Testing OO Distributed Systems with Temporal Logic Formalisms. In *18th International IASTED Conference Applied Informatics'2000*, Innsbruck, Austria, 2000.

[11] M. Richters and M. Gogolla. A Metamodel for OCL. In R. France and B. Rumpe, editors, *UML'99 – The Unified Modeling Language. Beyond the Standard. Second International Conference, Fort Collins, CO, USA*, volume 1723 of *Lecture Notes in Computer Science*, pages 156–171. Springer-Verlag, 1999.

[12] J. Ruf and T. Kropf. Symbolic Model Checking for a Discrete Clocked Temporal Logic with Intervals. In E. Cerny and D. Probst, editors, *Conference on Correct Hardware Design and Verification Methods (CHARME)*, pages 146–166, Montreal, Canada, October 1997. IFIP WG 10.5, Chapman and Hall.

[13] J. Warmer. The Draft 1.4 OCL Grammar, Version 0.1c. Technical report, Klasse Objecten, June 2000. URL: http://www.klasse.nl/ocl/ocl-grammar-01c.pdf (last visited on July 11th, 2001).

[14] J. Warmer. UML 1.4 RTF: OCL Issues – Changes from 1.3 to 1.4. Technical report, Klasse Objecten, March 2000. URL: http://www.klasse.nl/ocl/ocl-issues.pdf (last visited on July 11th, 2001).

Appendix A

Grammar

The here presented grammar in EBNF is for the definition of OCL predefined types based on the metamodel discussed in Section 4.1. A type definition consists of the type name, preceded by its mandatory metatype name, and succeeded by optional supertypes and the definition body. We have added a non-terminal umlStereotype to be able to declare types as "abstract" or as "enumeration". We allow sequences of names in the rule definitionBody to define enumeration types. The grammar rule returnType is modified in comparison to its OCL definition, as we allow parameter names and operation names in a return type, e.g., e.evaluationType.

Moreover, we had to modify the rule for operationName; logical operation names like implies and not can be removed (cf. [14], issue 3138).

```
typeDefinitions     ::= "<startTypeDef>" ( typeDefinition )*
                        "<endTypeDef>"
typeDefinition      ::=  metatypeSpecifier ( umlStereotype )?
                            typeSpecifier ( supertypes )?
                            "{" definitionBody "}"
metatypeSpecifier   ::= "CollectionConstructor" | "CollectionType"
                        | "OclBasicType" | "Class" | "DataType"
umlStereotype       ::= "<<" name ">>"
typeSpecifier       ::= simpleTypeSpecifier
                        | collectionType
supertypes          ::= "<supertype>"
                            typeSpecifier ( "," typeSpecifier )*
definitionBody      ::= ( operation | attribute )*
                        | ( name ( ',' name )* )?
operation           ::= operationName
                            "(" ( formalParameterList )? ")"
                            ( ":" returnType )? ";"
operationName       ::= name | "=" | "+" | "-" | "<" | "<="
                        | ">=" | ">" | "/" | "*" | "<>"
formalParameterList ::= name ":" typeSpecifier
                            ( "," name ":" typeSpecifier )*
returnType          ::= ( collectionKind
                            "(" pathName ( "." operationName )? ")"
                          )
                        | ( pathName ( "." operationName )? )
attribute           ::= name ":" simpleTypeSpecifier ";"
collectionType      ::= collectionKind "(" simpleTypeSpecifier ")"
collectionKind      ::= "Set" | "Bag" | "Sequence" | "Collection"
simpleTypeSpecifier ::= pathName
pathName            ::= name ( "::" name )*
```

Example

For the previous grammar, the definition of the generic type Set is specified as follows:

```
CollectionConstructor Set(T) <supertype> Collection(T) {
    =               (s : Set(T))          : Boolean;
    <>              (s : Set(T))          : Boolean;
    select          (e : OclExpression)   : Set(T);
    reject          (e : OclExpression)   : Set(T);
    including       (t : T)               : Set(T);
    excluding       (t : T)               : Set(T);
    union           (s : Set(T))          : Set(T);
    union           (b : Bag(T))          : Bag(T);
    intersection    (s : Set(T))          : Set(T);
    intersection    (b : Bag(T))          : Set(T);
    -               (s : Set(T))          : Set(T);
    collect         (e : OclExpression)   : Bag(e.evaluationType);
    symmetricDifference     (t : T)       : Set(T);
}
```

Set inherits all operations from Collection because of the subtype relationship. Note here that operations = and <> are explicitly listed because of their different semantics in the generic types Set, Sequence, and Bag.

Appendix B

This appendix gives a listing of all OCL rules that had to be modified for our extension with respect to OCL version 1.4 RTF [13].

1. Add a new keyword until to the list of logical operators. Note that we do not restrict the qualifiers to conform to a well-formed interval declaration here, although this can be easily realized.

    ```
    logicalOperator ::= "and" | "or" | "xor" | "implies"
                      | ( "until" (qualifiers)? )
    ```

2. Add the @-operator as a third property access facility to the grammar rule post-fixExpression. It may be used only for temporal operations.

    ```
    postfixExpression ::= primaryExpression
                          ( ( "." | "->" | "@" ) propertyCall )*
    ```

3. Remove the rule timeExpression from the OCL grammar, as @pre is now derived through postfixExpression. Note that we now regard pre as an operation defined in OclAny.

4. Remove the term (timeExpression)? from the rule propertyCall to obtain a consistent grammar again. The resulting rule is

    ```
    propertyCall ::= pathName (qualifiers)?
                     (propertyCallParameters)?
    ```

Statistical Constraints and Verification

John Knapman

IBM, Hursley Park, Winchester, Hampshire, SO21 2JN, England
knapman@uk.ibm.com

Abstract. Statistical constraints have been introduced to UML models to describe their most salient aspects, allowing a natural expression of what is usually
the case while tolerating exceptions. They are defined using well-known statistical constructs in terms of OCL collections. They offer more freedom and
flexibility than the standard logical quantifiers ('exists' and 'forAll'). This is
achieved in a way that is mathematically well formed so that such constraints
can be interpreted and verified at run time when a system (represented by a
UML model) has been deployed. To make the constraints intelligible to non-IT
people, a grammar has been defined that supports more than one syntactic style.
The syntax of OCL is supported in addition to other styles that are more accessible to persons without mathematical or computer-science training, and the
styles can be mixed. The paper shows examples of statistical constraints, particularly in cases where application systems are being extended by the addition
of new capabilities and a new software package for business-to-business (B2B)
trading on the Internet. The scenarios involve setting up routing and transformations using a message broker with verification on both extracted and sample
data. There are also examples of limiting the complexity of transformations by
constraining their definitions.

1   Introduction

Statistical or approximate constraints were recently introduced to UML models by
extending the OCL in two directions. The first was to build on OCL's provision of
collection classes; the second was to offer greater syntactic flexibility. Statistical constraints are designed to express the most salient aspects of a model or of the behavior
that it implies in a manner that has a precise meaning but still allows flexibility in the
degree of conformance. A constraint such as, "Most purchase orders go to Fulfillment," says something that can be verified statistically at execution time or through
model-based simulation if we give a straightforward meaning to such quantifiers as
"most" and "some" based on percentage ranges of cases. We can say that "most" implies $p>75\%$ while "some" implies $25\%\leq p\leq75\%$, where p stands for the proportion of
cases that satisfy the constraint. The choice of percentages to be associated with
quantifiers can be made by installers or amended in the light of usage statistics.

Statistical constraints can be used to characterize processes in a manner that is
comprehensible to people who are not IT specialists. They provide a dimension of ab-

A. Clark and J. Warmer (Eds.): Object Modeling with the OCL, LNCS 2263, pp. 172-188, 2002.
© Springer-Verlag Berlin Heidelberg 2002

straction that is distinct from the customary high and low-level views of application functions but which is complementary to, and compatible with, the more conventional OO design methods of UML. Statistical constraints typically describe what is usually or often the case. Examples can deal with logical flow, sequencing, timing and data relationships.

A monitoring tool can extract sample data from a running system such as a message broker and report on conformance or deviations, either in real time or off line. Such verification is possible also at design and development time if suitable sample data is available together with a model simulator or test bed. The aim is to report on exceptions over statistically or commercially significant periods (e.g., hours or days) rather than to enforce constraints rigidly.

To treat sample data adequately, an additional collection class is introduced. OCL offers three specializations of collection: bags, sets and sequences. A sequence is ordered and is the natural representation for a set of sequential messages containing data to trigger an operation. The order of a sequence is important for correlation with other sets of messages that are logically related, such as the input and output of an operation. However, it is not possible to include all the messages used or created by an operation, since that would entail knowing not just its complete usage history but its future usage as well. We must deal with sample data, either taken from monitoring deployed implementations or prepared by hand, by a simulator or by a test case generator. Starting with OCL collections, we define a *stream* as a collection of samples, each of which is a sequence. A constraint on a stream is taken to be a constraint on a (statistically significant) sample from the stream.

OCL provides a range of operators and quantifiers on collections. We define an operator

```
c->percent(x,y)
```

as constraining the size of a subcollection of c to be between x% and y% of the size of c. This can then be used to define other quantifiers such as ->some(), ->most() or ->few() as ->percent(25,75), ->percent(75,100) or ->percent(0,10), respectively. The exact numbers can be varied [1].

1.1   Semantics, Simulation, and Animation

Having defined the semantics in OCL terms, it is possible to map these constraints not only to operational systems but also to simulations. A convenient language in which to prototype this is PROLOG because of its natural support for constraint-based programming. Sample datasets can be represented in lists, and constraints appear as predicates. It is also possible to cast the graphical elements of a UML model in PROLOG with suitable additional clauses covering such basic rules as inheritance of methods and attributes in classes and types. Indeed, a UML model can itself be regarded as a set of constraints on its elements.

Modeling in this way with sample data makes it possible to verify the consistency of models (with their constraints) and their refinements, as far as the semantics of

UML allow. The models in this form are active, in that it is possible to perform or animate them. It is also possible to test and verify the concepts of statistical constraints themselves, as has been done for several examples. However, PROLOG models may not be suitable for dealing with operational data in any quantity; a Java implementation may be preferable.

1.2   Syntax and Grammar

When statistical constraints are added to OCL, the syntax becomes somewhat unwieldy. A generalized grammar has been defined that permits a choice of syntax, including OCL alongside other styles as exemplified by: "Most complaints give rise to management reports in 10 seconds." The intention is to make constraints readable to non–IT specialists while still giving them a precise meaning. For that reason, this extension to OCL has been named the Business-oriented Constraint Language (BCL).

The grammar permits operations to be defined as prefixes, suffixes, bracketed expressions and combinations of these. Users who are comfortable with a more mathematical style can adhere to conventional parenthesized expressions such as:

```
CorporateRequisitions->some()
    ->forAll(c | c.goTo (CorporateAuthorityCheck))
```

An alternative style for this constraint is, "Some corporate requisitions go to Corporate Authority Check." Software vendors, installers and users could all define operations of their own. The paper [2] gives UML state diagrams for the parser, including rules for ambiguous cases. The parser recognizes and assigns types for variables and expressions. These allow the avoidance of conventional parentheses in most cases. The parser is defined so that it requires look-ahead no further than one term, which is important for reasons of efficiency. It has been prototyped in PROLOG.

2   Example 1

The example illustrates an addition to the design of a system for catalogue sales so that Open Buying on the Internet (OBI) will be used for getting approval of requisitions from selected corporate customers. A software package for business-to-business (B2B) trading is to be used. The class diagram in Fig. 1 shows the design of a company's existing system. In Fig. 2, the designer has shown the new use of OBI. Figs. 3 and 4 are supposed to be generic samples provided with the B2B software package; they are not specific to a company.

Fig. 1 shows part of an order-entry system represented as a UML class diagram. This could be a web-based business-to-consumer (B2C) system that itself evolved from an earlier 3270-based system designed for taking orders over the telephone. In turn, that might have started life based on punched-card input or electronic date interchange (EDI) files on magnetic tape. Some of these earlier modalities may still be in use, complemented by a direct sales channel in which sales representatives use a client-server messaging system from mobile computers. The class diagram includes a statistical constraint: "Most corporate requisitions go to Corporate Authority Check." This describes the mainline actions and can also be regarded as an annotation. Many UML users confine themselves to class diagrams with annotations, and the annotations informally describe salient aspects of the behavior. It is possible to write some of these in BCL in a form in which they are machine readable and can be verified during later execution.

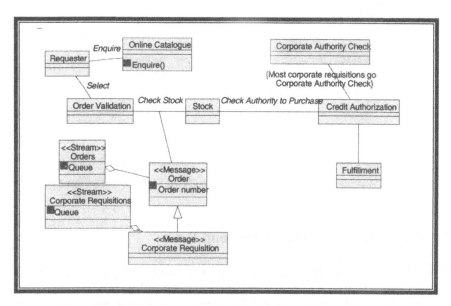

Fig. 1. Class diagram for part of an order entry system

As the B2B software package or infrastructure product is introduced, one of the changes will be that corporate requisitions raised by individuals from selected companies will be checked back to their corporate buying departments in real time using OBI. This will expedite their orders compared with the existing method of checking authority to purchase, which is done as part of the credit check.

Fig. 2 shows the amended class diagram as a designer could draw it to summarize at a fairly high level the changes needed to introduce OBI for this purpose.

A router has been introduced to intercept messages being passed from the Stock Check to Credit Authorization. This passes messages from selected corporate customers to the OBI Order Request Manager, which checks back with the relevant purchasing department over the Internet and then passes approved orders on to Fulfillment. This is an important alternative to what was previously the mainline route. Now routing is divided mainly between these alternatives, and so the first constraint says "some" instead of "most" and another one has been introduced.

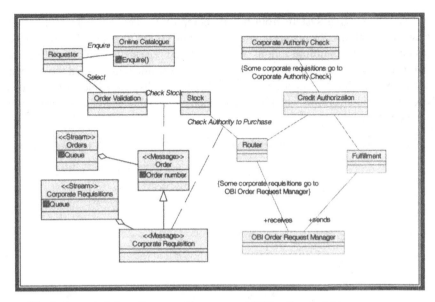

Fig. 2. Amended class diagram with router and OBI order requisition manager

3   Productivity of Development and Reuse

Most enterprises approach a new IT challenge, such as offering greater Internet access to their customers and trading partners, with a substantial legacy of existing systems. They generally find it expedient to reuse these assets when creating new systems. Techniques exist to extract statistical relationships between elements of existing systems by monitoring and correlating messages that flow between them (e.g., [3]). A major challenge is to help these enterprises speed up the development and deployment of such hybrid application systems. There are many efforts under way to do this, including a common model for visual programming as flow composition, standardized design and modeling methods based on UML profiles and the MOF, and continuing extension of Enterprise Java Beans (EJBs). Particularly relevant are the UML profiles for Enterprise Application Integration (EAI) [4] and Enterprise Distributed Object Computing (EDOC) [5].

Each of these and other advances establishes more patterns and standard ways of doing things. They improve the degree of streamlining and automation of the development process by speeding up the work that starts with a statement of requirements followed by a high-level design that is eventually refined to an implementation. In the B2B example, we might start with a set of flow diagrams representing existing business processes. We will also have access to new models and modeling elements that represent B2B capabilities. The task can be viewed as transforming the existing models by adding extra capabilities. Formally it is seen as a search problem. The idea is to hypothesize routing and transformation rules and test them, choosing the best combination found. There may be hundreds of process-flow diagrams, each capable of undergoing various changes.

Unfortunately, in commercially realistic scenarios, the number of combinations will be too great for conventional methods. Suppose a large enterprise has 30,000 application programs and there are several ways of invoking them (e.g., synchronously, asynchronously, via screen scraping, or wrapped in an EJB). If each interface has an average of 200 fields and we allow message augmentation (enrichment) from databases, the number of combinations is compounded to 2^{50}. Calculations, even with some simplifying assumptions (confined to derivations from up to four other fields with, say, eight operations drawn from a set of a dozen operators), increase the number of combinations by a further factor of 2^{16} to 2^{66}. These estimates are purely illustrative, but the numbers quoted are based on experience of large IT systems at a number of enterprises.

A well-established approach to the problems is to divide them into simpler subproblems. This can take the form of architectural decomposition, progressive topdown refinement, bottom-up composition from simpler elements, or a combination of these and other methods. Statistical constraints can be used for verification at intermediate stages of design and development using test data, sample data or extracts from operational data.

4   Example 2

The next level of refinement for part of the OBI scenario is shown in the next two diagrams. In Fig. 3, a purchase order request is raised and sent based on information about the trading partner held by the Trading Partners Manager.

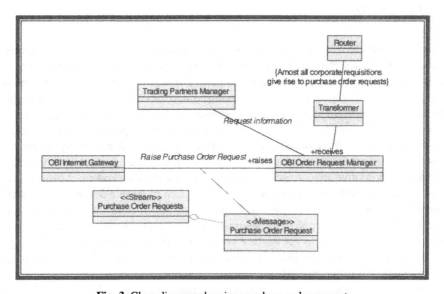

Fig. 3. Class diagram showing purchase order request

In Fig. 4, purchase orders are received from corporate customers, checked (including matching to purchase order requests) and passed to Fulfillment. Each diagram includes a statistical constraint with the respective quantifiers "most" and "almost all".

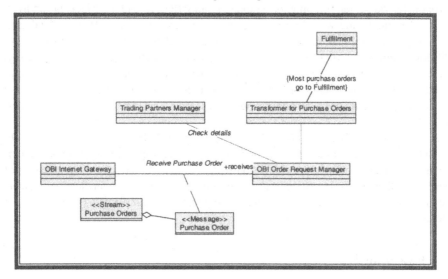

Fig. 4. Class diagram showing purchase order (response to requisition)

5   Structuring

Many enterprises have modeled their IT systems. Some are extending these models to connect with models of the business. Recent approaches to architectural modeling in UML [6] promise to enhance these possibilities. The idea of architectural modeling is to support precisely the kinds of composition and decomposition that are necessary to give structure to designs and to make implementations intelligible and manageable.

A problem that remains challenging is to streamline development approaches at the architectural level. Increasingly, departments create new capabilities by fitting together intermediate-level components, whether they be their own previously developed application programs or packages bought from software vendors. Software design and development tools are advancing to make such pluggable development easier. Statistical constraints provide additional high-level information about a process or system, and they can be applied to determine to what extent an implementation conforms to them. However, to get the best value out of them, we need to consider ways of checking the conformance and consistency of design refinements before a complete implementation has been created.

One means of doing this is to perform symbolic execution of models. This is sometimes known as 'animation' and has been demonstrated in the B tool [7] and in the design language Z [8]. Another could be to work at a more symbolic level, representing data by fuzzy sets or cross-correlated probability distributions. A complementary approach to evaluating prospective refinements or, ultimately, implementations of higher-level architectural or design constructs is to use sample data, preferably extracted from recently running systems. This is the method adopted here for verifying statistical or approximate constraints on a design change.

6   Functional Verification and Test Coverage

There is a considerable body of research on the design of test datasets that provide maximal coverage of a problem space for a given algorithm [9]. Our task can be related to that. We seek a tradeoff between complexity of evaluation of possibilities and the probability that we will achieve representative coverage of the problem space.

The context for this tradeoff is that alternative design decisions are being made. Consider the B2B examples. When a designer is considering the option of inserting or changing an element in a high-level design, we cannot evaluate all possible refinements or implementations of that design change. We can, however, test it against sample data and evaluate it against constraints, including statistical constraints. We can maximize the chances (and hence the estimated probability or evaluation function) by judicious choices of data extracted from live operations, from test runs and by running simulations of operations and application systems chosen from those already in use, supplied with a software package (including samples), generated using default values from a flow diagram or prepared by hand.

6.1   Characterizing Coverage Statistically

Most of the work on calculating coverage of test data and test cases is based on formal specifications such as Z. There is some work on UML, but UML's lack of rigorous formal semantics makes such work problematic. Alloy [10]), for instance, develops a formal graphical notation that allows models to be checked for self consistency, but it is not UML. Unfortunately, Z, VDL and similar methods are not widely used. They are extensively employed for safety-critical systems (e.g., air traffic control or monitoring of nuclear installations) but seem inaccessible to most commercial programmers, let alone business specialists or managers. This is true even for mission-critical applications that are essential to keeping commercial enterprises in operation, notwithstanding that some of these systems run vital parts of the global economy and deal with massive sums of money.

Characterizing operations by means of sets of input and output data is known formally as an *extensional* definition. The input may consist of parameters, a message, state and database value; the output may be the result, a state change and a database update. A persistent state held in a database can be treated much like a local state change. Defining operations algorithmically, logically or by program code is *intensional*. For most operations, a complete extensional definition is impractical and may well be infinite. However, sample datasets provide a natural and practical characterization that is equally applicable to low-level and high-level components. It is possible to construct sample datasets manually as part of the specification of new components or flows without worrying about the details of how the components are composed. In other words, we can create samples from the extensional definition whether or not we have the intensional definition. Moreover, subsetting is possible in two dimensions. A dataset is like a table. Each member (record, row, tuple or message) contains data elements (fields, columns, tagged values). At the design stage, a sample might not specify all the data elements that will eventually be needed. Hence, the sample table (see example in Table 1) might show only a few rows and columns compared with what could be obtained by extraction from a running operational system. Shortening the rows represents another kind of abstraction, since it means leaving out the details of many fields, just as UML diagrams do not usually show all the attributes of classes. Having fewer rows is like having fewer test cases; testing is much faster and data preparation is easier, but the coverage is a lot less.

Table 1. Sample dataset

Customer number	Requisition number	Code
1712144	787877	A772CA
8232890	787878	A783BB
3801411	787442	X227YY
3911880	787444	X387QQ
5650227	788020	B777TA

In many software practices, the principal way to decide whether a program (procedure, module, object, component) is fit for purpose is to test it. Often, testing is in two parts:

1. Functional verification: someone reads documentation on the program and constructs and runs test cases that exercise the functions. Errors or unexpected results are reported to the programmer who either corrects them or persuades the tester that they were legitimate. This process continues until the rate at which errors are found has fallen below a certain level.
2. System test: a group of people test a collection of programs to ensure that they work together. This may lead to the discovery of design errors or programming errors that were missed during functional verification. Again, test cases are created and run until the rate at which errors are found has fallen below a certain level.

A great deal of human and managerial judgement is involved in deciding what is an acceptable level, depending on the uses to which the software will be put and the consequent costs or penalties of errors being found in subsequent use. Essentially, though, testing is a statistical process in which it is assumed that some errors remain. Often, there is controversy about the classification of some exceptions, which may lead to changes in the documentation or even aspects of the design. Software may then be subject to trial runs with users or beta testing. After going into use (or commercial distribution) it is expected that the software will have to be serviced. Again, the errors reported will involve a mix of undisputed coding errors and judgements about how the software was intended to behave or is now required to behave. Servicing will also be monitored statistically, and this will affect decisions about the frequency with which updates are implemented. In some cases it can lead to withdrawal from use.

In safety-critical systems, the goal is absolute certainty. However, practitioners know that this goal is an unachievable ideal. Safety standards for aircraft systems, for example, are not set as absolutes but rather as extremely long mean times to failure. Duplex, triplex or even (in manned spacecraft) quintuplex redundancy may be incorporated to minimize the odds of system failure in the event of critical-component failure. Commercial IT systems may be built for mean times to failure of several years, depending on a cost-benefit analysis and an estimate of their likely obsolescence. In fast-moving industries, where obsolescence is rapid, shorter times to failure can be tolerated, whereas the mean time to failure for aircraft systems must be orders of magnitude greater.

6.2   Statistical Estimating

A real process, once implemented, has a lifetime during which it handles a finite set of input-output pairs. This set is a precise description of it, whereas the code is liable to undergo correction and maintenance and is a less definitive statement about a process. Essentially a procedure has a signature that constrains the input values, usually through type specifications, and a body that applies further constraints to the input (raising errors where necessary) and generates the output values. Given the practical impossibility for both human beings and machines to deal with such vast sets (important parts of which will be in the future) or even with the space of possible algorithms that might constrain and generate such sets, the customary design practice is to deal with abstractions. Popularly these take the form of UML diagrams with annotations and, sometimes, formal constraints. These are contrived to lead to implementations in a programming language, usually textual (e.g., Java or C++) but sometimes visual (e.g., message flows as in the message broker MQSeries Integrator Version 2 [11]). An important intermediate stage for complex processes is sometimes the use of a simulation tool such as that from Holosofx [12], which works with MQSeries Workflow [13].

Statistical constraints provide an additional succinct description of salient aspects. They have the virtue of being verifiable with running code but, compared with other kinds of constraints, typically need information to be extracted and accumulated statistically over a period of time. Such an accumulation is a sample from the total set of input-output pairs that the process deals with over its lifetime. As argued above, this total set defines the process. Samples, either drawn from an executing system or prepared by hand, are a useful and convenient means of describing the behavior or intended behavior of a process. They may be of varying size, right down to a brief sample that is almost as short as a process's signature.

There are well-known methods for assessing the reliability or likelihood of conclusions drawn from samples of varying sizes, such as the method of Pareto [14] (also called the 80-20 Rule). In general with samples, there is a tradeoff between the time and resources needed to perform evaluation and the reliability of the results.

When verifying that a design or its implementation satisfy given requirements, sample data can serve both to amplify the requirements and identify parts of the solution. It supplements other forms of information but is particularly tractable as a means of discriminating between hypotheses at high levels, where model-based evaluation or simulation of potentially very many alternative realizations at the next lower level is likely to be prohibitively expensive or exponentially slow.

A key issue with sample data sets is consistency. Consistent samples can be prepared in advance by hand or extracted from running systems. Data mining algorithms such as statistical analysis or token collection and matching can be used offline on both databases and audit trails of messages to compute the likelihood that fields in different message formats, databases and signatures are the same. Depending on the strength of the evidence, a procedure can select sample data sets that share a degree of overlap that reflects the degree of certainty about whether they should be identified with one another. Although in both cases there is a risk of false or accidental identification, the risk is mitigated by the use of larger data sets. The sample values provide a ready means to hypothesize and test transformations between messages, signatures and database schemas.

Consistency of sample data is harder to achieve in the case of a new system that is under design. Of course, the designer can always prepare test data by hand, just as programmers often have to. In some cases, a simulation can be used to create more test data, provided some extracted operational data is available. A commercially supplied software package may come with some samples, but it obviously cannot come with data from the customer's business. Again, though, if there is some extracted operational data, this can be used to drive the package and create output data for more evaluation and testing.

Of course, sample data is not the only method for evaluating and improving designs and other software artefacts. The use of samples supplements other methods, such as running simulations, executing stubs or using default options and settings.

7   Example 3

In the next example (Fig. 5), an investment banking system is shown that links Depositors to classes representing the main services offered when a deposit is received. Other investment services (e.g., foreign currency investments) are performed at a later stage and so are not linked directly. A statistical constraint identifies the mainline route for the majority of transactions.

The system is to be improved (Fig. 6) so that more options are available straight away. A message broker is to be used so that the routing rules can readily be amended in the light of experience and to minimize the amount of conventional application programming needed.

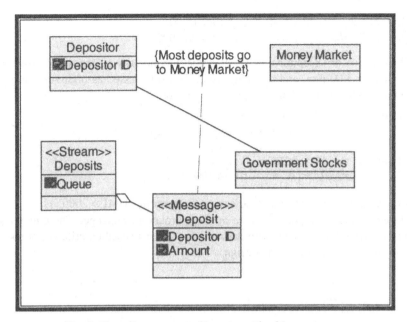

Fig. 5. Class diagram: part of investment banking system

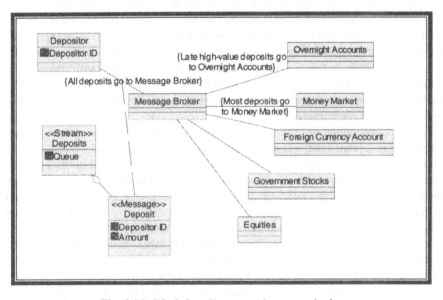

Fig. 6. Modified class diagram with message broker

This example includes a statistical constraint with the terms "late" and "high-value". These terms represent statistical concepts and are themselves defined using statistical constraints as follows:

Most *late* deposits have time stamp after 15:00.
Most *high-value* deposits have amount > 400,000.

These allow for exceptions. They state that the majority of deposits classed as late come in after 3:00 p.m. and the majority of deposits classed as high-value are worth more than 400,000 each. The OCL equivalents are:

```
((deposits->late())->most())
    ->forAll(d|after(1500,d.timeStamp))

((deposits->highValue())->most())
    ->forAll(d|d.amount>400000)
```

More examples of such statistical concepts appear in «UML» 2000 [1].

The exact rules incorporated in the message broker may change. There may also be manual override for selected customers or other actions based on criteria not specified at this level of abstraction in the design.

8   Defining Transformations

In a related task, we are interested in defining the rules and, in particular, the transformations to be performed by the message broker. Constraints (statistical or otherwise) can be applied with benefit at this stage as well as at run time. The approach to be taken is to treat the existing systems as black-box services and define routing and transformation rules to them. This could require quite complex transformations, including the augmentation of messages by referencing databases. A subsequent refinement might be to revise some of these systems, removing obsolete parts and incorporating the database references directly.

The black-box definitions are based on sample datasets. Transformations are constructed from a predefined set; these have a mixture of algorithmic and data-based definitions. Primitive transforms such as arithmetic operators could in theory be defined extensionally (as triples of arguments and results), but this would be inefficient. On the other hand, a table lookup or database reference (giving, e.g., a telephone number for a customer number) is naturally defined over datasets. (PROLOG programmers are familiar with this dichotomy.) Transformations may be only partly defined at first so that only some of the fields are dealt with, others being deferred for more detailed consideration later in the development cycle.

For the sake of consistency, samples need to be prepared from logically related data instances. Suppose that deposits arrive late in the day, are invested overnight and then are placed in other accounts or securities the next day. To be usable for verifying designs and constraints, samples must cover both days so that a representative set of transactions is present that covers the business processes that are taking place. This kind of requirement can still be expressed statistically in terms of data samples, even though it applies to an administrative operation rather than a direct business operation.

Statistical constraints, in common with other OCL constraints, can also be applied to models themselves or their refinements. Here they can govern the kinds of transforms that are acceptable. If nearly every field undergoes change during a transformation, we may decide that transformation between black-box operations is the wrong approach for some applications. Constraints of this kind can be one way for system administrators to keep a check on the complexity of transforms defined by application developers.

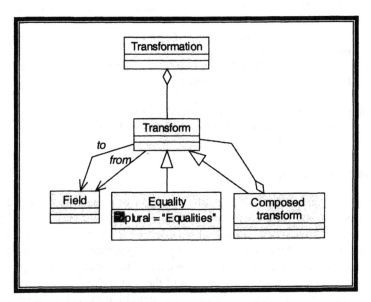

Fig. 7. Structure of transformations

As some of the other examples illustrate, constraints can be made quite succinct and readable by introducing new terms, which are illustrated in the class diagram. To begin with, we say that a *transformation* applies to a whole message or group of fields and results in an output message or group; a *transform* applies to an individual field or a small number of input fields but results in a single output field as shown in Fig. 7. We would like to express an expectation that most transformations carry over most of the fields unchanged and only a minority need transforms applied. Otherwise application programming would probably be preferable to use of a message broker, and the administrator would like to be alerted to the potential performance and maintenance problems that might ensue.

We decide to use the word "simple" to express this concept and then define it statistically. This can be expressed as follows:[1]

---

[1] Plurals can be defined by an optional tagged value *plural* and a little extra OCL:

```
        class.pluralName=class.allInstances.name
    if class.plural=""
      then class.pluralName=concat(class.name,"s")
      else class.pluralName=class.plural endif
```

Most transformations are simple.

Transformation T is *simple* **if** most transforms in T are equalities **and** few transforms in T are composed transforms.

Almost all composed transforms contain no more than 4 transforms.

In the third constraint, we have added a limit on the complexity of almost all composed transforms. The equivalent OCL is:

```
(transformations->most())->forAll(T|T.isSimple())

if (T.transforms->most())->forAll(R|R.oclType=equality)
    and (T.transforms->few())
        ->forAll(R|R.oclType=composedTransform)
    then T.isSimple() endif

(composedTransforms->almostAll())
    ->forAll(C|C.transforms->size()<=4)
```

8.1   Software Packages

A vendor-supplied software package obviously cannot come with sample data drawn directly from a customer's operational system, even though it may come with various samples that help to explain its use and provide a basis for it to be tailored to the particular requirements of the customer enterprise. To generate test datasets, the package must be run against some of the enterprise data. This entails setting up transformations between selected input message types of the package and messages or other data already in use in the customer's systems. The definition of such transformations can be governed or verified by statistical and other constraints, such as requiring that cost equals quantity times unit price, which is expected in the case of OBI messages.

A somewhat different kind of constraint can be applied to the matching of names between the package and the enterprise's message signatures, even though there will often be cases where the names are too obscure (e.g., CHB0787 coming from the days of eight-byte names). Suppose a thesaurus (or synonym table) for OBI has been defined like the one in Table 2. The customer might want to extend the thesaurus with names or even comments drawn from data-structure definitions.

The synonym table can be used to constrain likely transformations. We prefer those that map like-named or synonymous fields. In keeping with the BCL philosophy, we avoid long compound sentences by introducing approximate terms representing concepts that are statistical in nature. We can write the main constraint as:

Most transforms map similar names.

Detail to define *map(s) similar names* can then be added separately, as follows:

Transform T from field A to field B *maps similar names*
    ≡ tokens of A.name are similar to tokens of B.name.

Tokens, X, *are similar to* tokens, Y, **=** some X are like some Y.

X *is like* Y **if** X=Y **or** X is synonymous with Y.

Synonymity is defined in terms of the table.

Table 2. Part of an OBI-based thesaurus or synonym table

OBI Term	Near Synonym	OBI Term	Near Synonym
Order request	Requisition	Line item detail	Lines, items, line items, details
Selling organization	Seller, vendor, selling organization	Line item	Item
Name		Qty	Quantity, number
Code	Number, id	Units	Unit
Request	Requisition, order	Item	Part, component
#	Number	No.	Number, id
Buying organization	Customer, buyer, purchaser, buying organisation	Commodity code	
Requisitioner	Initiator, requester, requestor, purchaser, buyer	Description	
Email	E-mail	Mfg	Manufacturing
Receiving contact	Receiver, recipient	Unit price	
Phone	Telephone	Total price	Amount, cost
Payment		Special	
Information	Details	Chg	Charge, supplement, addition
Currency		Allow	Allowance, discount
Procurement card	Credit card	Tax	VAT, sales tax
Other		Total after tax	Amount, amount after tax, amount including tax, amount with tax
Expiration	Expiry	Special instructions	Comment
Authorization	Authorisation		

9   Conclusion

Statistical constraints can be used to characterize salient aspects of models that can be verified on operational data extracts. They constitute a dimension of abstraction that complements the abstraction represented by UML diagrams. Constraints of three kinds have been shown:

1. On sample or extracted data carried or represented as streams of messages
2. On transformations between streams of messages or other datasets, based on sample data
3. On transformations based on names appearing in a synonym table.

The use of statistical constraints has been extended from validation at execution time to such design and development tasks as verifying the plausibility or consistency of transformations of messages and other data.

The constraints can be cast in more than one syntactic form, including standard OCL and a style more accessible to non-IT staff using the flexibility of BCL.

References

1. J.Knapman "Statistical Constraints for EAI" in A.Evans, S.Kent, B.Selic (eds) "«UML» 2000 — The Unified Modeling Language, Advancing the Standard", Third International Conference, October 2000, Springer
2. J.Knapman "Business-oriented Constraint Language" in A.Evans, S.Kent, B.Selic (eds) "«UML» 2000 — The Unified Modeling Language, Advancing the Standard", Third International Conference, October 2000, Springer
3. Bristol Technology's eSleuth, see http://www.bristol.com/esleuth/
4. UML Profile for Event-based Architectures in Enterprise Application Integration (EAI), at http://www.omg.org/techprocess/meetings/schedule/UML_Profile_for_EAI_RFP.html
5. UML Profile for Enterprise Distributed Object Computing, at http://cgi.omg.org/techprocess/meetings/schedule/UML_Profile_for_EDOC_RFP.html
6. T.Weigert, D.Garlan, J.Knapman, B.Møller-Pedersen, B.Selic, "Modeling of Architectures with UML" in A.Evans, S.Kent, B.Selic (eds) "«UML» 2000 — The Unified Modeling Language, Advancing the Standard", Third International Conference, October 2000, Springer
7. B and B-Toolkit at http://www.b-core.com/
8. J.Wordsworth, "Software Development with Z: A Practical Approach to Formal Methods in Software Engineering", Addison-Wesley, 1992
9. W.Howden, "Systems testing and statistical test data coverage", Proc. 21st Annual International Computer Software and Applications Conference (COMPSAC'97), Washington, DC, USA, Aug.1997
10. D.Jackson, I.Schechter, I.Shlyakhter, "Alcoa: the Alloy Constraint Analyzer", Proc. International Conference on Software Engineering, Limerick, Ireland, June 2000
11. IBM MQSeries Integrator Version 2.0.1, at http://www-4.ibm.com/software/ts/mqseries/library/manualsa/#Integrator Version 2.0.1
12. Holosofx Enterprise Process Management Suite, at http://www.holosofx.com
13. IBM MQSeries Workflow, at http://www-4.ibm.com/software/ts/mqseries/library/manualsa/#Workflow
14. V.Pareto, "d'économie politique", 1896-7

«Java»OCL Based on New Presentation of the OCL-Syntax

Bernhard Rumpe

Technische Universität München,
Arcisstr. 21, D-80333 Munich, Germany,
Rumpe@in.tum.de

Abstract. The Object Constraint Language (OCL) is a part of the Unified Modeling Language (UML) – an emerging standard language for object-oriented analysis and design. OCL is designed as a formal language for specifying constraints that cannot be expressed conveniently using UML's diagrammatic notation.

This article describes results of a careful analysis of the syntactic structure of OCL, resulting in a number of improvements of the OCL-syntax. In particular, a new and better readable grammar describing OCL is defined. The paper enhances not only the language OCL itself, but in particular its presentation.

Given the new grammar, a Java-style variant of OCL with essentially the same abstract grammar is defined, which should be more comfortable to Java-programmers.

1 Introduction

The Unified Modeling Language (UML) [17] has become the de-facto standard for modeling object-oriented systems. The UML is a graphical description language and therefore, similar to most other graphical languages, limited in its expressiveness. The Object Constraint Language (OCL) [16] is a precise textual specification language used to complement graphical modeling languages. OCL was designed to express logical constraints within a UML model that cannot or not conveniently enough be expressed with the mainly diagrammatic UML. In particular, OCL supports specifying invariants of classes in a class model and describing pre- and postconditions of operations and methods.

OCL is a textual supplement of UML. As such, it needs to be pragmatic in use, but still concise enough in its definition to be assisted by tools, such as a parser and a type or consistency checker.

The history of language definitions shows, that it is impossible to define a sufficiently useful language in perfect shape from the very beginning. Many different syntactic, semantic, and methodical issues have to be resolved, and different stake-holders want a language adapted for particular needs. Therefore, it is not surprising that the relatively young OCL has some syntactic and semantic flaws that need to be fixed. Fortunately, OCL can build on a large basis of work on already defined languages, starting from the programming languages

A. Clark and J. Warmer (Eds.): Object Modeling with the OCL, LNCS 2263, pp. 189–212, 2002.
© Springer-Verlag Berlin Heidelberg 2002

like Modula-2 [21] or Java [9], including OCL's own predecessor [6], up to textual specification languages such as VDM [7] and Spectrum [3]. The research on language definition shows that not only the language itself, but also its presentation can be improved to make it more amenable for tools as well as for reading and understanding the language.

The purpose of this article is not to provide OCL with semantics. Instead this article concentrates on the syntax and the presentation of this syntax of OCL. In Section 2 separation between syntax and its presentation is discussed in detail. Section 3 furthermore discusses how to use OCL at the meta-level without explicitly including the meta-level of OCL. In Sections 4 and 5 the original OCL grammar given in the OCL specification is re-formulated and the context conditions are adapted based on the insights gained before. Section 6 then presents a syntactic variant of OCL that is oriented towards Java. It is called ≪Java≫OCL and might be regarded as Java-profile of OCL.

It is assumed that the reader is somewhat familiar with OCL as well as with UML class diagrams.

2   Langauges and Their Presentation

This paper restructures the presentation of the expression part of OCL so that its grammar rules are structurued in a way similar to that of Java (and C++). To understand the impact of such a restructuring, it is necessary to look at how language definition works in general. Formally, a textual *language* is a set of *well-formed sentences* over a basic alphabet. This holds for natural languages as well as for Java and OCL.

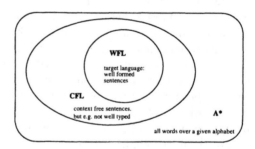

Fig. 1. The hierarchy of language definition

Given an alphabet A (e.g. the ASCII or Unicode character sets), a language is a subset of all words over that alphabet. Among others, Java, Pascal and OCL are examples. Due to the fact that these languages have infinite numbers of sentences (i.e. possible class definitions in Java), a finite, compact and understandable characterization of such a language is necessary.

Normally a compact definition is achieved in two steps. In a first step the so called *context free language* is defined using a grammar. The grammar of a language therefore *presents* a language. The extended Backus-Naur-Form (EBNF) is a comfortable way to describe the grammar. Its conventions are[1]:

- Identifiers included in ⟨ ⟩ brackets denote nonterminal symbols.
- **Underlined boldface** font denote terminal symbols.
- The empty word is denoted by ε.
- Brackets {...} are used for grouping.
- Alternatives are separated by a vertical bar |.
- Constructs followed by a Kleene star, such as ⟨identifier⟩* and {...}* can be repeated zero or more times.
- Optional parts are expressed by a question mark ?.

The context free grammar of a language defines the set of context free sentences, called CFL. However, still many ill formed OCL-expressions may exist. Well known examples are violated typing rules or variables that are used, but not declared or have a wrong type. Therefore, in a second step, context conditions further constrain the CFL, resulting in a set of well-formed sentences (WFL). Standard examples for context conditions are typing rules as well as rules for variables declarations and uses. Unfortunately, there is no simple technique similar to a context free grammar to describe context conditions and therefore these context conditions are usually presented as informal, textual description together with examples. In summary, there are three sets of sentences (see Fig. 1) including each other: WFL $\subset$ CFL $\subset$ A*. In the context of OCL this means, the set of well formed, useful OCL expressions is identified with WFL.

The following sections concentrate on the context free language definition of OCL (called CFL) and the improvement and reformulation of the context conditions is left to others (see related publications in this proceedings).

Context conditions are often referred to as *semantic conditions*. This is partially a historic fault, because context conditions are the last step to define the language. They are heavily influenced by the intended language semantics, but nevertheless they are defined in form of purely syntactic and therefore checkable criteria. In particular, context conditions do not define the semantics of a language. E.g. from a given set of context conditions on a language like OCL or C++ the semantics of the and-operator on undefined values or non-terminating calculations cannot be inferred. The reader is referred to [12] for a general discussion of semantics for modeling languages such as the OCL.

Furthermore, the separation between context free grammar and context conditions is floating. Although, context conditions exist that can clearly not be expressed in a context free grammar, there are other issues that can be defined in context free grammars, but usually aren't. Among them are the priorities of infix operators. The OCL book defines them in context free form, but gets blurred through a number of additional nonterminals (⟨expression⟩,

---

[1] EBNF provides further operators that serve as notational shortcuts, but aren't used here.

⟨ifExpression⟩, ⟨logicalExpression⟩, ⟨relationalExpression⟩, ⟨additiveExpression⟩, etc.). It's more compact, readable and equally precise to use an explicit precedence table, like the one in Table 1 that expresses the same information in a more compact way. Therefore, the relationship between WFL and CFL of a language can strongly be influenced by an intelligible definition.

Table 1. Precedence for OCL operations (highest to lowest).

Name	Syntax	Associativity
Unary operations	`-, not`	right
Multiplication and division	`*, /`	left
Addition and subtraction	`+, -`	left
Relational operations	`<, >, <=, >=`	left
Relational equality	`=, <>`	left
Logical operations	`and, or, xor`	left
Logical implies	`implies`	right

Furthermore, a distinction between the grammar that characterizes a language and the language itself is important. There are numerous grammars that describe the very same (context free) language. As a simple example, the grammar ⟨X⟩ ::=<u>a</u> { <u>b</u> ⟨X⟩ <u>a</u> }* <u>b</u> describes alternating ab-structures. Another grammar for the very same "language" can be defined by:

$$⟨Y⟩ ::= ⟨ADAM⟩^* ⟨ADAM⟩ ⟨ADAM⟩^*$$
$$⟨ADAM⟩ ::= \underline{a} \ ⟨EVE⟩$$
$$⟨EVE⟩ ::= \underline{b} \ ⟨ADAM⟩^?$$

Both grammars present the same language <u>ab</u>{<u>ab</u>}*, but strongly differ in their structure. One important purpose of this article is to restructure the given context free grammar of OCL. These changes aim at an improvement of the grammar of OCL to become more amenable to an interested reader, as well as to be more compact for a tool implementation. Along the way of improving the grammar, there will also be a number of language improvements that will be discussed in the next sections.

3   The Use of OCL. What Are Meta-levels Good for?

3.1   Fitting OCL into a Language Category

The Object Constraint Language (OCL) defines itself as "an expression language that enables one to describe constraints on object-oriented models and other modeling artifacts." ([20], pg. xix). Heavily based on the *constraint* concept, it explicitly gives its own interpretation of this term in an object-oriented setting by "a constraint is a restriction on one or more values of (part of) an object-oriented model or system." ([20], pg. 1).

However, OCL exhibits some characteristics of other kinds of languages and lacks some standard concepts of constraint languages. Therefore, a short comparison of OCL to other languages seems appropriate. The main language categories that are not necessarily disjoint are:

Modeling language allows abstract characterizations of the modeling domain, which may be a system as well as business or other forms of environment.

Object-oriented language encompasses the concept of *object*, together with dynamic creation, identity, and normally also inheritance and classes.

Programming language is primarily characterized through being executable in such a way that it constructively transforms its input (and internal data structures) into an output result.

Logic language provides logic concepts, such as Boolean operators and quantifiers to describe properties of systems and their data structures.

Functional language is an highly compact, executable language that operates without side-effects.

OCL exhibits some characteristics of most of these languages. However, it is not a full modeling language, because OCL does not provide concepts to define new data structures. New classes, methods, or constants cannot be introduced. Therefore, OCL is only intended to be used together with an existing modeling language, such as UML, that needs a supplement for describing constraints. In this combination OCL also exhibits the characteristics of an object-oriented language, because it incorporates the UML typing system.

The relationship of OCL to logic is somewhat difficult. Yes, OCL provides Boolean operators, like and, etc., but these are present in programming languages, like Java, as well. The basic question here is, how OCL treats undefined values. To show the differences, Fig. 2 gives an overview of possible semantics of the and-operator, where some are useful for logic and some are useful for execution. Differences in the presented truth tables are underlined. E.g. in C++ A and B and its commutative B and A are distinguished, where in logic languages this hampers the usability of a language. Current definitions of OCL take different and sometimes inconsistent approaches [20].

Yes, OCL provides two quantifiers, forall and exists, but only for finite domains. Therefore, OCL is only a propositional logic. This means that without further concepts, OCL is neither capable of specifying the transitive closure of the subclass relation ([5]) nor many other recursive or loop based properties. Fortunately, OCL provides some built in data types such as Integer or Strings and can rely on UML based data types as well. Based on given method implementations of the UML model it is possible to specify many constraints beyond propositional logic. In summary, OCL is a propositional specification language that exhibits additional power through data structures and operations provided by UML.

OCL is not a general programming language. It is widely believed, that OCL is executable. This belief is correct in the sense that there are algorithms that can decide on constraints written in propositional logic. However, there are a number of subtle problems among others with non-terminating operations provided by

Classic 2-valued Logic:

a ∧ b	True	False
True	True	False
False	False	False

Strict, implementation:

a and b	True	False	Undef
True	True	False	Undef
False	False	False	Undef
Undef	Undef	Undef	Undef

Parallel implementation and Kleene-Logic:

a ∧ b	True	False	Undef
True	True	False	Undef
False	False	False	False
Undef	Undef	False	Undef

Sequential, for implementation (Java):

a && b	True	False	Undef
True	True	False	Undef
False	False	False	False
Undef	Undef	Undef	Undef

Lifting (Undef treated as False):

a ∧ b	True	False	Undef
True	True	False	False
False	False	False	False
Undef	False	False	False

Fig. 2. Possible implementations of the **and**-operator

UML. Assuming that OCL is executable, it unfortunately cannot constructively change any data structure, because it can only compute Boolean values that tell, whether some constraint is violated or not. E.g. if a post-condition of form a<b is given, then it can check whether that condition holds. However, it cannot easily correct that condition. It may increase b or it alter a, or both? Although, there are standard solutions for particular cases, e.g. there cannot be a solution for general constraints. For example in f(a)=g(b) there is no general solution if it is assumed that both methods are provided by underlying UML models and OCL doesn't know anything about them.

Under the assumption that OCL is executable, it is very similar to the expression part of a functional language. It calculates values without changing the underlying data structures and therefore without side-effects. If an executable version of OCL was embedded in an ordinary language, e.g. by using OCL as expression sublanguage then a compact general programming language would be given. GOS [19] is an example for such a successful combination.

3.2 Where to Use OCL?

Being a mixture of propositional logic and functional language that heavily depends on the underlying UML models OCL can serve a number of different purposes.

OCL code may be added to a running system for testing purposes. The OCL constraints are then used like assertions in C++ or Eiffel's contracts in form of pre- and postconditions.

This may be a very effective means of defining model based tests. If direct generation of code from OCL is feasible and this is ideally accompanied by code generation from the UML model itself, then the *Extreme Modeling* approach [2, 14] becomes feasible. The basic idea of the Extreme Modeling approach is the replacement of an ordinary programming language for coding and test specification by a high-level graphical approach, based on UML and OCL. OCL then plays a vital role in the software development process as a constraint definition language for the description of automated tests. This can greatly enhance the productivity of the programmers. Furthermore, modeling and programming become one combined activity.

It is worthwhile to distinguish development-time and runtime. During *development-time* the system is being developed. The source code and models of the system are available and these artifacts are iteratively enhanced, detailed and transformed. During *runtime* the source code has been translated into object code and is executed. Above the usefulness of OCL during runtime was discussed. The benefits of OCL during development-time and which OCL constraints can be executed during development is discussed below.

For stability of the running application, for efficiency and a number of other reasons, it makes sense to restrict reflective access and modifiability of systems during runtime. Although there are systems that allow dynamic adaptation, and this is sometimes very useful, in most cases this kind of runtime adaptability is rather restricted and deals with coarse modifications only. E.g. Java allows dynamic load of complete classes or packages with well defined interfaces, but not to adapt single methods or attributes within a class. Common Smalltalk systems of course are exceptions to that rule, because they allow rather unrestricted access to their own meta-levels. However, this feature should not be used widely as it is dedicated to experienced programmers mainly. Further drawbacks of reflective access are the increased complexity for understanding the code and the lack of a typing system.

However, reflection in sequential programming languages is generally understood by now. In a specification language, such as OCL, the access of the meta-level directly within OCL is widely unclear and unnecessary. First, it is widely unclear, because it allows to specify weird statements, such as class `Car` does exist exactly, if the attribute `age` of object `tim:Person` is not 5:

```
tim.age <> 5   xor   OclType.allInstances( x | x.name <> "Car" )
```

How is that to be implemented? a) ensure `tim` is older than 5, b) ensure `tim.age=5` and don't implement class `Person`, or c) delete class `Person` when `tim` becomes 5?

`tim.age <> 5` is an expression to be executed during runtime, the other part is to be evaluated during development-time where objects like `tim` aren't yet available. OCL, therefore, mixes evaluation times by providing direct access on the meta-level.

The primary purpose of the OCL meta-level is to allow the developer to talk about properties of a UML (and OCL) model during development-time, such as: "If class `Person` provides method `foo()`, then so does class `Child`". Fortunately meta-level access is not necessary within OCL itself. The trick is to provide this meta-level access through the underlying UML meta-model. `OclType` then becomes an ordinary UML class and is not part of OCL itself.

Furthermore, a specification language for describing runtime behavior e.g. in form of pre- and postconditions and another specification language that describes restrictions on the modeling elements must be strictly distinguished. The idea is to use OCL at both levels and to call them *meta-OCL* and *runtime-OCL*. Both are entirely disconnected and just by coincidence have the same look-a-like. The English language e.g. can be described using the English language itself, but it could also be described using an entire different language. Many other examples, where languages are used to describe themselves can be found. E.g. the EBNF to describe context free grammars can itself be defined using EBNF – both appearances of EBNF are fully separated.

Runtime-OCL talks about objects and values. The term `tim.age <> 5` belongs to this language. Meta-OCL talks about classes, their attribute structure and associations. The term `OclType.allInstances(x|x.name<>"Car")`, which can easily be checked during development-time, would belong to Meta-OCL. A combination of both expressions would be syntactically disallowed. OCL would be type checked and executable at both levels separately.

At development-time OCL can describe constraints that may not be violated by UML models. E.g. if a class is tagged by a certain stereotype ≪EJB≫, then it should provide certain functionality. OCL is surely feasible here. However, it would be of interest to link meta-OCL constraints with procedures at the meta-level that help to repair violated constraints, e.g. through automatically or interactively adding required functionality. Meta-level procedures act during development-time, where the developer is still available.

In summary, it becomes clear that a meta-level needs not be accessible within OCL. As a conclusion the meta-level of OCL is removed in the following. The OCL grammar is in the following restructured and the OCL context conditions are re-formulated appropriately, so that this flaw in the presentation of OCL can be amended. Furthermore, OCL becomes much simpler and more understandable to programmers.

4   The New OCL Grammar

OCL can be described by a context free grammar like any other language. In this section, an enhanced version of such a grammar through refactoring of the grammar originally given in [16] will be provided.

One of the most important changes concerns the strict separation of logic level and meta-level discussed in Section 2. In specification languages, e.g. SPECTRUM [3] and in all strongly typed programming languages, meta-level and logic level are never mixed.

The redefined grammar below is partly supplied with an explanation where considered necessary. Please note that is is assumed that the reader has some familiarity with OCL as provided in [16]. The following grammar rules are all formulated in EBNF as introduced in the previous section.

In the grammar's restructuring the identifiers ⟨className⟩, ⟨attributeName⟩, ⟨roleName⟩, ⟨methodName⟩, ⟨packageName⟩, ⟨stateName⟩, and ⟨varName⟩ were introduced supplementary. They are equal to ⟨name⟩. Using these identifiers instead of ⟨name⟩ makes the grammar easier to read.

Note that the grammar restructuring to a large extent focuses on a better grammar presentation, not on the language adaptation, even if some changes are made. The following section 5.4 discusses these changes on the language itself.

A constraint can either specify an invariant or describe pre- and/or postconditions but never do both at the same time. This is made explicit in the redefined grammar. Furthermore, the order of appearance for pre- and postconditions has been defined. Moreover, empty context declarations are allowed when neither the keyword **self**, nor any alternative single object occurs within the constraint expression.

$$
\begin{aligned}
\langle\text{constraint}\rangle ::= \ &\textbf{context} \ \langle\text{clContext}\rangle \ \underline{\textbf{inv}} \ \{ \ \langle\text{name}\rangle \ \}^{?} \ \underline{:} \ \langle\text{exprList}\rangle \\
&| \ \underline{\textbf{context}} \ \langle\text{opContext}\rangle \\
&\quad \{ \ \underline{\textbf{pre}} \ \{ \ \langle\text{name}\rangle \ \}^{?} \ \underline{:} \ \langle\text{exprList}\rangle \ \}^{?} \\
&\quad \{ \ \underline{\textbf{post}} \ \{ \ \langle\text{name}\rangle \ \}^{?} \ \underline{:} \ \langle\text{exprList}\rangle \ \}^{?} \\
&| \ \langle\text{exprList}\rangle \\
\langle\text{clContext}\rangle ::= \ &\{ \ \langle\text{name}\rangle \ \underline{:} \ \}^{?} \ \langle\text{class}\rangle \\
\langle\text{opContext}\rangle ::= \ &\{ \ \langle\text{name}\rangle \ \underline{:} \ \}^{?} \ \langle\text{class}\rangle \ \underline{::} \ \langle\text{methodName}\rangle \ \underline{(} \ \langle\text{fParamList}\rangle^{?} \ \underline{)} \\
&\quad \{ \ \underline{:} \ \langle\text{typeExpr}\rangle \ \}^{?} \\
\langle\text{fParamList}\rangle ::= \ &\langle\text{fParam}\rangle \ \{ \ \underline{,} \ \langle\text{fParam}\rangle \ \}^{*} \\
\langle\text{fParam}\rangle ::= \ &\langle\text{varName}\rangle \ \underline{:} \ \langle\text{typeExpr}\rangle
\end{aligned}
$$

The OCL specification [16] allows an alternative name for **self** within the class context specification, whereas within the operation context specification such an alternative is not allowed. This can be more systematic, by allowing alternative names in both cases.

To reduce the number of required non-terminals and grammar rules, the precedence rules for operations are given by a separate table. A complete precedence rules table is given separately in Section 5.3. As already discussed in Section 2 these could be expressed within grammar rules as well, but their presentation is more compact and readable within the precedence rules table.

$$
\begin{aligned}
\langle\text{expr}\rangle ::= \ &\langle\text{unaryExpr}\rangle \ \{ \ \langle\text{infixOp}\rangle \ \langle\text{unaryExpr}\rangle \ \}^{*} \\
\langle\text{unaryExpr}\rangle ::= \ &\langle\text{unaryOp}\rangle^{*} \ \langle\text{primeExpr}\rangle \\
\langle\text{unaryOp}\rangle ::= \ &\underline{-} \ | \ \underline{\textbf{not}} \\
\langle\text{infixOp}\rangle ::= \ &\underline{\textbf{and}} \ | \ \underline{\textbf{or}} \ | \ \underline{\textbf{xor}} \ | \ \underline{\textbf{implies}} \\
&| \underline{=} | \underline{>} | \underline{<} | \underline{\geq} | \underline{\leq} | \underline{<>} | \underline{+} | \underline{-} | \underline{*} | \underline{/}
\end{aligned}
$$

Unfortunately, the description of ⟨primeExpr⟩ and related non-terminals in [16] is rather confusing. This makes it quite difficult for the reader to understand what exactly expressions are and what their meaning is. After a detailed analysis of ⟨primeExpr⟩ the following restructuring was developed. Due to its many variants, the grammar rules for ⟨primeExpr⟩ are presented in several parts:

> ⟨primeExpr⟩ ::= ⟨letExpr⟩
> | ⟨ifExpr⟩
> | (⟨expr⟩)
> | ⟨collectKind⟩ { { ⟨collItem⟩ { , ⟨collItem⟩ }* }? }
> | ⟨property⟩
> | ⟨primeExpr⟩ . ⟨property⟩
> | ⟨primeExpr⟩ . ⟨collectFeature⟩
> | ...

In [16], the literal collection allows either a single range of values or a list of individual values, but not all in one, e.g. Set {1, 4..7, 11..13, 2}. The grammar was extended accordingly, by enhancing the ⟨collItem⟩ later on.

The original specification uses an arrow symbol -> for calling a collection operation. The operations of the other types however, are called like a usual property with a dot between both arguments, like e.g. i.abs (absolute value of an integer i). This lack of uniformity adds unnecessary complexity to OCL. This complexity was removed by replacing the arrow with a dot. The often heard argument, that it is necessary to distinguish normal features from OCL-features using arrows, simply does not hold, because a type system can easily resolve name clashes.

> ⟨primeExpr⟩ ::= -- continued
> | ⟨type⟩
> | ⟨literal⟩
> | self
> | result
> | ...

Not only constants, but also the special keywords self and result, types, and in particular class names may be used at expression position. A class name used as expression is interpreted as the set of all existing objects of that class at that time. This replaces the superfluous OCL feature allInstances. Class names can then be used in two functions. They are allowed, both where types or set values are appropriate and their position can be resolved because of a well structured grammar. As the new grammar distinguishes between ⟨typeExpr⟩ and ⟨expr⟩, this approach works.

⟨primeExpr⟩ ::= -- continued
    | ⟨primeExpr⟩ **.oclAsType** (⟨typeExpr⟩)
    | ⟨primeExpr⟩ **.oclIsKindOf** (⟨typeExpr⟩)
    | ⟨typeifExpr⟩
    | ⟨primeExpr⟩ **.oclIsInState** (⟨stateName⟩)
    | ⟨primeExpr⟩ **.oclIsNew**
    | ...

The special operation p.oclAsType(T) means the type of expression p is changed to T. The second special operation p.oclIsKindOf(T) evaluates to true exactly if the value denoted by p is of type or a subtype of T.

The four OCL specific constructs oclIsKindOf, oclAsType, oclIsInState, and oclIsNew are explicitly included in the ⟨primeExpr⟩ grammar rule. This shows that these properties are not normal functions, but special *control constructs*. For example, in programming languages like Java, the casting of objects differs syntactically from ordinary method invocation. Unfortunately, OCL syntax did not distinguish this and, therefore, OCL is confusing here, because it tried to fit every concept into method call structure. Now this principal distinction is demonstrated at least in the presentation of the syntax. Furthermore, this rearrangement makes it unnecessary to treat their arguments as objects. Therefore, meta-level type OclType is not needed here anymore.

Unfortunately the casting construct oclAsType has the drawback that it needs to deal with cast failures. This may not result in a raised exception, as logic doesn't raise exceptions at all. The newly introduced alternative construct ⟨typeifExpr⟩ combines the cast with an if-then-else construction that allows to specify both cases and should largely replace oclAsType (see below).

In the last part, timed expressions, qualified associations and usage of roles are defined in the same way as it had been given in original OCL.

⟨primeExpr⟩ ::= -- continued
    | ⟨primeExpr⟩ **@pre**
    | ⟨primeExpr⟩ [⟨exprList⟩]
    | ⟨primeExpr⟩ [⟨roleName⟩]

The definition of the let expression is extended by multiple bindings. It is now possible to declare more than one variable at the same time. Furthermore, a let expression can be used within other let expressions.

The ⟨typeifExpr⟩ rule allows a variable to be introduced and bound to an expression. The variable has the casted type in the then-part and its original type in the else-part.

⟨letExpr⟩ ::= **let** ⟨declList⟩ **in** ⟨expr⟩

⟨ifExpr⟩ ::= **if** ⟨expr⟩ **then** ⟨expr⟩ **else** ⟨expr⟩ **endif**

⟨typeifExpr⟩ ::= **typeif** ⟨decl⟩ **isof** ⟨typeExpr⟩ **then** ⟨expr⟩ **else** ⟨expr⟩ **endif**

⟨property⟩ ::= ⟨attributeName⟩
 | ⟨methodName⟩ (⟨exprList⟩$^?$)
 | ⟨roleName⟩

⟨literal⟩ ::= ⟨char⟩ | ⟨string⟩ | ⟨number⟩ | ⟨bool⟩
 | ⟨enumTypeName⟩ :: ⟨name⟩

Predefined operations applicable to the basic types `Integer`, `Real`, `String` and `Character`, such as `abs`, `floor`, or `size` are treated like ordinary method calls. In case they don't have arguments, they are like attributes. See [16] for a full list of operators.

In [16], the possibility of specifying with Boolean values was missing and has been added here.

The definition of the enumeration types in [16] exhibits some inconsistency when compared to the UML enumerations. All enumeration types and their values must be defined in the underlying UML model. Therefore, each enumeration type already has a name. The redefined grammar uses the same notation as for class pathnames to refer to a certain enumeration type. If the enumeration type `Color` among others contains the element `red`, then `Color::red` is a qualified enumeration value.

The nonterminal ⟨collectFeature⟩ describes the features of collection types. For brevity in the following only a few examples of each category are listed, i.e. operations without parameter, operations with one parameter of type ⟨expr⟩, but all the special constructs with their specific parameters. A complete list of the normal features can be inferred from the official OCL definitions.

⟨collectFeature⟩ ::= **size** | **isEmpty** | ...
 | **includes** (⟨expr⟩) | **union** (⟨expr⟩) | ...
 | **select** (⟨var⟩ | ⟨expr⟩)
 | **reject** (⟨var⟩ | ⟨expr⟩)
 | **collect** (⟨var⟩ | ⟨expr⟩)
 | **forAll** (⟨varList⟩ | ⟨expr⟩)
 | **exists** (⟨varList⟩ | ⟨expr⟩)
 | **iterate** (⟨var⟩ ; ⟨decl⟩ | ⟨expr⟩) | ...

The special constructs `select`, etc. have been redefined in their structure. They are not treated as ordinary functions anymore, but explicitly introduced through the grammar. In the presented grammar each of them has a *block* as body. A block at first introduces and binds one or several new variables and then allows to express a constraint over that variables. So far the OCL definition has treated these bodies wrongly as ordinary arguments. This adaptation is a good example for a grammar restructuring that does not affect the language, but makes the language presentation more conform to standard language definitions. But finally these constructs have got two changes: In official OCL it was allowed to omit the explicit introduction of a variable, in which case the variable `self` was newly introduced and bound implicitly. This can easily lead to misunderstanding in more complex formulae and is therefore abandoned. On the other hand, for some of these operators it is now possible to introduce several variables at once.

The non-terminals used in the above control structures look like this:

$$\langle\texttt{varList}\rangle ::= \langle\texttt{var}\rangle \; \{ \, , \langle\texttt{var}\rangle \; \}^{*}$$
$$\langle\texttt{var}\rangle ::= \langle\texttt{varName}\rangle \; \{ \, : \langle\texttt{typeExpr}\rangle \; \}^{?}$$
$$\langle\texttt{declList}\rangle ::= \langle\texttt{decl}\rangle \; \{ \, , \langle\texttt{decl}\rangle \; \}^{*}$$
$$\langle\texttt{decl}\rangle ::= \langle\texttt{var}\rangle \equiv \langle\texttt{expr}\rangle$$
$$\langle\texttt{exprList}\rangle ::= \langle\texttt{expr}\rangle \; \{ \, , \langle\texttt{expr}\rangle \; \}^{*}$$
$$\langle\texttt{collItem}\rangle ::= \langle\texttt{expr}\rangle \; \{ \, .. \langle\texttt{expr}\rangle \; \}^{?}$$

Unlike the grammar of [16] this grammar explicitly allows class names to be qualified by a package name in the non-terminal ⟨class⟩. This guarantees that a package name may be given wherever ⟨class⟩ appears. This feature is essential for dealing with identical class names in different packages.

$$\langle\texttt{class}\rangle ::= \{\langle\texttt{packageName}\rangle \; :: \; \}^{*} \; \langle\texttt{className}\rangle$$
$$\langle\texttt{collectKind}\rangle ::= \underline{\textbf{Set}} \mid \underline{\textbf{Bag}} \mid \underline{\textbf{Sequence}} \mid \underline{\textbf{Collection}}$$
$$\langle\texttt{typeExpr}\rangle ::= \langle\texttt{collectKind}\rangle \; (\; \langle\texttt{type}\rangle \;) \mid \langle\texttt{type}\rangle$$
$$\langle\texttt{type}\rangle ::= \langle\texttt{class}\rangle \mid \langle\texttt{basicType}\rangle \mid \langle\texttt{enumTypeName}\rangle$$
$$\langle\texttt{basicType}\rangle ::= \underline{\textbf{Integer}} \mid \underline{\textbf{Real}} \mid \underline{\textbf{Boolean}} \mid \underline{\textbf{String}} \mid \underline{\textbf{Character}}$$

The well known and often used type `Character` was missing in OCL and therefore newly added to the basic types. Its operations are given in 5.2.

The rule for numbers that allows floating-point constants is extended, because numeric constants were missing in [16]:

⟨digit⟩ ::= [**0** − **9**]

⟨digits⟩ ::= ⟨digit⟩ { ⟨digit⟩ }*

⟨number⟩ ::= ⟨digits⟩ { **.** ⟨digits⟩ }? { { **e** | **E** } { **+** | **−** }? ⟨digits⟩ }?

⟨letter⟩ ::= [**a** − **z A** − **Z** _]

⟨name⟩ ::= ⟨letter⟩ { ⟨letter⟩ | ⟨digit⟩ }*

⟨char⟩ ::= **'** valid Unicode character **'**

⟨string⟩ ::= **"** ⟨char⟩* **"**

⟨bool⟩ ::= **True** | **False**

The resulting language is now rather conform to standard ways of presenting expression syntax. It indeed improves readability and eases tool implementation.

5   Additional Adaptations Based on the New Grammar

The previously defined context free grammar describes a language quite similar to the official OCL. It enhances or restricts some constructs, but largely focuses on better presentation of its context free grammar.

As a next step, it is necessary to adapt the context conditions to the new grammar where necessary. This will not be done in this article, but a small set of these issues will be tackled here.

5.1   Type Hierarchy

In the OCL specification [16] OclAny is a supertype of both model and basic types. On the one hand, this gives rise for some subtle type conformance problems. On the other hand, it would be more convenient to have the possibility to address the universe of all objects, without basic values such as numbers included. Therefore, OclAny now is the supertype of all class types, but excludes the basic types and all collection types.

This also means, that Set(OclAny) is not included in OclAny anymore, but the universe of sets, distinct from the universe of objects. The corrected type hierarchy is given in Fig. 3.

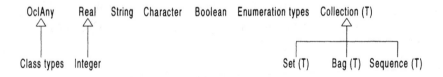

Fig. 3. OCL type hierarchy

5.2 Predefined Operations

As already mentioned, logic level and meta-level are strictly separated. In the grammar as given in [16], the basic types Integer, Real, String and Boolean are on the same level as OCL specific meta-types, namely OclExpression and OclType. These meta-types were used in the grammar to describe specific kinds of arguments for a number of special constructs. After the restructuring presented in this paper, these types become superfluous. Access to the meta-level is no longer necessary. Therefore, OclExpression and OclType can be removed.

Please note that parentheses are used within the definitions of the infix operations to improve readability.

OclAny. Here, object is a variable of type OclAny. OclAny has the following signature:

```
object = (object1 : OclAny) : Boolean
object <> (object1 : OclAny) : Boolean
```

Both operations are heterogeneous. Therefore, variables object and object1 do not need to be of the same type, but may be arbitrary class types.

Basic types. For the sake of brevity only a few Integer operators are shown.

Due to the type system re-arrangements, the overall equality does only accept class types as arguments, but not basic types. Therefore, several additional equality functions on each basic type are needed. These functions can be additionally defined, because in typed languages the syntactic overloading of methods can be resolved statically. This means the compiler can determine, which equality is to be used.

Here, i is a variable of type Integer.

```
i = (i1 : Integer) : Boolean
i <> (i1 : Integer) : Boolean
i + (i1 : Integer) : Integer
...
```

Enumeration types. Enumerations defined in a UML model have to be represented within OCL constraints. There may exist various different enumerations in a model. Therefore, the attempt of [16] to describe all enumerations with only one enumeration type does not work properly. Instead, enumerations are treated as individual, non-further related types. In UML, each enumeration is defined as a special datatype and accordingly has a type name and the belonging values. Within OCL an enumeration value is referred to by the enumeration type name and the value name. Let enum be a variable of a given enumeration type E.

```
E::enum = (E::enum1 : E) : Boolean
E::enum <> (E::enum1 : E) : Boolean
```

In languages like C++, further functionality exists for enumeration types: for example, a linear order or a successor function.

Please note that the built-in type Boolean can be regarded as a two-valued enumeration type.

Collection types. Below the signatures of collection types are introduced as polymorphic types. The key idea is that if an operation *doesn't care* about the value type, then it reacts uniformly regardless of what these values are.

This section deals with the predefined features on the parameterized collection types `Collection(T)`, `Set(T)`, `Bag(T)`, and `Sequence(T)`, where the type variable T denotes any type except collection types.

In the grammar provided by this article, these features are included by the construct

⟨primeExpr⟩ . ⟨collectFeature⟩

As already mentioned, in the grammar of [16] all possible features for collections were treated as method calls. This was not quite correct. In fact, they mix both method calls and specialized control structures. The grammar defined above realizes this difference, because the control structures are explicitly mentioned in the grammar. This now allows to explicitly mention the variable lists in the grammar that are separated from the normal expression syntax.

Collection-based control structures usually evaluate a particular expression for each element in the collection. Again inspired by Smalltalk the syntax of these control structures as defined in [16] is somewhat misleading. According to [16] the argument of such a control structure is of type `OclExpression`. As the redefinition of the grammar already shows that the binding of new variables should be allowed in blocks consisting of a declarative part and an expression part.

A block is an introduction of a new variable together with an expression that uses the variable. The standard syntax for the `forAll` function:

`Collection(T).forAll(t : T | expr : Boolean)`

Quantification can range over a number of variables:

`Collection(T).forAll(t1 : T, ... , tn : T | expr : Boolean)`

A block consists of one or several defined variables and then, separated by a vertical bar |, a Boolean expression follows. Functional languages would regard this block as a function definition based on a λ-abstraction.

OCL from [16] does allow to omit an explicit introduction of a variable. In this case, the block looks like an expression, but it still serves the duties of a block, as implicitly the variable `self` is introduced. As already mentioned, the restructured grammar does not allow implicit binding of `self` anymore.

5.3   Precedence Rules

For the reasons of completeness, a list of precedence rules is included here. Although the rules can be modeled by the grammar itself, it is more compact and equally precise to use an explicit precedence table.

Table 2. Precedence for OCL operations (highest to lowest).

Name	Syntax	Associativity
Pathname	`::`	left
Time expression	`@pre`	left
Dot operation	`.`	left
Unary operations	`-, not`	right
Multiplication and division	`*, /`	left
Addition and subtraction	`+, -`	left
Relational operations	`<, >, <=, >=`	left
Relational equality	`=, <>`	left
Logical operations	`and, or, xor`	left
Logical implies	`implies`	right

The associativity of an operator specifies the order that operations of the same precedence are performed in. Left associativity means that operations are grouped from left-to-right. For example:

```
a.b.c                = (a.b).c
a / b / c            = (a / b) / c
a and b and c        = (a and b) and c
a implies b implies c = a implies (b implies c)
```

Please note that dependent on the semantics of the and operator, it is not necessarily the case that and is associative, i.e. according to Fig. 2 it can be wrong to replace

```
a and (b and c)    by    (a and b) and c
```

5.4   Summary of Grammar Adaptations

Three categories of adaptations can be identified. Some grammar adaptations affect the language, other changes affect the predefined operations, and a third group is introduced through adaptations of the context conditions. This is a short summary of the according changes. The new grammar was compared to [16].

Grammar based language changes. Often, but not always, changes of the grammar effect the language. A number of such grammar based language changes is listed below.

- The consistency of the grammar was improved: previously some nonterminals were enclosed in angle brackets, and others not.

- Separation of invariants and pre-/postconditions within the constraint definition.
- Clarification of the order in which pre- and postconditions appear.
- Correction of the class context specification. It is now possible to deal with identical class names in different packages by qualifying the class context specification with an optional pathname.
- The grammar of the context declaration was enhanced, allowing an alternative name for self also for the operation context.
- The type of method parameters as well as the return type of a method was changed to ⟨typeExpr⟩, which additionally contains collection and enumeration types. This allows the underlying UML model to provide methods for OCL constraint specifications with that according types.
- Method parameters are now separated by comma instead of semicolon.
- Precedence rules have been removed from the grammar and given in a precedence table.
- Unary operators are now allowed to occur repeatedly.
- The grammar for the non-terminal ⟨primeExpr⟩ was largely restructured.
- The syntax for the literal collection was changed to allow more general enumeration and number constants.
- The arrow symbol, used for calling a collection operation, was replaced by a dot.
- The let-expression was extended so that firstly, multiple bindings are allowed and secondly, more than one let-expression may occur in an expression.
- Nonterminal ⟨literal⟩ now contains the Boolean values.
- The definition of the enumeration types was corrected, since in [16] it is inconsistent with the UML meta-model.
- Whenever a class name is used, this class can be qualified using a path name.
- Numbers now include floating-point constants.
- Along with the introduction of the new type Character the notation of strings was adapted. In the redefined grammar, strings have to be enclosed by double quotes.

Change of the Predefined Operations

- The operator <> was added to the operations of Integer, String, Boolean and the three concrete collection types.
- Integer and String were additionally completed by the operations <, <=, >, and >=.
- The operations on collection types where divided in method calls and control structures.
- The block concept was introduced for the control structures.
- For the operations includes, excludes and count the type of the called argument was changed to the type of the collection elements.
- The forAll operation has an extended variant.

Change of the Context Conditions

- The type hierarchy of OCL was adapted: the type `OclAny` is not a supertype of the basic types or the collection types anymore.
- For a strict separation of logic level and meta-level, the meta types `OclType` and `OclExpression` have been removed.
- The explicit possibility of building all type instances was removed. Instead of `allInstances` the class name can be used directly now.
- The type `Character` was newly introduced.

6 ≪Java≫OCL: The Java-Variant of OCL

≪Java≫OCL has almost the same abstract syntax as standard OCL. However, variable declarations, method calls, type casts and some other concepts have been given a different syntactic shape. ≪Java≫OCL is conform to Java and therefore is more familiar to Java developers. Some small differences occur due to available operations and e.g. due to the change of the cast into an infix operation.

For a detailed description of the differences, the previously defined OCL grammar and the new ≪Java≫OCL grammar are listed on the left resp. right hand side. Small adaptations are explained below.

OCL	≪Java≫OCL
⟨constraint⟩ ::=	
context ⟨clContext⟩	**context** ⟨clContext⟩
inv { ⟨name⟩}$^?$: ⟨exprList⟩	**inv** { ⟨name⟩}$^?$: ⟨exprList⟩
| **context** ⟨opContext⟩	| **context** ⟨opContext⟩
{ **pre** { ⟨name⟩ }$^?$: ⟨exprList⟩ }$^?$	{ **pre** { ⟨name⟩ }$^?$: ⟨exprList⟩ }$^?$
{ **post** { ⟨name⟩ }$^?$: ⟨exprList⟩ }$^?$	{ **post** { ⟨name⟩ }$^?$: ⟨exprList⟩ }$^?$
| ⟨exprList⟩	| ⟨exprList⟩
⟨clContext⟩ ::=	
{ ⟨name⟩ : }$^?$ ⟨class⟩	| ⟨class⟩ { ⟨name⟩ }$^?$
⟨opContext⟩ ::=	
⟨clContext⟩ :: ⟨methodName⟩	{ ⟨typeExpr⟩ }$^?$ ⟨class⟩ .
(⟨fParamList⟩$^?$) { : ⟨typeExpr⟩ }$^?$	⟨methodName⟩ (⟨fParamList⟩$^?$)
⟨fParamList⟩ ::=	
⟨fParam⟩ { , ⟨fParam⟩ }*	| ⟨fParam⟩ { , ⟨fParam⟩ }*
⟨fParam⟩ ::=	
⟨varName⟩ : ⟨typeExpr⟩	| ⟨typeExpr⟩ ⟨varName⟩

Due to the switched nonterminals in the ⟨clContext⟩ rule, it becomes confusing to allow relabelling of the object in the ⟨opContext⟩. Therefore, this is omitted in ≪Java≫OCL.

OCL	«Java»OCL
⟨expr⟩ ::= ⟨unaryExpr⟩ { ⟨infixOp⟩ ⟨unaryExpr⟩ }*	⟨unaryExpr⟩ { ⟨infixOp⟩ ⟨unaryExpr⟩ }*
⟨unaryExpr⟩ ::= ⟨unaryOp⟩* ⟨primeExpr⟩	| ⟨unaryOp⟩* ⟨primeExpr⟩
⟨unaryOp⟩ ::= − | **not**	− | **not** | ~ | ! | (⟨typeExpr⟩)
⟨infixOp⟩ ::= **and** | **or** | **xor** | **implies** | = | ≥ | ≤ | ≥= | ≤= | <> | + | − | * | /	**&&** | **||** | **xor** | **implies** | == | ≥ | ≤ | ≥= | ≤= | != | + | − | * | /

An additional unary operator has been added that allows type casts. It replaces the `oclAsType` operation. New binary operators stem from additional functionality on basic Java types.

OCL	«Java»OCL
⟨primeExpr⟩ ::= ⟨letExpr⟩	⟨letExpr⟩
| ⟨ifExpr⟩	| ⟨ifExpr⟩
| (⟨expr⟩)	| (⟨expr⟩)
| ⟨collectKind⟩ { { ⟨collItem⟩ {, ⟨collItem⟩ }* }? }	| ⟨collectKind⟩ { { ⟨collItem⟩ {, ⟨collItem⟩ }* }? }
| ⟨property⟩	| ⟨property⟩
| ⟨primeExpr⟩ . ⟨property⟩	| ⟨primeExpr⟩ . ⟨property⟩
	| ⟨class⟩ . ⟨methodName⟩ (⟨exprList⟩?)
| ⟨primeExpr⟩ . ⟨collectFeature⟩	| ⟨primeExpr⟩ . ⟨collectFeature⟩
	| ⟨collectExpr⟩
| ⟨type⟩	| ⟨type⟩
| ⟨literal⟩	| ⟨literal⟩
| **self**	| **this**
| **result**	| **result**
| ⟨primeExpr⟩ .**oclAsType** (⟨typeExpr⟩)	
| ⟨primeExpr⟩ .**oclIsKindOf** (⟨typeExpr⟩)	| ⟨primeExpr⟩ **instanceOf** ⟨typeExpr⟩
| ⟨typeifExpr⟩	| ⟨typeifExpr⟩
| ⟨primeExpr⟩ .**oclIsInState** (⟨stateName⟩)	| ⟨primeExpr⟩ .**isInState** (⟨stateName⟩)
| ⟨primeExpr⟩ .**oclIsNew**	| ⟨primeExpr⟩ .**isNew**
| ⟨primeExpr⟩ **@pre**	| ⟨primeExpr⟩ '
| ⟨primeExpr⟩ [⟨exprList⟩]	| ⟨primeExpr⟩ [⟨exprList⟩]
| ⟨primeExpr⟩ [⟨roleName⟩]	| ⟨primeExpr⟩ [⟨roleName⟩]

As there are many OCL specific operations that don't have "ocl" as prefix, this was also removed from the above mentioned special operations. A useful alternative might be to write `OCL.isNew(o)` instead of `o.isNew`. As Java generally allows to use static methods, this possibility was added to «Java»OCL as

well. Then a number of OCL specific operations might be provided by a special
"class" called OCL.

The new nonterminal ⟨collectExpr⟩ was added, to allow a syntactic differen-
tiation between method calls and special constructs such as `forall`.

OCL	≪Java≫OCL
⟨letExpr⟩ ::= let ⟨declList⟩ in ⟨expr⟩	| let ⟨declList⟩ in ⟨expr⟩
⟨ifExpr⟩ ::= if ⟨expr⟩ then ⟨expr⟩ else ⟨expr⟩ endif	| if ⟨expr⟩ then ⟨expr⟩ else ⟨expr⟩ | ⟨expr⟩ ? ⟨expr⟩ : ⟨expr⟩
⟨typeifExpr⟩ ::= typeif ⟨decl⟩ isof ⟨typeExpr⟩ then ⟨expr⟩ else ⟨expr⟩ endif	| typeif ⟨decl⟩ instanceof ⟨typeExpr⟩ then ⟨expr⟩ else ⟨expr⟩ | ⟨decl⟩ instanceof ⟨typeExpr⟩ ? ⟨expr⟩ : ⟨expr⟩
⟨property⟩ ::= | ⟨attributeName⟩ | ⟨methodName⟩ (⟨exprList⟩?) | ⟨roleName⟩	| ⟨attributeName⟩ | ⟨methodName⟩ (⟨exprList⟩?) | ⟨roleName⟩
⟨literal⟩ ::= ⟨char⟩ | ⟨string⟩ | ⟨number⟩ | ⟨bool⟩ | ⟨enumTypeName⟩ :: ⟨name⟩	⟨boolean⟩ | ⟨char⟩ | ⟨int⟩ | ⟨String⟩ | ... | ⟨class⟩ . ⟨name⟩

In Java an `endif` is not used. Therefore, in nested `if`-expressions it might
become necessary to add brackets. The .?.:. variant for expressions is added
as additional alternative for `if`-expressions. Java handles enumeration types as
ordinary integer constants. However, a tricky way of denoting these constants
gives a look and feel as if they would be true enumeration types. ≪Java≫OCL
handles enumeration types in a similar manner.

OCL	≪Java≫OCL
⟨collectFeature⟩ ::= size| isEmpty | ... | includes (⟨expr⟩) | ... | union (⟨expr⟩) | select (⟨var⟩ | ⟨expr⟩) | reject (⟨var⟩ | ⟨expr⟩) | collect (⟨var⟩ | ⟨expr⟩) | forAll (⟨varList⟩ | ⟨expr⟩) | exists (⟨varList⟩ | ⟨expr⟩) | iterate (⟨var⟩ ; ⟨decl⟩ | ⟨expr⟩) | ...	size| isEmpty | ... | includes (⟨expr⟩) | ... | union (⟨expr⟩)

Special constructs, like `forall` are rearranged such that their syntax immediately differs from method calls. Previously `select` was written as

```
Person.select( p | p.age > 5 )
```
and is now formulated as
```
select p=Person | p.age > 5
```

as well as (select p=Person | p.age > 5). Inversion of the first argument makes the constructs much more flexible, as it is now possible to use different expressions for different variables within one quantifier:

exists p=Person, f=p.father | f.age < p.age + 18

OCL	≪Java≫OCL
	⟨collectExpr⟩ ::=
	__select__ ⟨decl⟩ | ⟨expr⟩
	| __reject__ ⟨decl⟩ | ⟨expr⟩
	| __collect__ ⟨decl⟩ | ⟨expr⟩
	| __forAll__ ⟨declList⟩ | ⟨expr⟩
	| __exists__ ⟨declList⟩ | ⟨expr⟩
	| __iterate__ (⟨var⟩ , ⟨decl⟩) ⟨expr⟩

The iterate operator resembles a Java while/for loop as close as possible.

OCL	≪Java≫OCL
⟨varList⟩ ::=	
⟨var⟩ { , ⟨var⟩ }*	| ⟨var⟩ { , ⟨var⟩ }*
⟨var⟩ ::=	
⟨varName⟩ { : ⟨typeExpr⟩ }?	| { ⟨typeExpr⟩ }? ⟨varName⟩
⟨declList⟩ ::=	
⟨decl⟩ { , ⟨decl⟩ }*	| ⟨decl⟩ { , ⟨decl⟩ }*
⟨decl⟩ ::=	
⟨var⟩ = ⟨expr⟩	| ⟨var⟩ = ⟨expr⟩
⟨exprList⟩ ::=	
⟨expr⟩ { , ⟨expr⟩ }*	| ⟨expr⟩ { , ⟨expr⟩ }*
⟨collItem⟩ ::=	
⟨expr⟩ { .. ⟨expr⟩ }?	| ⟨expr⟩ { .. ⟨expr⟩ }?

OCL	≪Java≫OCL
⟨class⟩ ::=	
{⟨packageName⟩ :: }* ⟨className⟩	| {⟨packageName⟩ . }* ⟨className⟩
⟨collectKind⟩ ::=	
__Set__ | __Bag__ | __Sequence__ | __Collection__	__Set__ | __Bag__ | __Sequence__ | __Collection__
⟨typeExpr⟩ ::=	
⟨collectKind⟩ (⟨type⟩) | ⟨type⟩	⟨collectKind⟩ (⟨type⟩) | ⟨type⟩
⟨type⟩ ::=	
⟨class⟩ | ⟨basicType⟩ | ⟨enumTypeName⟩	⟨class⟩ | ⟨basicType⟩
⟨basicType⟩ ::=	
__Integer__ | ...	__int__ | ...

Of course Boolean values, digits etc. differ between OCL and Java, but their detailed definition is omitted here. Further changes appear in the context conditions. For example the type OclAny should be replaced by Java's Object.

7   Conclusion

In this article, a number of syntactical and semantic inconsistencies of OCL have been revealed and corrected. One important change concerns the strict separation of logic level and meta-level. Furthermore, the given grammar of the OCL specification [16] was changed in a manner that achieves an improved grammar structure, allowing easier readability and a better implementation of tools. The improved OCL presentation using the restructured grammar is now more in line with standard programming language grammars. Accordingly, it allows an easier comparison and translation of OCL to standard programming languages. Furthermore, this conformance increases readability.

In a last step ≪Java≫OCL was introduced as a Java-like variant of OCL. It has (almost) the same abstract syntax as the enhanced version of OCL presented in this paper, but its syntactic sugar is given in the flavor of Java.

Acknowledgements. This work was partially funded by the Bayerisches Staatsministerium für Wissenschaft, Forschung und Kunst under the Habilitation-Förderpreis program and by the Bayerische Forschungsstiftung under the FORSOFT research consortium. Many thanks go to my colleagues Manfred Broy, Peter Braun, Steve Cook, Heinrich Hußmann, Jos Warmer, and in particula Manuela Scherer for fruitful input and discussion on this topics.

References

1. Aliprand, J., Allen, J., Becker, J., Davis, M., Everson, M., Freytag, A., Jenkins, J., Ksar, M., McGowan, R., Moore, L., Suignard, M., Whistler, K., *The Unicode Standard, Version 3.0.* Addison Wesley Longman Publisher, 2000.
2. Boger, M., Baier, T., Wienberg, F., *Extreme Modeling*, In: XP'2000 conference proceedings, Ed. Michele Marchesi (to appear), Addison-Wesley, 2001.
3. Broy, M., Facchi, C., Grosu, R., Hettler, R., Hussmann, H., Nazareth, D., Regensburger, F., Slotosch, O., Stolen K., *The Requirement and Design Specification Language SPECTRUM. An Informal Introduction. Version 1.0. Part ii* . Technical Report TUM-I9312, Technische Universität München. Institut für Informatik, TUM, München, Germany, May 1993.
4. Church A, *A formulation of the simple theory of types.* Journal of Symbolic Logic, 5:56-68, 1940.
5. Cook, S., Kleppe, A., Mitchell, R., Rumpe, B., Warmer, J., Wills, A., *The Amsterdam Manifesto on OCL*, Technical Report, Technische Universität München, Computer Science, 1999.
6. Cook, S., Daniels, J. *Designing Object Systems–Object Oriented Modeling with Syntropy.* Prentice-Hall, 1994.
7. Fitzgerald, J., Larsen, P. G., *Modelling Systems: Practical Tools and Techniques in Software Development.* Cambridge University Press, 1998.
8. Gogolla, M., Richters, M., *On Constraints and Queries in UML.* In M. Schader and A. Korthaus, editors, *Proc. UML'97 Workshop 'The Unified Modeling Language - Technical Aspects and Applications'*, pages 109-121. Physica-Verlag, Heidelberg, 1997.
9. Gosling, J,. Joy, B., Steele, G., *The Java Language Specification*, Addison-Wesley, 1996.
10. Hamie, A., Civello, F., Howse, J., Kent, S., Mitchell, R., *Reflections on the Object Constraint Language.* In P. Muller and J. Bézivin, editors, Proc. of UML'98 International Workshop, Mulhouse, France, June 3-4, 1998, pages 137-145.

11. Hamie, A., Howse, J., Kent S., *Interpreting the Object Constraint Language*. In Proceedings of Asia Pacific Conference in Software Engineering. IEEE Press, July 1998.

12. Harel, D., Rumpe, B., *Modeling Languages: Syntax, Semantics and All That Stuff*, The Weizmann Institute of Science, Rehovot, Israel, MCS00-16, 2000.

13. Hussmann, H., OCL Compiler. Technische Universität Dresden. Available from http://www-st.inf.tu-dresden.de/ocl, 2001.

14. Jacobi, C., Rumpe, B., *Hierarchical XP – Improving XP for large scale projects*, In: XP'2000 conference proceedings, Ed. Michele Marchesi (to appear), Addison-Wesley, 2001.

15. OCL Parser, Version 0.3. Available from http://www.software.ibm.com/ad/standards/ocl-download.html, 1999.

16. OMG. Object Constraint Language Specification. In *OMG Unified Modeling Language Specification, Version 1.3 (June 1999)*, chapter 7. Available from http://www.rational.com.

17. OMG Unified Modeling Language Specification, Version 1.3 (June 1999). Available from http://www.rational.com.

18. Richters, M., Gogolla, M., *On Formalizing the UML Object Constraint Language OCL*. In Tok-Wang Ling, Sudha Ram, and Mong Li Lee, editors, Proc. 17th Int. Conf. Conceptual Modeling (ER'98), pages 449-464. Springer, Berlin, LNCS 1507, 1998.

19. Rumpe, B., *Gofer Objekt-System – Imperativ Objektorientierte und Funktionale Programmierung in einer Sprache*, Technical Report, Universität Passau, MIP-9519, 1995.

20. Warmer, J., Kleppe, A., *The Object Constraint Language: Precise Modeling with UML*. Addison Wesley Longman, Reading, Massachusetts, 1999.

21. Wirth, N., *Programming in Modula-2*, Springer Verlag, 1982.

The Semantics of the OCL Action Clause

Anneke Kleppe[1] and Jos Warmer[2]

Klasse Objecten, The Netherlands, www.klasse.nl
[1]A.Kleppe@klasse.nl
[2]J.Warmer@klasse.nl

Abstract. The proposal for the 2.0 version of the UML's Object Constraint Language provides the modeller of object-oriented systems with a way to express the fact that a signal has been send, or an operation has been called. This type of expression is called an Action Clause. This paper defines the Action Clause based on a model of the values in the semantic domain of UML models. In order to define the semantics of the Action Clause a small kernel of the semantic domain of every UML model needs to be specified. This paper uses a specification of the semantic domain based on local object states. These local object states includes a 'virtual' input and output queue that may contain signals. The Action Clause is defined using the signals in the in- and output queues.

Keywords. UML, OCL, constraints, pre- and postconditions, invariants, actions, operations, dynamic semantics, action clause.

1 Introduction

The Unified Modeling Language [1], the standard set by the Object Management Group for object-oriented modeling and design, has rapidly gained acceptance amongst system analysts and designers. The Object Constraint Language is a language that has been defined as part of the UML. It provides the modeller of object-oriented systems with ways to express the semantics of an object-oriented model in a very precise manner. These semantics can be expressed in invariants, and pre- and post-conditions, which are all forms of constraints.

In "Extending OCL to Include Actions" [5] we proposed a new type of constraint: the action clause, which is a way to express that signals are or will be send, or that operations are or will be called. This is an important, and very useful extension to the OCL, e.g. for doing business modeling, as in Eriksson and Penker [3], and specifying outgoing events of components.

Note that we use the term 'signal' in a more generic way that the UML 1.4 definition. Both asynchroneous UML signals and UML operation calls are included in our definition of signal.

This paper defines the semantics of the action clause in terms of a semantic domain described by a set of meta classes. The first section introduces the action clause, because not many readers will be already familiar with it. The second gives the abstract syntax, and the third states the semantics, in terms of the relation between elements from the semantic domain and elements from the abstract syntax. The semantics section includes

A. Clark and J. Warmer (Eds.): Object Modeling with the OCL, LNCS 2263, pp. 213–227, 2002.
© Springer-Verlag Berlin Heidelberg 2002

a definition of the semantic domain of a small subset of the UML. The final section of this paper contains our conclusions.

The work in this paper an adapted version of the part of the report on the unification of static and dynamic semantics of UML [6].

2   Introduction to the Action Clause

An action clause contains three parts:

1. the set of target instances to which the signal (or signals) is send, called targetSet,
2. the set of signals that has been (or should be) send to this targetSet, called signal-Set,
3. a condition, which is optional.

As concrete syntax for an action clause we use the following:

```
action: when <condition> to <targetSet> send <signalSet>
```

The targetSet is a list of objects reachable from the executing object, separated by comma's. The signalSet is a list of names with actual parameters between brackets, also separated by comma's. The condition can be any OCL expression of Boolean type.

Action clauses connected to an operation will be evaluated at postcondition time. Postconditions define what has been achieved by the operation, and so does the action clause. The action clause specifies that the set of signals have been send by the operation to the objects in the target set if the condition is true. An example of the usage of an action clause with an operation is:

```
context CustomerCard::invalidate()
pre    : none
post   : valid = false
action: when customer.special to customer send politeInvalidLetter()
action: when not customer.special to customer send invalidLetter()
```

Another part of a system specification where the action clause is useful, is as an invariant to a classifier (e.g. a class, interface, or component). An invariant states what should be true "at all times" for an instance of that classifier. In practice, violation of invariants will happen. Some of these violations could be fatal, that is, the system can not function correctly if the invariant does not hold. Other violations may be acceptable and only need some "mending" of the instance for the system to function properly again. There is a need to specify what should happen when such an invariant fails. We call this type of invariant action-invariant. An example of an action clause for a classifier:

```
context CustomerCard
inv    : validFrom.isBefore(goodThru)
action: when goodThru.isAfter(Date.now) to self send invalidate()
```

The action-invariant clause specifies that the signals are sent to the specified targets whenever the condition becomes true (i.e. changes from false to true).

Now to understand the meaning of the action clause in detail, assume we have an operation, where we want to specify that, as a result of the operation, some signals has been sent. We use the notation @post to indicate the point in time of the after snapshot of the operation. We can make the following observations.

- We can not guarantee that a signal that was send by the operation to a certain target, was received by that target @post (asynchronous messages). The transport mechanism might take a long time.
- We can not guarantee that a signal that was send by the operation to a certain target, and that was received by that target, is still in the input queue of that target at operation@post. It may be dispatched or removed in some other way.
- We can not guarantee that the postcondition of an operation called by this operation is still true at operation@post. Attribute and other values could have been changed in a number of ways after the called operation has finished.
- We can not guarantee that a signal that was send by the operation is still in the output queue of the operation@post.

Concluding, we may say that the only thing that can reasonably be guaranteed @post, is that an outgoing signal has been in the virtual outputqueue during the execution of the operation. Therefore our natural language definition of an action clause is:

> *An action clause evaluates to true if, and only if, whenever the condition holds, the virtual outputqueue of the instance that executes the operation has contained at some point in time during execution of the operation, all <target, signal> pairs that are specified by the combination (Carthesian product) of the targetSet and the eventSet.*

Note that we use the notion of a virtual output queue, similar to the virtual input queue defined in the UML 1.4 semantics.

3   Abstract Syntax

The abstract syntax concepts for the Action Clause are shown in figure 1. It defines four new concepts:

- OclExpression: the supertype of all ocl expressions. Every OCL expression has a (one) type, a reference to a Classifier, which is defined in UML 1.4 [1].
- ActionClause: an expression that states that a signal should be (or has been) send. It has two associations with different OCL expressions, the condition, and the target set. Note that although in the concrete syntax we spoke of a list of targets, in the abstract syntax this can be represented by one OCL expression: the union of all target objects.
- ActionRef: a reference to an Action (as defined in UML 1.4), including an association to the actual arguments.
- InvariantDef: a definition of an invariant, that has a name, and a body that is an OCL expression.

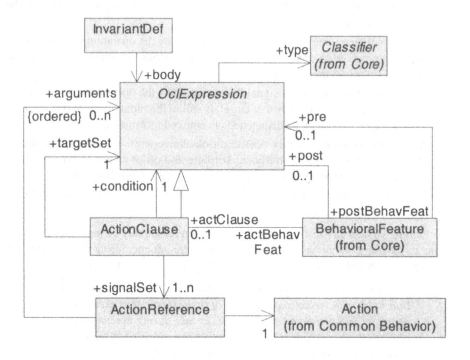

Fig. 1. The abstract syntax concepts

The associations from BehavioralFeature and Classifier to the newly defined concepts, *pre, post, actClause*, and *invariants*, are more specific forms of the association between ModelElement and Constraint as defined in UML 1.4.

3.1   Well-Formedness Rules

The following well-formedness rules must apply for the abstract syntax concepts.

1. The targetSet of an ActionClause is a collection of objects.

```
context ActionClause inv:
      targetSet.type.isKindOf( Collection )
```

2. The condition of an ActionClause is of Boolean type.

```
context ActionClause inv:
      condition.type.isTypeOf( Boolean )
```

4   The Semantic Domain

In order to define the semantics of the action clause in a more precise manner than natural language, a semantic domain, i.e. a set of values, needs to be identified. However, the OCL uses a UML model to define its types, i.e. classes and data types. Therefore, the semantic domain of the OCL overlaps with that of the UML (or maybe it is identical to that of the UML). A problem is that the semantic domain of the UML, until now, has not been generally agreed upon. The UML 1.4 specification [1] does not specify a semantic domain, and the Action Semantics [2] that does specify a semantic domain, has been criticized for being to specific on this issue. Because we can not do without, we specify the semantic domain of the smallest subset of the UML that would fit the OCL.

4.1   A Kernel Semantic Domain for UML Models

A model of the kernel semantic domain for UML models is shown in . It introduces the fundamental domain elements, the things we can reason about using the UML. The

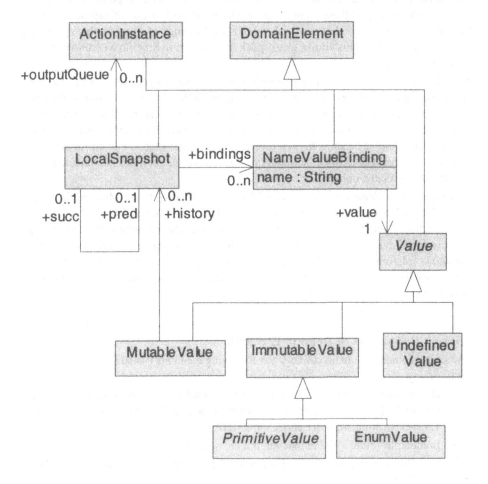

Fig. 2. The kernel semantic domain

most important notion is that of Value, of which there are mutable and immutable versions. The most obvious subclass of MutableValue is Object, but there may be others, e.g. Component, or Agent could in an extension of this kernel be defined as another subclass of MutableValue. The most obvious subclass of an ImmutableValue is PrimitiveValue, i.e. integer, string, boolean values, etc, but there could be an extension in which an immutable structured type, e.g. a C language struct, or an SQL tuple, is defined. Every value has an identity, which can not be changed. Because PrimitiveValues have no other structure than their identity, their identity is in general regarded to be identical to the value, e.g. 3 equals 3.

Mutable values may contain references to other values. These references are bindings at a certain point in time of a name (the reference) to a value, which is represented by the metaclass NameValueBinding. Because the bindings may change from moment to moment, the history of these changes are captured in a list of LocalSnapshots held by the MutableValue. Each LocalSnapshot holds all bindings of one MutableValue at a certain point in time. This allows us to speak of 'changes in time' to a certain object or component.

Note that the concept named LocalSnapshot in our approach is different from the concept called snapshot in the meta modeling language MML [4], but it is like to the definition of the concept given in the Action Semantics [4]. A LocalSnapshot is purely local to an object, it is not an instance of a complete package (as it is in MML). A LocalSnapshot contains only the names known directly to its owner object, e.g. all its attributes and associations. It does not contain any names known indirectly to the object, e.g. attributes of associated objects.

As in the Action Semantics time is considered to be relative to the MutableValue, i.e. each MutableValue has it own notion of time. Time is considered to pass in discrete steps, each step being represented by another snapshot. The real time between the snapshots is not relevant in this kernel. Note that this view on time is in accordance within Einstein's relativity theory. Every space-continuum, in our case every mutable value, has its own time. Furthermore, every mutable value has its own specific view of the total universe: it sees only the values that are associated with it.

4.1.1   Definitions of Domain Elements

The kernel semantic domain contains the following elements (listed in alphabetical order).

- DomainElement: an element that can be reasoned about (specified, modelled) using the UML. This class serves the same purpose as ModelElement in the UML 1.4 specification, all other classes inherit from this class.
- ImmutableValue: a Value that can not change, or be changed.
- LocalSnapshot: a collection of NameValueBindings for a certain MutableValue at a certain point in time.
- MutableValue: a Value that has bindings of which the value may change. A MutableValue that has a state, represented in a LocalSnapshot, and is able to change that state, thereby creating a new LocalSnapshot.

- NameValueBinding: a combination of a Name (reference) and a Value.
- ActionInstance: an Instance of an Action.
- UndefinedValue: a Value that represents void (null, nul, nil) or undefined.
- Value: a DomainElement that represents one of the elements of the world that can be modeled using the UML.

4.1.2   Well-Formedness Rules and Additional Operations

The following well-formedness rules and additional operations are defined for the concepts in the kernel semantic domain:

1. The history of an object is ordered. The first element does not have a predecessor, the last does not have a successor.

```
context MutableValue
inv: history->oclIsTypeOf( Sequence(LocalSnapShot) )
inv: history->last().succ->size() = 0
inv: history->first().pre->size() = 0
```

2. The additional operation *allPredecessors* returns the collection of all snapshots before a snapshot, *allSuccessors* returns the collection of all snapshots after a snapshot.

```
context LocalSnapshot
def: Let allPredecessors : Set(LocalSnapshot) =
          if pred->notEmpty then
              pred->union(pred.allPredecessors)
          else
             Set {}
          endif
def: Let allSuccessors : Set(LocalSnapshot) =
          if succ->notEmpty then
              succ->union(succ.allSuccessors)
          else
             Set {}
          endif
```

3. The additional operation *getCurrentValueOf* results in the value that is bound to the *n-th* parameter in the latest snapshot in the history of an object value. Note that the value may be the UndefinedValue.

```
context MutableValue
def: Let getCurrentValueOf(n: String): Value =
                  history->last().bindings->any(name = n).value
```

4. The additional operation *bindings* results in all name-type combinations in the last snapshot of the history of a mutable value.

```
context MutableValue
def: Let bindings() : Set(NameValueBindings) =
        history->last()->collect( bindings )
```

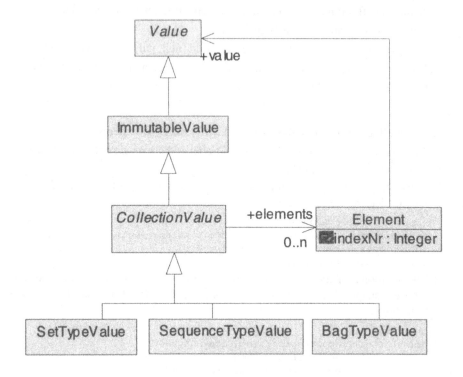

Fig. 3. The collection values in the semantic domain

4.2   Ocl Collection Values in the Kernel Semantic Domain

In order to define the semantics of OCL expressions, the kernel semantic domain will not suffice. We need to introduce an extension: the values that are specified by the OCL collection types, shown in figure 3 .

4.2.1   Definitions

The definitions of the concepts needed to define the collection values are:

• BagTypeValue: A bag type value is a collection value which is a multiset of elements where each element may occur multiple times in the bag. The elements are unordered.

• CollectionValue: A collection value is a list of values. Part of every collection value are the values of its elements.

• Element: An element represents a single component of a tuple value, or collection value. An element has an indexNr, and a value. The purpose of the indexNr is to uniquely identify the position of each component, when it is used as an element of a SequenceValue.

- SequenceTypeValue: A sequence type value is a collection value which is a list of values where each value may occur multiple times in the sequence. The values are ordered by their position in the sequence. Part of a sequence value are the values of its elements.
- SetTypeValue: A set type value is a collection value which is a set of elements where each distinct element occurs only once in the set. The elements are not ordered. Part of a set value are the values of its elements.

4.2.2   Well-Formedness Rules

1. All elements belonging to a sequence value have unique index numbers.

```
context SequenceTypeValue inv:
self.element->isUnique(e : Element | e.indexNr)
```

4.3   Ocl Evaluations in the Kernel Semantic Domain

This section defines the evaluations of OCL expressions. The evaluations package mirrors the abstract syntax package by providing an evaluation for each OCL expression in the abstract syntax, as shown in figure 4. Evaluating an OCL expression always results in a value. The 'meaning' (semantics) of an OCL expression is the value yielded by its evaluation within an environment, this value is named *resultValue*. Note that there may be multiple evaluations associated with one expression, yet every evaluation results in exactly one value.

Every OCL expression is evaluated within a certain name space. The evaluation of an OCL expression is named *OclExpEvaluation*, the name space is named *environment*. Some OCL expressions, postconditions and action clauses used as postcondition, also need information about a previous point in time. This is also represented by a name space called *beforeEnvironment*.

The evaluation of an action clause expression is called *ActionClauseEval*. The *ActionClauseEval* is a subtype of the *OclExpEvaluation*, with additional associations to represent the values for *condition*, *targetSet* and *actionRef*. The evaluation of a reference to an action is called *ActionRefEval*. This is a very general concept that represents an instance of an action.

4.3.1   Definitions

- ActionClauseEval: the evaluation of an action clause expression.
- ActionRefEval: the evaluation of an action reference.
- NameSpace: a domain element that holds a series of name value bindings.
- NameValueBinding: a domain element that binds a name to a value.
- OclExpEvaluation: the evaluation of an OCL expression.

4.3.2   Well-Formedness Rules

1. All names in a name space must be unique.

```
context NameSpace inv:
bindings->isUnique(name)
```

2. The value referenced by the keyword 'self' must be the same in both beforeEnvironment and environment.

```
context OclExpEvaluation inv:
environment.getValueOf('self') =
                        beforeEnvironment.getValueOf('self')
```

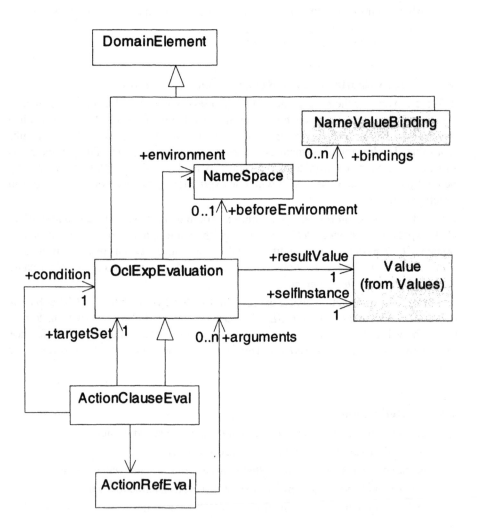

Fig. 4. The domain elements representing evaluations

4.3.3   Well-Formedness Rules That Specify the Name Space Environment

Each expression is evaluated in a defined environment. Which are the name value bindings that are in the environment in which an OCL expression is evaluated, is therefore an important issue to resolve. Before a postcondition or action clause is evaluated, the *beforeEnvironment* needs to be established. Note that the *beforeEnvironment* can be seen as a minimal system snapshot, including all values that can be reached from the object for which the expression is evaluated, but not more. The following rules state how the name value bindings in the *environment* are defined. Although they are not stated here, the same rules hold for the *beforeEnvironment*.

1. The environment of an OCL expression contains at least the (object) instance for which the expression is evaluated, and its bindings.

```
context OclExpEvaluation inv:
self.environment
    ->includes( new NameValueBinding('self', selfInstance)
      ->union( selfInstance.bindings() ) )
```

2. The environment of the condition, the targetSet, and the arguments of the signalSet of an ActionClauseEval are all equal to the environment of that ActionClauseEval.

```
context ActionClauseEval
inv: condition.environment = self.environment
inv: targetSet.environment = self.environment
inv: signalSet.arguments->forAll( environment = self.environment )
```

4.3.4   Additional Operations

1. The operation *getValueOf* results in the value that binds to the *name* parameter in the bindings of a name space. Note that the value may be the UndefinedValue.

```
context NameSpace
def: Let getValueOf(n: String): Value =
     bindings->one(name = n).value
```

2. The operation *replace* replaces the value of a name, by the value given in the *nvb* parameter.

```
context NameSpace::replace(nvb: NameValueBinding): NameSpace
pre: -- none
post: result.bindings = self.bindings
    ->excluding( self.bindings->any( name = nvb.name) )
      ->including( nvb )
```

3. The operation *add* adds the name and value indicated by the NameValueBinding given by the *nvb* parameter.

```
context NameSpace::add(nvb: NameValueBinding): NameSpace
pre: -- none
post: result.bindings = self.bindings->including( nvb )
```

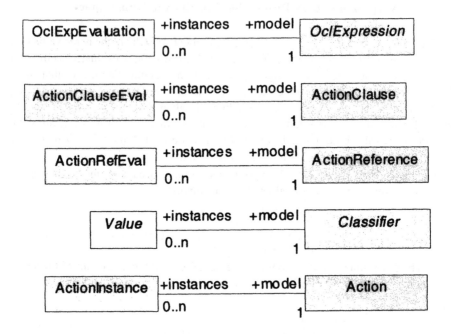

Fig. 5. The relations between abstract syntax and semantic domain

5   The Semantics for the Action Clause

Once the semantic domain has been established, it is rather easy to define the semantics of the action clause expression. The semantics model is shown in figure 5. It simply maps OclExpression to OclExpEvaluation, and ActionClause to ActionClauseEval. Likewise the values are mapped to their type counterparts. For example, in the context of Object the expression *self.model* represents a Classifier (probably a Class, which is a subtype of Classifier).

5.1   Well-Formedness Rules

1. The meaning of the action expression is that an ActionInstance with the specified Action as its model must have been in the output queue of the self instance at some time between 'now' and a reference point in time. 'Now' is represented by the environment of the expression, the reference point in time is represented by the before environment. The Lets in the invariant below are convenient to indicate the list of all snapshots between the 'now' and the reference time point.

   The above must be true for each action specified in the action clause.

```
context ActionClauseEval inv:
Let start: LocalSnapshot = beforeEnvironment.getValueOf( 'self' )
                                        ->history->last() in
```

```
Let end: LocalSnapshot = environment.getValueOf( 'self' )
                                     ->history->last() in
Let inBetween: Sequence( LocalSnapshot ) =
    start.allSuccessors->excluding( end.allSuccessors)
                                 ->including( start ) in

resultValue = condition implies
self.model.signalSet.action->forAll(a : Action |
                    inBetween->collect(outputQueue)
                        ->exists( ai : ActionInstance | ai.model = a))
```

2. All elements in a collection value must have a type that conforms to the element-Type of its corresponding CollectionType.

```
context CollectionValue inv:
elements->forAll( e: Element |
                    e.value.model.conformsTo( model.elementType ) )
```

3. The additional operation *isInstanceOf(c : Classifier)* of Value returns true if this value is an instance of the specified classifier.

```
context Value::isInstanceOf( c: Classifier ): Boolean
pre: -- none
post: result = self.model.conformsTo( c )
```

4. The result value of the evaluation of an ocl expression must be an instance of the type of that expression.

```
context OclExpEvaluation inv:
    resultValue.isInstanceOf( model.type )
```

5. When an OCL expression is used as postcondition, the environment also contains the parameters of the behavioral feature. Note that we can not identify the value of these parameters, all we can state is that there must be a binding of the parameter name to a value present in the environment of an OCL expression.

```
context OclExpEvaluation inv:
    model.postBehavFeat->size() = 1
        implies self.environment.bindings.name
                        ->includesAll( model.behavFeat.parameter.name )
```

6. When an action clause is connected to a behavioral feature, the environment also contains the parameters of the behavioral feature. Note that we can not identify the value of these parameters, all we can state is that there must be a binding of the parameter name to a value present in the environment of an OCL expression.

```
context ActionClauseEval inv:
    model.actBehavFeat->size() = 1
        implies self.environment.bindings.name
                        ->includesAll(model.behavFeat.parameter.name )
```

7. When an OCL expression is used as postcondition, the beforeEnvironment is present.

```
context OclExpEvaluation inv:
    model.postBehavFeat->size() = 1 implies
                                beforeEnvironment->size()=1
```

8. When an action clause is connected to a behavioral feature, the beforeEnvironment is present.

```
context ActionClauseEval inv:
  model.actBehavFeat->size() = 1 implies
                          beforeEnvironment->size() = 1
```

9. Signals may be send to objects only, not to data values.

```
context ActionClause inv:
  targetSet.instances->forAll( e | e.isKindOf( MutableValue ))
```

10. If an element in the signalSet of an ActionClause refers to an operation call, the corresponding operation should be defined in the Classifier of each target in the targetSet.

```
context ActionClause inv:
    signalSet.action->isKindOf( CallAction ) implies
    targetSet->forAll(
      model.features->includeAll( signalSet.action.operation) )
```

Note that rule 1, which is the core of the semantics defininition is not fully complete. It currently defines that there is at least one action instance for each specified action. For completeness it should state that for each specified action there should be one action instance for each object in the target set. This requires an extension to the semantic domain from figure 2. ActionInstance should have an association to MutableValue with rolename 'target' at the mutable value side.

6   Conclusions

Our conclusions after having formalized the natural language definition of the action clause expression into a more formal semantics describes using the UML and OCL, are:

- The semantics of the action clause given in this paper, are not formal in the traditional sense that a mathematical formalism is used to describe them. Still they are much more formal, more clear, less prone to ambiguities, etc. than the natural language semantics given in the introduction. Yet they are understandable to people working with the UML.

- Metamodeling is a good way to describe the abstract syntax and the semantic domain of an object language like UML. The semantics, i.e. the mapping from abstract syntax concepts to semantic domain values, is defined by associations from abstract syntax concepts to the semantic domain concepts.

- A generally agreed upon kernel that contains a definition of a semantic domain and semantics of UML must be established in order to define extensions, like the action clause, to the UML and the OCL. The semantics of the action clause as given in this paper highly depend on that kernel, and may therefore be subject to change. Superimposing this conclusion on the whole of the UML, raises doubts on the current standardisation efforts. The RfP [9] send out by the OMG for extensions to the UML, or 'superstructure', is bound to produce unrelated language constructs, as long as the RfP [8] for a kernel language, or 'infrastructure', has not been properly answered.

References

[1]   OMG Unified Modeling Language Specification, Version 1.4, May 2001
[2]   Response to OMG RFP ad/98-11-01 *Action Semantics for the UML*, March 24, 2001,
        available from www.kc.com/as_site/home.html
[3]   Hans-Erik Eriksson and Magnus Penker, *Business Modeling with UML, Business Patterns
        at Work*, 2000, Wiley
[4]   Tony Clark, Andy Evans, Stuart Kent, Steve Brodsky, Steve Cook, *A feasibility Study in
        Rearchitecting UML as a Family of Languages using a Precise OO Meta-Modelling Ap-
        proach*, version 1.0, September 2000, available from www.puml.org
[5]   Anneke Kleppe and Jos Warmer, *Extending OCL to Include Actions*, in Proceeedings of
        the <<UML>> 2000 - The Unified Modeling Language, 2000, Springer Verlag
[6]   Anneke Kleppe and Jos Warmer, *Unification of Static and Dynamic Semantics of UML*,
        version 0.2, July 2001, available from www.klasse.nl/english/uml/semantics
[7]   Jos Warmer and Anneke Kleppe, *The Object Constraint Language, Precise Modeling with
        UML*, 1999, Addison-Wesley
[8]   Request for Proposal: UML 2.0 Infrastructure RFP, OMG document ad/2000-09-01, Sep-
        tember 2000
[9]   Request for Proposal: UML 2.0 Superstructure RFP, OMG document ad/2000-09-02, Sep-
        tember 2000

Constraint Trees

Stuart Kent[1]* and John Howse[2]*

[1] University of Kent, Canterbury, UK
sjhk@ukc.ac.uk,
http://www.cs.ukc.ac.uk/people/staff/sjhk
[2] University of Brighton, Brighton, UK
John.Howse@brighton.ac.uk

Abstract. OCL's contribution to the definition of constraint languages
is twofold: the identification of core concepts for a constraint language
suitable for object-oriented modeling; a developer-friendly notation for
that language, as an alternative to traditional mathematical syntax.
Whilst the former is an important contribution the latter is more questionable. Not only is notation often a matter of taste, but it would also
be desirable to freely mix notations, allowing the most appropriate notation to be chosen for the task at hand or for notations to be seamlessly
interchanged. A further problem when writing constraints is scalability:
the number and complexity of constraints can be overwhelming for a
model of a real-sized system, and current techniques for organizing the
constraint space of a model are limited. The contribution of this paper
is to provide a notation, *constraint trees*, which can be used both for
mixing different notations and for organizing the constraint space of a
model. Constraint trees achieve this by revealing aspects of the underlying abstract syntax structure of a constraint. The paper demonstrates
the utility of the notation using an example from the telecomms networks
domain, and shows how constraint trees can be used to write a constraint
involving a mix of textual OCL notation, constraint diagrams, object diagrams and rich pictures. This also demonstrates the organizational role
of constraint trees. An outline meta-model definition of constraint trees
is provided and issues surrounding their tooling is discussed.

1   Introduction

OCL's contribution to the definition of constraint languages is twofold: the identification of core concepts for a constraint language suitable for object-oriented
modeling; a developer-friendly notation for that language, as an alternative to
traditional mathematical syntax. Whilst the former is an important contribution
the latter is more questionable. Not only is notation often a matter of taste, but
it would also be desirable to freely mix notations, allowing the most appropriate
notation to be chosen for the task at hand or for notations to be seamlessly
interchanged. An example of mixing constraint notations is given in [KH99],

---

* Partially funded by the UK EPSRC, grant number GR/M02606

A. Clark and J. Warmer (Eds.): Object Modeling with the OCL, LNCS 2263, pp. 228–249, 2002.
© Springer-Verlag Berlin Heidelberg 2002

where we explored how constraint diagrams [Ken97,KG98] could be mixed with the textual notation of OCL. The motivation for this was twofold: firstly, constraint diagrams are not powerful enough to express all parts of a constraint; secondly, constraint diagrams provide a more natural rendering of some parts of a constraint whilst a textual notation seems more appropriate for others. In this paper, we show how constraint trees provide a more unified solution to mixing notations than the one proposed in [KH99], and then extend their use to bringing object diagrams and rich pictures into the mix.

A further problem when writing constraints is scalability. The number and complexity of constraints can be overwhelming for a model of a real-sized system. Current techniques for organizing the constraint space of a model are limited: all one is able to do is locate a list of conjuncts in a class. In this paper, we show how constraint trees can be used to organize the constraint space of a model. The organization need not follow the class structuring, and conjuncts are not the only way in which a constraint may be subdivided into clauses.

The paper is organized as follows. Section 2 motivates constraint trees. It motivates the need for organizing constraints across a model, other than by class or by conjunct, and the need for intermingling diagrammatic notations, such as constraint diagrams, with the textual notation. The section also introduces the running example, which is taken from the modeling of networks and services in the telecomms domain. Section 3 introduces constraint trees and shows how they can be used to give different presentations of the examples in Section 2. Section 4 introduces the idea that object diagrams can be used to notate part of constraints, and shows how constraint trees facilitate this. It also discusses how casting object diagrams as "rich pictures" could provide a relatively lightweight approach to developing more domain specific notations for constraints. Section 5 discusses the facilities that tools could provide for viewing and managing constraints, using the constraint tree concept. Finally, Section 6 draws some conclusions and outlines further work. In particular it discusses work required to complete the formalization of constraint trees using the meta-modeling approach, and how this could contribute to the development of tools.

2   Motivation

The motivation for constraint trees comes from two sources: a desire to mix constraint diagrams with textual OCL notation; a desire for a more flexible approach to organizing constraints in a model. We deal with each in turn, after introducing two examples, one drawn from the domain of modeling telecomms networks and one a simplistic library system. The former is substantive; the latter is needed to support one case which is not naturally supported by the networks example.

2.1   Examples

This section introduces the class diagrams on which the constraints formulated throughout the remainder of the paper are based.

Mapping service descriptions to IP network configurations. This example has come from the telecomms domain, where there is a desire to model services delivered over a network independent of any particular network technology, and separately provide a model of the mapping of that abstraction to particular network technologies.

Figure 1 shows a fragment of the model of a virtual network, which is the model independent of a particular technology. In this model, a network is viewed as a set of virtual connections, each of which connects a source and target point of access to the network (so a virtual connection is directed). Each access point may have a set of hosts attached to it. A virtual connection may have associated with it a set of services, where a service connects two hosts (indicated by its signature) which must be connected to the access points of the virtual connection with which the service is associated, one at each end. A service is also associated with a service level. A service level has a priority – the higher the priority the better QoS (Quality of Service) the service should receive.

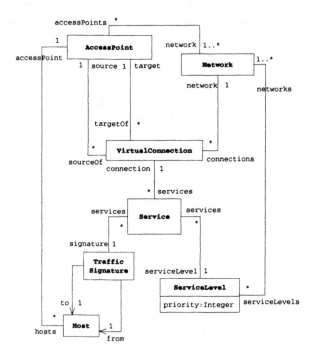

Fig. 1. Virtual network

The mapping from the virtual network to the particular technology can also be modeled. Figure 1 is the class diagram for a model of the fragment of that mapping relevant to this paper. The dashed boxes carry no meaning – they have been inserted just to distinguish between the virtual network layer, the mapping layer and the IP network layer. This distinction can be made in UML using packages; we have not done so here as it would introduce an additional layer of concepts that is not relevant to this paper.

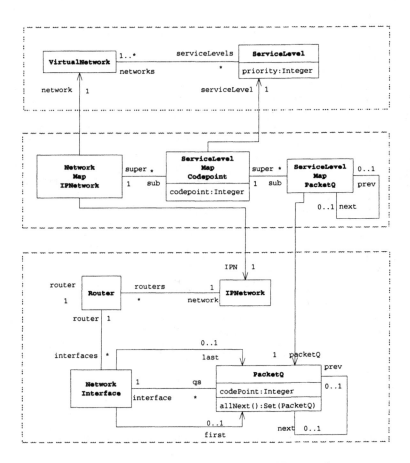

Fig. 2. Mapping virtual networks to IP networks

The details of the model are, perhaps, best explained through a particular instance, which can be found in Figure 3. This shows a fragment of the state of a virtual network, which has two service levels defined. These get mapped down to the IP network layer using intermediate mapping objects, as follows. Every network interface on every router (in this case there is only one of each) must have a packet queue (and only one) corresponding to each service level, plus an additional queue to handle default service. In the example, pq3 is the queue handling default service for interface ni4. A service level also maps to a codepoint, and any queues corresponding to that service level must be marked by that codepoint. Thus sl1 maps to codepoint 8 and so pq2 must also be marked by codepoint 8. Packet queues are themselves held in a queue, and the ordering of this queue corresponds to priorities on the corresponding service levels. So pq2 comes next after pq1, because sl1 has a lower priority than sl2.

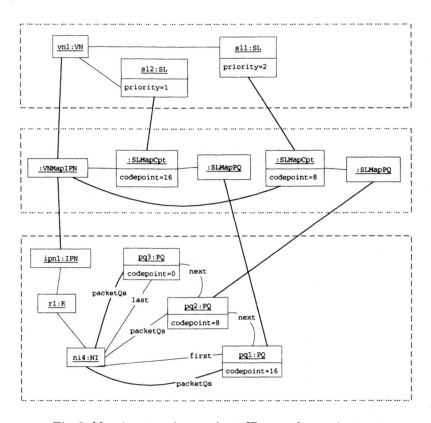

Fig. 3. Mapping virtual networks to IP networks - an instance

The idea behind this mapping is that when data packets enter the IP network at the edge, they get classified by marking them with the codepoint corresponding to the quality of service they receive. When they reach a network interface during their traversal across the network, this mark is used to decide on which packet queue they should be placed. Packet queues are serviced in order, with queues higher in the order being served more frequently. Hence packets placed on a queue higher in the order are likely to get sent on their way more quickly, so receive a better quality of service.

Only a small piece of the mapping has been shown here. There are also mapping rules to handle classification of packets at the edge of the network, to handle mapping of virtual connections to routes through the network, and mapping of configuration information on routers to ensure that packets are correctly routed.

Library. The class diagram for the library system is given in Figure 4. A library keeps a record of the copies in its collection and of loans made. A loan records the copy lent out and the user to which it is/was lent out. The library keeps a record of both current and past loans. A copy may be associated with its current loan, if that copy is out on loan.

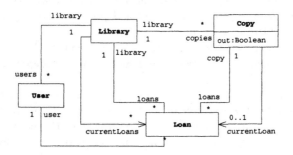

Fig. 4. Library

2.2   Structuring and Organizing Constraints

The scalability of a notation is dependent, in part, on the facilities provided in that notation for breaking a large artifact into a well-defined structure of smaller, comprehensible pieces. In object modeling, scalability issues traditionally have been addressed using the notion of class, and, more recently, by allowing classes to be collected together into packages. In UML, structuring of OCL constraints is achieved in two ways: firstly, by riding piggy-back on classes (OCL invariants are attached to classes) and by allowing separate conjuncts to be listed separately. An illustration of the former is given by constraints (1) and (2), below. Constraint (3) illustrates why the latter is not an effective tool for organizing constraints.

1. *Two services on a virtual connection must link different pairs of hosts.*
   context vc:VirtualConnection **inv**:
   > vc.services->forAll(s1,s2|
   > s1.signature.from<>s2.signature.from or
   > s1.signature.to<>s2.signature.to)
2. *Hosts for a service must be connected to access points of the*
   virtual connection that the service is on
   context s:Service **inv**:
   > s.signature.to.accessPoint=s.connection.target and
   > s.signature.from.accessPoint=s.connection.source

3. `context vnip:VirtualNetworkMapIPNetwork inv:`
     `let sls=vnip.sub.serviceLevel in`
        there is a submapping for each service level of the network,
        and only these submappings
        `(sls=vnip.virtual.serviceLevels->asBag`
        the codepoints associated with each network service level are unique
        `and vnip.sub.codepoint->size=sls->size`
        and zero is reserved (for default service)
        `and vnip.sub.codepoint->excludes(0)`
        the interface on every router of the target IP network has a queue
        for each service level of the network plus an additonal queue for
        codepoint 0 which is always serviced last
        `and vnip.IP.routers.interfaces->forAll(i|`
           `i.queues->size=sls->size+1 and i.lastQ.codepoint=0))`

Constraints (1) and (2) are constraints which are related in the sense that they are constraints on signatures of services. However, they are grouped under two different classes, as (1) needs to be expressed in the context of a virtual connection, not a service. In organizing the constraint space for this model, one could argue that it would be more understandable if these constraints were grouped together and not separated. Whilst one can perceive of a tool that would support such groupings, e.g. as a view on the constraint space, the tendency with tooling is to group things by some containment hierarchy of model elements. Thus classes tend to be grouped in packages, operations/methods and attributes in classes and so on. Indeed, some tools which have placeholders for constraints (e.g. Rational Rose), group invariants in classes and pre/post conditions as part of an operation definition. Interestingly the USE tool [RG00], which is designed to support OCL, groups constraint by package, suggesting that there, constraints are viewed as being as part of packages, not classes (we have some sympathy with this view). Constraint trees allow constraints to be organized by any of these methods. We believe they could provide a means for notating different views on a constraint space, by defining (reasoning) rules for deriving one constraint tree from another.

Constraint (3) illustrates the case where structuring as a list of conjuncts has limited usefulness when organizing constraints. The problem here is that there are four conjuncts appearing inside the scope of a let statement. Each of these conjuncts refers to a different aspect of behaviour, and it would be desirable to separate these out, giving each their own label. One way of doing this would be to treat each conjunct as a separate constraint, repeating the let statement preamble each time. This has two undesirable properties: if it was decided that the defining expression of the let statement needed to be changed, then it would have to be changed four times; when reading the constraint the let statement has to be parsed four times. If the preamble was more complex than in this case, then both these drawbacks would become more severe. An alternative would be to allow subclauses of an expression to be explicitly labeled. This would work with appropriate tool support. That is, when a list of constraints appears in the tool, one should be able to open a constraint to receive a list of its named subclauses, and so on. Indeed, one might view a list of constraints as being a single constraint with a number of labeled conjuncts, and then this would be the only mechanism needed to structure a collection of constraints. This is essentially the mechanism supported by constraint trees, noting that disjuncts and other kinds of clauses are also supported.

2.3   Mixing Constraint Diagrams and OCL

The motivation for wishing to mix constraint language notations has come from our work on the visual constraint notation, constraint diagrams [Ken97,KG98]. Sample constraint diagrams are given in Figures 5 and 6.

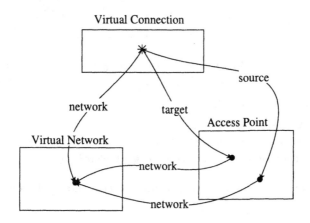

Fig. 5. Constraint diagram 1

Spiders (blobs and stars) represent elements, a star a universally quantified element. Contours (boxes and ellipses) represent sets. Venn/Euler/Peirce diagram notation is used to show the relationships between sets and elements. Arrows represent navigation. A navigation expression is represented by a sequence of arrows, where the target of the final arrow in the sequence represents the element or set of elements arrived at by navigating that path.

A key to reading a constraint diagram is to know where to start. A good rule of thumb is to start at the outermost universally quantified element(s) (i.e. those elements not in scope of other elements). Sometimes this can be difficult to locate, as there can be mutual recursion. Work is ongoing to resolve such issues.

The corresponding OCL for these diagrams is given by:

4. **context vn:VirtualNetwork inv**:

   vn.network=vn.target.network **and** vn.network=vn.source.network
   and not(vn.source=vn.target)

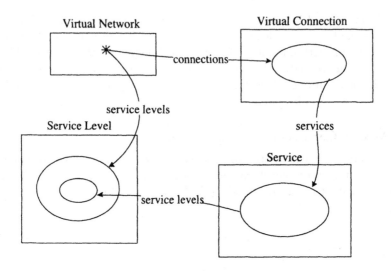

Fig. 6. Constraint diagram 1

5. **context vn:VirtualNetwork inv:**
   vn.serviceLevels->includesAll(
   vn.connections.services.serviceLevels->asSet)

We have made four observations, in our experiments with constraint diagrams, which are relevant to this paper:

– Some constraints, or parts of a constraint, are more naturally expressed as constraint diagrams than others.
– Some people find the constraint diagram version of a constraint (or part thereof) more intuitive and easier to understand, than the textual variant. Some do not.
– Constraint diagrams provide a useful compliment to the textual form, and vice-versa. Having both can be a valuable cross-check.
– It is hard, if not impossible, to visualize some constraints using constraint diagrams.

These observations led us to consider in [KH99] how to mix constraint diagrams with textual OCL notation. Two ideas emerged from that paper, illustrated by Figures 7 and 8, respectively.

Figure 7 embodies the idea of adding a textual annotation to constraint diagrams, where these annotations use free variables that are bound by the constraint diagram. The figure represents the constraint 3 in Section 2.2. There is no notation in constraint diagrams for representing the size of sets or bags (all contours denote sets). The requirement for bags has been avoided by explicitly showing distinct elements in `vnip.subs` mapping to distinct elements in `sls`.

diagram 1

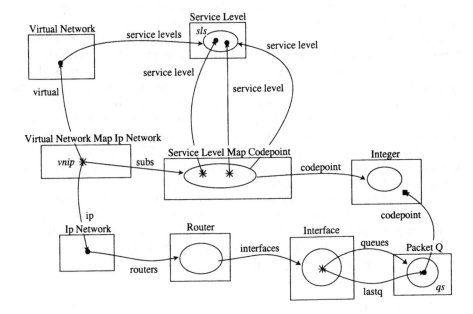

context diagram 1 inv: qs->size=sls->size+1

Fig. 7. Annotated constraint diagram

context lib:Library inv:
  let outCopies=lib.copies->select(c|c.out=true) in

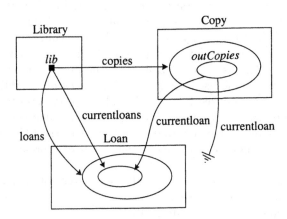

Fig. 8. Embedded constraint diagram

However, the only way to ensure that the size of sls and qs are appropriately related is to add a textual annotation. This is done by naming the diagram and using the context clause in the OCL to refer to that name.

Figure 8 embodies the idea of embedding a constraint diagram in a textual constraint, where, again, free variables are bound by the text in which the constraint diagram is embedded. This is an extract from the model of a library system. The constraint ensures that copies of a library which are in the out state (i.e. out on loan) are associated with a loan object, whereas copies which are not out are not. The OCL text introduces a subset of copies in the let statement, which is selected from all the copies of the library. Select statements can not be expressed in current OCL syntax (though see [KH99] for a suggestion of how they might be and [Ken97] for an alternative way of modeling states that is supported by constraint diagrams).

Constraint trees, introduced in the next section, unify these two approaches, by revealing directly in the notation parts of the underlying structure of a constraint, thereby providing placeholders for textual or diagrammatic rendition of subexpressions. In addition, they support the ability to place one expression in the context of another, with appropriate binding of free variables in the latter.

3   Constraint Trees

Constraint trees are a notation that reveal aspects of the underlying abstract syntax structure of a constraint. Not only do they provide a unified solution to the mixing of textual and graphical constraint notations, as described in the previous section, they can also be used as a tool for organizing and viewing the constraint space of a model.

The general form of a constraint tree is illustrated by Figure 9. It consists of nodes, which are rendered as boxes, each containing a diagrammatic or textual expression. Boxes may optionally be annotated with a comment – we have chosen to use the UML note notation for this purpose, and/or may have a label. Labels may be chosen by the user, or a labeling scheme may be adopted, such as the sequence number scheme used for labeling messages on a UML collaboration diagram. Nodes are organized in a tree. Simple lines are used to connect nodes. A generalization of this is to allow trees to share the same nodes, which allows different perspectives on a constraint space to be constructed.

A node can contain one of three different kinds of expression:

1. the introduction of a variable through a let statement or quantifier
2. the representation of a boolean formula
3. a logical connective (AND, OR, XOR, NOT)

Nodes of kind (1) and (2) must have one and only one child. Nodes of kind (3) must have two or more children. One could no doubt define other variations (e.g. for implication), but we posit that the above will be sufficient for most purposes.

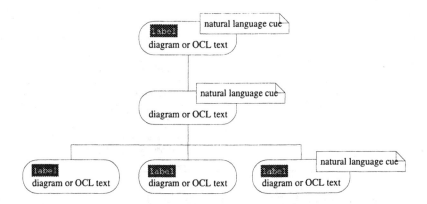

Fig. 9. General form of constraint trees

Each kind of node is illustrated by rendering the examples introduced in the previous section as constraint trees. This will also illustrate how constraint trees can be used to mix constraint diagrams with OCL textual notation in a uniform manner, and provide a flexible notation for organizing a constraint space.

3.1 Nodes

Let statements and quantification. Nodes serving as let statements and quantification are illustrated by rendering Figure 8 as a constraint tree, as in Figure 10. The interpretation of this diagram is as expected. The given set outCopies in the constraint diagram is defined by the let expression in the node that precedes it. The given element lib in the constraint diagram is the same as that used in the let expression which is bound by the quantifier appearing in the parent node of the node containing the let expression. There are two points of note here, with regard to the OCL syntax.

- We have changed the concrete syntax of OCL for let and forAll: constraint trees remove the need to have notation (e.g. keywords such as in) to indicate nesting.
- We have replaced the **context** ... **inv**: expression in OCL with a forAll quantifier over the class referred to in the context expression. This is the effective meaning of **context** ... **inv:**, and avoids unnecessary proliferation of concepts.

Representation of a boolean formula. Nodes serving as a representation of a boolean formula are illustrated by rendering Figure 7 as a constraint tree, as in Figure 11. The interpretation of this diagram works by binding the free variables (representing both sets and elements) in the tree whose root is the child of this node. Thus, in the example, qs and sls in the bottom node are bound to the sets with these labels as defined in the top node.

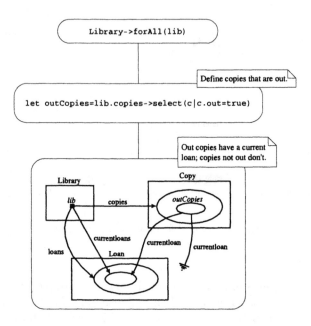

Fig. 10. Embedded cd with constraint trees

Logical connectives. Nodes serving as logical connectives are illustrated by Figure 12. This combines constraints 1 and 2 in Section 2.2 into a single tree.

3.2   Mixing Constraint Diagrams with Text

Embedding of constraint diagrams in OCL textual notation (see Section 2.3), is illustrated by Figure 10. Annotation of constraint diagrams with OCL textual notation is illustrated by Figure 11. These demonstrate that constraint trees provide a uniform approach to the mixing problem.

3.3   Organizing the Constraint Space

Constraint trees provide a more flexible way of organizing constraints over an object-oriented model, than the approach currently used. Figure 13 illustrates how constraint trees can be used to break down a constraint into small, digestible chunks, in a way that is not possible when the only structuring mechanism at your disposal is to provide a list of conjuncts.

This is an expansion of the constraint 3 in Section 2.2, which was previously rendered as the constraint tree in Figure 11. The two expanded conjuncts together provide an alternative rendering to the latter. The tree shows clearly the overall structure of the constraint, being careful to separate out easily digestable subclauses and any commonality between these subclauses. For example, node

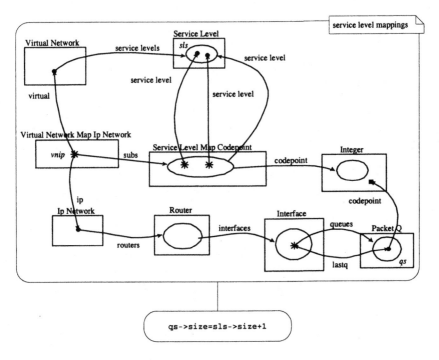

Fig. 11. Annotated cd with constraint trees

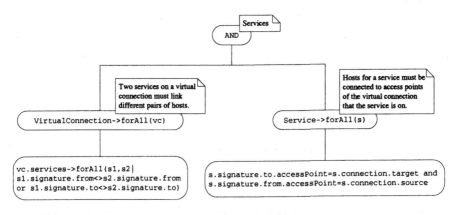

Fig. 12. A ct with AND and OR

submappings of vn map ip identifies a set subs that is common to the two conjuncts beneath this node. Notes provide a natural language cue to the meaning of what is contained in each node (and their subnodes). Diagrams have been used where we feel they are most effective, that is to show Venn-diagram style relationships between sets and to show navigation paths. It should be stressed

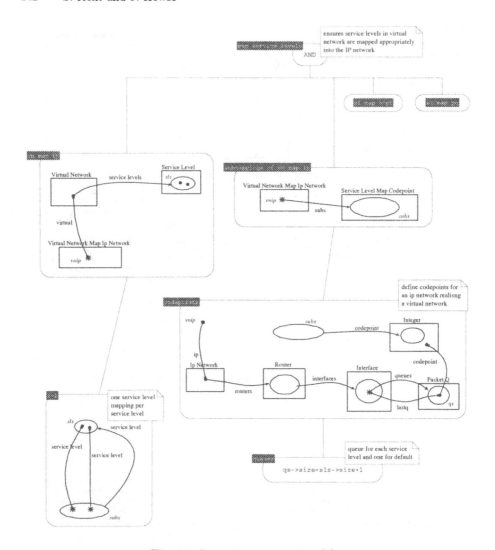

Fig. 13. Organising constraints (1)

that this is our choice; a modeler would be free to use text or diagrams and break up a constraint into pieces as little or as much as they wished.

Both expanded conjuncts are constraints on the class

`VirtualNetworkMapIPNetwork`

(a universal quantifier is introduced in this class). Two other (collapsed) conjuncts are shown, with roots labeled sl map c'pt and sl map pq. These conjuncts represent constraints on other classes. The latter has been expanded in Figure

14. This tree has further examples of connective nodes and the use of OCL textual notation to express a part of constraint that is awkward with constraint diagrams (ordering of priorities, which are integers).

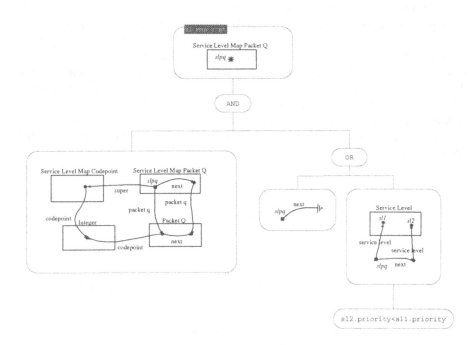

Fig. 14. Organizing constraints (2)

Thus Figure 13 demonstrates how constraint trees can be used to group constraints from different classes. The tree in Figure 12 provides a second example.

One can imagine situations where one would wish to maintain multiple views on the same constraint space: trees which group constraints by topic rather than class, and trees which group constraints by class. In principle, this could be achieved by selecting from a tree or set of trees all subtrees which share root nodes that contain equivalent expressions. Thus, to identify all the constraints that apply to the class ServiceLevelMapPacketQ, one could traverse the set of trees representing the constraint space to collect together all subtrees with root nodes containing expressions equivalent to sl map pq. These subtrees could then be merged, by merging their root nodes into one (and inserting an appropriate AND node), to form the constraint tree representing all the constraints on that class.

4   Embedding Object Diagrams

So far we have shown how constraint trees can be used to mix constraint diagrams with textual notation. This section expands on this idea by noticing that some parts of a constraint can be rendered as object diagrams.

Figure 15 shows an alternative rendering to Figure 12. The clause on the left hand-side of that constraint has been replaced by a constraint diagram, to introduce the quantified variables, followed by an OR clause, whose subclauses have been rendered as a constraint diagram and object diagram, respectively. This is intended to illustrate how an object diagram can be used in place of certain kinds of constraint diagram (the left and right disjuncts are very similar in their meaning), namely one with only elements and no sets, and, therefore embedded in a constraint tree. The right hand conjunct of the constraint could have been broken down in a similar way.

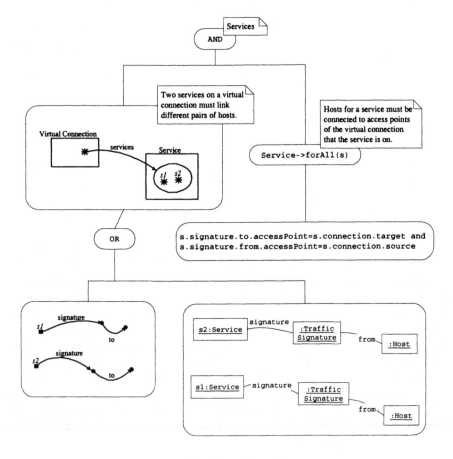

Fig. 15. Embedding object diagrams

In many domains, it is usually quite a simple matter to render an object diagram in a more domain specific way as a rich picture. This is in contrast to, say, developing a domain-specific notation for general OCL expressions, class diagrams or constraint diagrams. This observation, in conjunction with the observation that object diagrams can be used to notate fragments of a constraint, leads to a systematic approach to the development of constraint languages with a domain specific flavour. Thus Figure 16 shows yet another alternative to Figure 12, which replaces the object diagrams in Figure 15 with rich pictures that might be appropriate for the telecomms domain.

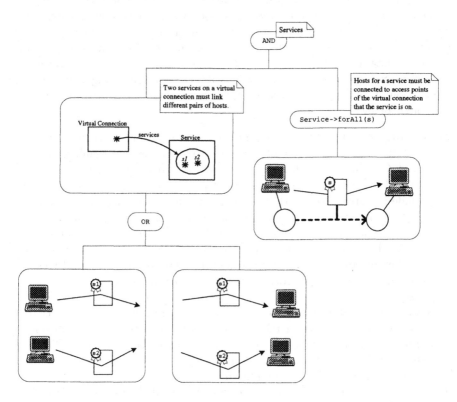

Fig. 16. Embedding rich pictures

A rich picture essentially replaces objects with domain-specific icons, and enriches links with formatting that might be more meaningful to the domain expert. It is also possible to replace object/link patterns with a single symbol. In this example, a service is represented as a document with a ribbon on one corner, and an arrow through the service represents its traffic signature, with the from and to hosts, represented as PC's, at the source and target of the arrow, respectively. A virtual connection is represented as a dotted arrow, with source and target access points as circles and at the source and target of the arrow, respectively. The attachment of a service to a virtual connection and of hosts to access points is represented as a plain link.

5   Tools

One way of using visual notations is as a communication aid during whiteboard discussions, or as an investigatitive aid when trying to work out a constraint in rough. In which case, tools are not required. However, as soon as one wishes to maintain the diagrams, use them in formal documentation, check their correctness, and so on, then tool support is essential. For example, our experience with trying to draw constraint diagrams (which are not typical box and line diagrams) with standard drawing tools led to the development of a specialized constraint diagram editor, which cured the problems we were encountering. Visual notations can also open up new possibilities for presenting and managing information stored in a tool. Some of the possibilities for constraint trees are elaborated below.

Organizing constraints. Constraint trees provide a convenient notation through which the constraint space of a model can be organized and presented. Currently tools that support constraints tend to organize them in lists attached to model elements, typically the class or package. Constraint trees provide an alternative to these lists. Each class or package has a constraint tree that organizes the constraint space for that model element. Putting constraints at the package level allows the constraints to be grouped other than by class. In this context, Section 3.3 has already discussed a mechanism for collecting together the constraints for a class by traversing all trees and looking for appropriate subtrees which can then be merged.

Zooming. Of course for any non-trivial system it would be impossible to fit a whole constraint tree on a single screen. A means, therefore, has to be provided for zooming in on and zooming out from parts of a tree. The obvious approach is to provide a way of exploding and collapsing nodes. There are two senses in which this can be done:
- Hiding and revelation of children.
- Hiding and revelation of the representation of the expression appearing in the node.

Both are illustrated by Figures 13 and 14, where the latter explodes one of the nodes of the former to reveal both the children and the contents of the node. It is worth noting that if one wished to explode the children of a node without revealing its contents then (probably) it would make little sense to reveal the contents of the children.

When a node is collapsed, the attached label or note might be used as a cue to the modeler about the contents of the node (this was done in Figure 13. When trying to fit many nodes on one screen, one could use the labels to identify the node and turn the notes into pop up descriptions which appear as the mouse moves over a node.

Notation interchange. It would be desirable for a tool to interchange the notation used to present the contents of a node, for example converting a constraint diagram into textual notation, and vice-versa. The main issue here is the laying out of diagrams when these are created from the text, and perhaps some way of persisting notation layout will be required. A slight extension of this idea is to collapse a whole subtree into a single node containing a textual or diagrammatic representation of the collapsed tree. This is unlikely to cause any problems when a textual representation is required, but only some subtrees will be convertible to, say, a constraint diagram. To see how this might work compare Figure 11 (collapsed form) with Figure 13.

Rich pictures. It would be desirable for a tool to support rich pictures. At its simplest, this requires an ability to replace a particular kind of object with some appropriate iconic representation. However, more generally one would wish to allow patterns of objects and links to be replaced with a picture, as illustrated in Section 4.

Integration with class and package diagrams. Finally, it would be interesting to integrate the constraint tree idea with class and package diagrams. That is, there would be an icon (say a tree) which could be placed on a class or package, and, when clicked, would reveal the constraint tree associated with it. The trees associated with a class may be calculated by traversing the tree in its containing package, as discussed on page 243.

6   Conclusions

The constraint tree notation was introduced and motivated by a desire to use different constraint notations to render different fragments of the same constraint, and a desire to provide a more flexible means for organizing and structuring a constraint space. An industrial-based example was used to illustrate the ideas. A rigorous, though informal, description of the constraint tree notation was provided. A systematic approach to developing notations with a domain specific flavour for constraints was proposed, the essence of which involves rendering nodes in constraint trees as rich pictures.

To carry this work forward three tasks need to be completed.

Formalization serves two purposes: to uncover any subtleties in the notation and ensure that it is well-defined; as a step towards providing tool support. Formalization requires various components to be defined. First, we must define a semantics domain which is common to all notations - this will, mostly likely, involve notions of object, slot and link. Next we must define an abstract syntax for each notation (these may overlap, but are unlikely to be the same) and render the semantics of each by a mapping into the semantics domain. Last (but not least) we must define the concrete notations and map those into their corresponding abstract syntaxes. We would also like to detail (reasoning?) rules that allow expressions in one notation to be rendered, where possible, in a different notation. We are keen to render the definitions as a OO meta-models, using a framework which we are involved in developing [EK99,CEF⁺99,CEK⁺00,CEK01]. Not only should this provide a quick route to tools (see below), it will also allow the notations to be easily integrated with industry-standard languages such as UML, which have also been defined using a meta-modeling approach.

Tools. A tool is being developed to support the precise meta-modeling approach mentioned above. This supports the "execution" of the meta-models and the mappings, so immediately we should be able test the correctness of our definition. However, the real potential of the notation will not be realised without putting considerable effort into usability issues. This means implementing many of the ideas in 5.

Evaluation of the notations is important but notoriously hard. In particular, it is very hard to separate a visual notation from the tool used to support it, and, for visual notations, tools such as specialized editors and viewers are essential to realize the potential of the notation. This suggests that one should construct the tools before attempting an evaluation. Even then, evaluation is difficult because it is hard to set up a controlled experiment: imagine getting together two teams to work on the same suitably complex problem, one using plain OCL with UML, and the other using constraint trees. Apart from anything else, the cost would be prohibitive. An alternative approach is to use analytical techniques, such as [YBDZ97]. These measure properties such as how directly the notation conveys the underlying meaning. This is certainly something we are considering. Finally, when all is said and done, the success of these ideas will stand or fall on the basis of market acceptance, for example whether one can get venture capital to build such tools, and then whether companies are prepared to buy these tools.

References

[CEF⁺99] A. Clark, A. Evans, R. France, S. Kent, and B. Rumpe. The puml response to the omg uml 2.0 rfi. Available from http://www.puml.org/, December 1999.

[CEK⁺00] A. Clark, A. Evans, S. Kent, S. Brodsky, and S. Cook. A feasibility study in rearchitecting uml as a family of languages using a precise oo meta-modeling approach. http://www.puml.org/mmt.zip, September 2000.

[CEK01] A. Clark, A. Evans, and S. Kent. The meta-modeling language calculus: Foundation semantics for uml. In *ETAPS FASE Conference 2001*, LNCS. Springer-Verlag, April 2001.

[EK99] A. Evans and S. Kent. Core meta-modelling semantics of UML: The pUML approach. In Robert France and Bernhard Rumpe, editors, *UML'99 - The Unified Modeling Language. Beyond the Standard. Second International Conference, Fort Collins, CO, USA, October 28-30. 1999, Proceedings*, volume 1723 of *LNCS*, pages 140–155. Springer, 1999.

[Ken97] S. Kent. Constraint Diagrams: Visualizing Invariants in OO Modelling. In *Proceedings of OOPSLA97*, pages 327–341. ACM Press, October 1997.

[KG98] S. Kent and Y. Gil. Visualising Action Contracts in OO Modelling. In *IEE Proceedings: Software*, number 2-3 in 145, pages 70–78, April 1998.

[KH99]   S. Kent and J. Howse. Mixing visual and textual constraint languages. In R. France and B. Rumpe, editors, *UML'99 - The Unified Modeling Language. Beyond the Standard. Second International Conference, Fort Collins, CO, USA, October 28-30. 1999, Proceedings*, volume 1723 of *LNCS*, pages 384–398. Springer, 1999.

[RG00]   M. Richters and M. Gogolla. Validating UML models and OCL constraints. In A. Evans and S. Kent, editors, *The Third International Conference on the Unified Modeling Language (UML'2000), York, UK, October 2-6. 2000, Proceedings*, LNCS. Springer, 2000.

[YBDZ97]   S. Yang, M. Burnett, E. Dekoven, and M. Zloof. Representation design benchmarks: A design-time aid for vpl navigable static representations. *Journal of Visual Languages and Computing*, 8:563–599, 1997.

Using OCL and UML to Specify System Behavior

Shane Sendall and Alfred Strohmeier

Swiss Federal Institute of Technology Lausanne (EPFL)
Department of Computer Science
Software Engineering Laboratory
1015 Lausanne EPFL
Switzerland
{Shane.Sendall, Alfred.Strohmeier}@epfl.ch

Abstract. Use cases are an excellent tool for capturing behavioral requirements of software systems, but they are not an ideal work product for driving design activities. We believe that there is value from complementing use case descriptions with pre- and postcondition descriptions, not only to better support reasoning about system properties and a basis for testing and debugging, but also to better support a predictable decomposition level on which one can base a systematic transition to design. Nevertheless, we recognize that pre- and postcondition descriptions are not widely used in practice. We believe this is in part due to the formalism used. Either the formalism is too heavy to learn and use, or the formalism does not offer sufficient abstraction from the vocabulary of implementation.

Via an example, the paper highlights our approach for specifying system behavior, which uses the Unified Modeling Language (UML) and its Object Constraint Language (OCL). We focus the paper on pre- and postconditions descriptions and in particular propose a number of enhancements and interpretations to OCL that we made while refining our approach. In particular, we describe a number of issues that cover areas such as the frame problem, incremental descriptions, structuring schemas, and events and exceptions.

Keywords: Unified Modeling Language, Object Constraint Language, Pre- and Postcondition Assertions, Software Specification, Requirements Analysis.

1 Introduction

Software development projects are subject to many factors, software and non-software related. It is a balancing act to get the right combination for a given project and its context—there are always trade-offs to make, according to priorities. For example, time-to-delivery and budget typically have a higher priority than rigor of development and quality assurance for most web-based systems [9], where the inverse is normally the case for systems that are human-life critical.

There are more and more projects that are somewhere inbetween safety-critical at the one end and non-critical at the other end. We believe that there is an increasing need for approaches that can provide a reasonable level of quality assurance and rigor in development but still must obey a restrained schedule and budget. For example, at the mid-to-upper range there are many e-business applications, which are "24-7" and mission-critical.

A. Clark and J. Warmer (Eds.): Object Modeling with the OCL, LNCS 2263, pp. 250–279, 2002.
© Springer-Verlag Berlin Heidelberg 2002

Our goal is to produce an approach for specifying reactive system behavior that can be used in the development of systems that lie in the mid-to-upper range. As a consequence, we have developed a software development method called Fondue [33] that covers the whole software development cycle, uses the UML notations, and is based on the Fusion process [6]. In this paper, we cover an important part of the analysis phase of Fondue.

We have defined a number of criteria that we believe need to be taken into account while developing an approach for the analysis phase:

- The proposed model should be compatible with industry practices and standards.
- The proposed model should be precise so that it can be used as a clear and unambiguous contract for later design activities, as a basis for understanding and documenting the application under development, and to precipitate hidden behavior.
- The proposed model should be targeted towards ease of use for the developer, i.e., it should be simple to learn and use, concise, understandable, etc.
- The proposed model should allow one to manage complexity and size of the description in a modular way that also allows one to localize the effects of change.
- The proposed model should allow one to contain design complexities.
- The proposed model should be conducive to verification activities—via and with the support of tools.
- The proposed model should express "quantifiable" non-functional requirements, such as performance constraints, in an integrated way with the functional requirements.
- The proposed model should be capable of capturing inherent concurrent properties of the system and quality of service properties.

Currently, we believe our approach fulfils, more or less, the first five criteria and goes someway in fulfilling the last three criteria—part of our current and future work.

Our Fondue analysis approach has three principal views:

- a model composed of descriptions of the effects caused by operations, which uses pre- and postcondition assertions written in UML's Object Constraint Language [29], called Operation Schemas [27];
- a model of the allowable temporal ordering of operations, called the System Interface Protocol (SIP) [23]; and
- a model that describes the system state used in the Operation Schemas, called the Analysis Class Model (ACM) [23].

The principal purpose of this paper is the proposition of a number of enhancements and interpretations to OCL that, we believe, make it less laborious to write pre- and postcondition assertions in Operation Schemas and that result in more readable and usable schemas. In particular, we describe a number of issues that cover areas such as the frame problem, incremental descriptions, structuring schemas, and events and exceptions.

The paper is composed of 8 sections. Section 2 provides the motivation for our approach and some justifications for some of the decisions that were made in coming up with Operation Schemas. Section 3 gives a brief overview of Operation Schemas and discusses how OCL is used in schemas. Section 4 presents an elevator case study that is used as an example throughout the paper. Section 5 makes a number of proposals for enhancing and interpreting OCL for use in pre- and postcondition descriptions; there is a continuous thread of proposals throughout. Section 6 discusses some issues related to the work presented and poses some open questions about OCL. Section 7 discusses related work and section 8 draws some conclusions.

2 Motivation for Operation Schemas

The ability of use cases to bridge the gap between the customers and the developers, or more precisely between the non-technical and technical stakeholders, has led to their wide and almost unanimous use in practice. However, use cases are not necessarily the ideal work product for driving design activities due, in part, to their focus on user intentions, which can lead to the unnecessary description of situations that cannot be detected or acted upon by the system. Furthermore, they do not offer sufficient guidelines for obtaining a description with a consistent level of precision, and they are prone to ambiguity and redundancy in their descriptions [17]; consequently they are only supported by tools that are limited to the analysis capabilities of word processors. In addition, use cases do not provide adequate means for dealing with interaction between use cases [13], cannot express state-dependent system behavior adequately [13], and can lead to naïve object-oriented designs in the hands of novice developers if care is not taken [11][12].

One of our first goals was to provide an additional, more precise model to which use cases can be systematically mapped, and which offers fixes to some of the problems encountered with use cases. This proposed model consists of Operation Schemas and a System Interface Protocol (SIP). The mapping process from use cases to Operation Schemas is described in [24]. In short, the use case descriptions are analyzed for events that would trigger system-level operations, these operations are then described using Operation Schemas, and the temporal ordering of those operations is defined in the System Interface Protocol. The advantages of such an approach are the following:

- Consistency of precision is better regulated: the combination of the Analysis Class Model, which defines the vocabulary from which Operation Schemas are defined, and OCL's restricted calculus allow a more consistent level of precision than the natural language descriptions of use cases. Furthermore, iteration between use cases and Operation Schemas focus the developer on refactoring use cases at a more consistent level of precision.
- Use cases are less likely to be over-decomposed (this poses problems, such as, premature design details, and a bias towards functional decomposition designs) because we decompose use cases until we get to the system operation level, and Operation Schemas provide better heuristics on what grain-size a system operation should be.
- Ambiguity is minimized by the calculus of OCL which is based on first-order predicate logic and set theory.
- Redundancy is reduced due to the (decision-making) process of mapping use cases to Operation Schemas.
- Operation schemas and the System Interface Protocol provide a precise means to deal with feature/service interaction (use case interaction at the use case level) and can express state-dependent system behavior.

Ultimately, we hope it is possible to show that the value added by mapping use cases to Operation Schemas is of greater value than the time spent in addition to produce the Operation Schemas.

To improve our chances of achieving this goal we put particular focus on making the Operation Schemas concise and precise, yet simple and easy to use for developers. We found that declarative pre- and postcondition descriptions were a good choice for achieving the first two points, because they offer the ability to specify the essential problem by focusing on what functionality is required—the abstract responsibilities provided/required—rather than its realization. The advantage is that one can abstract above the detail of how the operation is realized in terms of object collaborations for an object-oriented system, for example. Provision for the latter two points was made by enhancing the chosen language for writing pre- and postconditions, i.e. OCL, with a procedural programming language-like style. Also, we made the observation that procedural programming languages are more commonly used in practice compared to declarative ones. We concluded that most developers would therefore be more familiar with this style, as opposed to a declarative style. Our idea was therefore to experiment with a procedural programming language-like facade for Operation Schemas and OCL, and also to provide practical guidelines to some grey areas of pre- and postcondition descriptions such as the frame problem, incremental descriptions, concurrency, etc.

We chose OCL as our formalism for writing Operation Schemas because (1) as we are committed to using UML, OCL is an obvious choice for writing constraints on UML models; (2) OCL already had a operational style that is one step towards what we imagined a procedural style facade in a declarative language to be; and (3) OCL is relatively easy to learn and use, even though we admit that it is sometimes verbose, due to its simple navigation style for constructing constraints—everything, more or less, is achieved by working with and manipulating sets, bags and sequences. The downside that we face with taking OCL on board for Operation Schemas is that it is still a young language and there are therefore still a few unresolved questions on its semantics [22]. Tool support for OCL is progressing and becoming more common (see [31] for a full list of tools), although we admit that major CASE tool vendors still have not shown a lot of interest in OCL, even though it is part of the UML standard [32].

3 Operation Schemas and OCL

An Operation Schema declaratively describes the effect of the operation on an abstract state representation of the system and by events sent to the outside world. It describes the *assumed* initial state by a precondition, and the required change in system state after the execution of the operation by a postcondition, both written in UML's OCL formalism. Moreover, we use the same correctness interpretation as the Larch family of specification languages [14]: when the precondition is satisfied, the operation must terminate in a state that satisfies the postcondition. Operation schemas as we define them here specify operations that are assumed to be executed atomically and instantaneously, hence no interference is possible.

The system model is reactive in nature and all communications with the environment are achieved by asynchronous input/output events. All system operations are triggered by input events, usually of the same name as the triggered operation.

The change of state resulting from an operation's execution is described in terms of objects, attributes and association links, which conform to the constraints imposed by the Analysis Class Model of the respective system. The postcondition of the system operation can assert that objects are created, attribute values are changed, association links are added or removed, and certain events are sent to outside actors. The association links between objects act like a network, guaranteeing that one can navigate to any state information that is used by an operation.

The Analysis Class Model is used to describe all the concepts and relationships in the system, and all actors that are present in the environment, and thus should not be confused with a design class model. Classes and associations model concepts of the problem domain, not software components. Analysis objects do not have behavior and are more closely related to entities from Entity-Relationship models [5] than to design objects.

The standard template for an Operation Schema is shown in figure 1. The various subsections of the schema were defined by the authors, and are not part of the OCL. However, all expressions are written in OCL and conform to our proposals presented in section 5. Each clause is optional except the first. **Pre** and **Post** clauses that are not included default to true and an omitted **Scope** clause defaults to the operation's context, which is the system. The **Declares** clause allows all declarations to be made in a separate and single place, which is in line with the proposal of Cook et al. [7], in contrast to standard use of the *let* construct in OCL, which form part of the expression. A more detailed description of the grammar and usage of Operation Schemas can be found in [27][34].

Operation: This clause displays the entity that services the operation (aka the name of the system of focus), followed by the name of the operation and parameter list.
Description:A concise natural language description of the purpose and effects of the operation.
Notes: This clause provides additional comments.
Use Cases: This clause provides cross-references to related use case(s).
Scope: All classes, and associations from the class model of the system defining the name space of the operation. (Note that it would be possible to have a tool generate this clause automatically from the contents of the other clauses.)
Declares: This clause provides two kinds of declarations: aliasing, and naming. Aliases are name substitutions that override precedence rules (i.e., treated as an atom, and not just macro expansions) and refer to the pre-state value of the variable, and thus no time expressions (e.g. @pre) are needed. A name declaration designates an object reference that denotes a unique object with respect to all other object name declarations in the schema.
Sends: This clause contains three subclauses: **Type**, **Occurrence**, and **Order**. **Type** declares all the events that are output by the operation together with their destinations, the receiving actor classes. **Occurrence** declares event occurrences and collections of event occurrences. **Order** defines the constraints on the order of events output by the operation.
Pre: The condition that must be met before executing the operation. It is a boolean expression written in OCL.
Post: The condition that will be met after the execution of the operation. It is a boolean expression written in OCL.

Fig. 1. Operation Schema Format

3.1 Presentation of OCL

OCL is a semi-formal language for writing expressions whose principles are based on set theory and first-order predicate logic. OCL can be used in various ways to add precision to UML models beyond the capabilities of the graphical diagrams. Two common uses of OCL are the definition of constraints on class models and the statement of system invariants. As we will see, it can also be used to define pre- and postconditions for operations.

OCL is a declarative language. An OCL expression has no side effects, i.e. an OCL expression constrains the system by observation rather than prescription. OCL is a typed language; it provides elementary types, like Boolean, Integer, etc., includes collections, like Set, Bag, and Sequence, and has an assortment of predefined operators on these basic types. It also allows user-defined types which can be any type defined in a UML model, in particular classes. OCL uses an object-oriented-like notation to access properties, attributes, and for applying operators.

4 Elevator Control Example

For illustrating our approach and for use as a common example throughout this paper, we describe an elevator control system, adapted from [24]. The system controls multiple lifts that all service the same floors of a building. There is a button to go up and one to go down on each floor, which are used to request a lift. Inside each cabin, there is a series of buttons, one for each floor. The arrival of the cabin at a floor is detected by a sensor. The system may ask a cabin to go up, go down or stop. In this example, we assume that a cabin's braking distance is negligible (or that at least the action of stopping the cabin is harmonized with the signal from the floor sensor). The system may ask a cabin to open its door, and it receives a notification when the door is closed; the door closes automatically after a predefined amount of time, when no more people get on or off at a floor. However, neither the automatic closing of an elevator door nor the protection associated with the door closing, stopping it from squashing people, are part of the system to realize.

A scenario for John using the elevator could be: John calls the lift from the 5th floor, choosing to go up. An available lift comes from the 10th floor to the 5th floor to pick him/her up and stops and opens its door. The user gets in and requests the 20th floor. The lift closes its door and goes to the 20th floor. Once it arrives it stops and opens its door. John leaves the lift. A use case that encompasses all scenarios related to a user using the elevator to go from one floor to another can be found in [24].

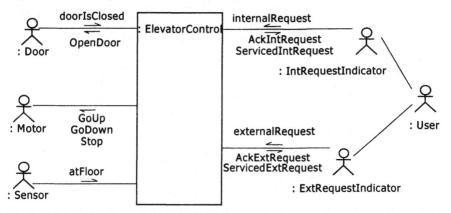

Fig. 2. Collaboration diagram summarizing the interaction between the system and its actors

The system operations for the elevator control system are derived from use case descriptions of the system. How this mapping activity is achieved is not discussed in this paper; interested readers are referred to [24]. The result of this mapping activity from a use case that describes a user taking the lift from one floor to another is shown in figure 2. A (specification-level) collaboration diagram shows four different input events: externalRequest, internalRequest, doorIsClosed, and atFloor, and eight different types of output events: AckExtRequest, AckIntRequest, ServicedExtRequest, ServicedIntRequest, OpenDoor, GoUp, GoDown, and Stop.

The diagram also shows that there is some form of communication between the User actor type and the external request indicator (ExtRequestIndicator) and internal request indicator (IntRequestIndicator) to clarify that the requests originally come from the user. Although we admit this may not be valid UML, strictly speaking, we think showing external communications paths often clarifies the overall working of a system and the consistent exchange of events in the system context.

One could imagine that the indicators control button lights to highlight a pending request.

The Analysis Class Model for the elevator control system is shown in figure 3. It shows all the concepts and relationships between them, the combination of which provide an abstract model of the state space of the system. Inside the system there are five classes, Cabin, Floor, Request, IntRequest, and ExtRequest, and outside six actor classes, Motor, Door, IntRequestIndicator, ExtRequestIndicator, User, and Sensor. The system has five associations: IsFoundAt links a cabin to its current floor, HasIntRequest links a set of internal requests to a particular cabin, HasCurrentRequest links a cabin to its current request, HasExtRequest links the set of all external requests issued by users to the system, and HasTargetFloor links requests to their target floor (source of call or destination). Finally, an <<id>> stereotyped association means that the system can identify an actor starting from an object belonging to the system, e.g., given a Cabin, cab, we can find its corresponding motor via the HasMotor association, denoted in OCL by cab.movedBy. The reason for the <<id>> stereotyped association is that the system can only send an event to an actor that can be identified. Identifying an external actor from inside the system strictly requires an <<id>> stereotyped association.

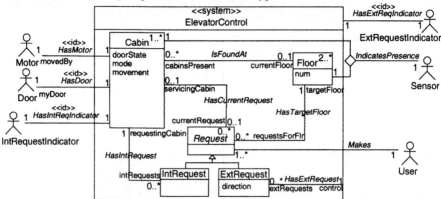

Fig. 3. Analysis Class Model of the Elevator Control System

The System Interface Protocol (SIP) defines the temporal ordering of system operations. An SIP is described with a UML state diagram. A transition in the SIP is triggered by an input event only if the SIP is in a state to receive it, i.e., there exists an arc with the name of the input event. If not, the input event that would otherwise trigger the operation is ignored. A transition from one state to another that has an event as label indicates the execution of the system operation with the same name as the input event.

The Elevator Control SIP is shown in figure 4. It consists of two parallel sub-states. The top-most sub-state models the activity of processing external requests. The dashed line shows that it works in parallel with the lift activities. The Lift submachine, the bottom-most state, is an auto-concurrent statemachine, indicated by a multiplicity of many ('*') in the upper right hand corner. There is a statemachine for each lift[1] but their number is not predefined, hence the multiplicity many. A Lift submachine consists itself of two parallel submachines. The submachine, on the left, models the activity of processing internal requests for the lift. The submachine, on the right, models the functioning of the lift cabin itself.

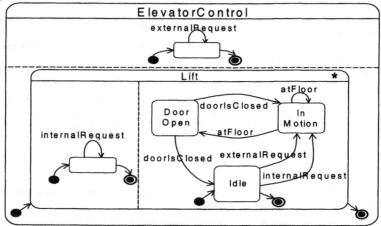

Fig. 4. Elevator Control System Interface Protocol

Each system operation, externalRequest, internalRequest, atFloor, and doorIsClosed, are described by Operation Schemas. However for reasons of size, we highlight just the atFloor Operation Schema, shown in figure 5. The atFloor Operation Schema describes the atFloor system operation. The atFloor system operation occurs as a consequence of a floor sensor detecting the arrival of an elevator cabin at a floor. The system must decide at this point whether there are any requests for the floor that it should service (this will depend on its mode); if so, it will drop off and/or pick up the requesting user(s), otherwise the system will let the lift continue.

The dot notation of OCL usually indicates the traversal of an association, in which case the result is a collection of objects, or the traversal to a property, in which case the result is value of the property. When navigating on association links, the dot notation is used together with the role name, e.g. cab.currentFloor. If there is no explicit role name, then the name of the target class is used as an implicit role name. For example, self.cabin denotes the set of cabins that can be reached by navigating from self, denoting the system instance, on the composition association between the system and the class Cabin.

---

1. We use the term lift to mean the cabin and it facilities.

The arrow operator is used only on collections, in postfix style. The operator following the arrow is applied to the previous "term". For instance, cab.intRequests->select (r | r.targetFloor = f) results in a set consisting of all internal requests r of the cabin, cab, that have the floor f as destination. Note also that we make use of the fact that an IntRequest inherits all the associations of its parent. For instance, it will inherit the association HasTargetFloor that links it to a Floor.

The **Declares** clause defines four aliases that are used for reasons of reuse and to make the postcondition less cluttered. The fourth alias, makeStop, (when substituted) results in true if there is an internal request and/or external request for the supplied floor f that should be serviced by the cabin. The second, third and fourth alias make use of the other aliases and the first alias uses a function calls, detailed in section 5.6.

Operation: ElevatorControl::atFloor (cab: Cabin, f: Floor);
Description: The cabin has reached a particular floor, it may continue or stop depending on its destination and the requests for this floor;
Notes: The system can receive many atFloor events at any one time, each for a different cabin;
Use Cases: take lift;
Scope: Cabin; Floor; Request; IntRequest; ExtRequest; HasIntRequest; HasExtRequest; HasCurrentRequest; HasTargetFloor; IsFoundAt;
Declares:
  reqsToStopFor: Set (Request) **is**
                    calcAllowedStops (cab, f, cab.intRequests->select (r | r.targetFloor = f),
                              self.extRequests->select (r | r.targetFloor = f));
  pickUpRequest: Set (ExtRequest) **is** reqsToStopFor->select (r | r.oclIsType(ExtRequest));
  dropOffRequest: Set (IntRequest) **is** reqsToStopFor->select (r | r.oclIsType(IntRequest));
  makeStop: Boolean **is** reqsToStopFor->notEmpty ();
Sends:
  Type: Motor::{Stop;}; Door::{OpenDoor;};
      ExtRequestIndicator::{ServicedExtRequest;}; IntRequestIndicator::{ServicedIntRequest;};
  Occurrence: stop: Stop; open: OpenDoor;
  Order: <stop, open>; -- the output events are delivered in the order "stop followed by open"
Pre:
  cab.movement <> Movement::stopped; -- cab was moving
Post:
  cab.currentFloor = f & -- new current floor for the cabin
  if makeStop **then** -- someone to drop off or pick up
      (cab.movedBy).**sent** (stop) & -- stop sent to cab motor
      cab.movement = Movement::stopped &
      (cab.myDoor).**sent** (open) & -- open sent to door
      cab.doorState = DoorState::open &
      self.request->excludesAll (reqsToStopFor) & -- removed all serviceable requests for this floor
      if pickUpRequest->notEmpty () **then**
          (self.extReqIndicator).**sent** (ServicedExtRequest (
          (callingFlr => pickUpRequest->any (true).targetFloor,
          dir => pickRequest->any (true).direction)))
      endif &
      if dropOffRequest->notEmpty () **then**
          (self.intReqIndicator).**sent** (ServicedIntRequest (
          (destFlr => dropOffRequest->any (true).targetFloor))) --inform int. request is serviced
      endif
  endif;

Fig. 5. atFloor Operation Schema for the Elevator Control System

The **Sends** clause shows that instances of the event types Stop, OpenDoor, ServicedExtRe-quest, ServicedIntRequest may be sent to the indicated actors (**Type** subclause) and that Stop and OpenDoor have named instances (**Occurrence** subclause). It also defines a sequencing constraint on the output events that states that the two event instances are delivered to their respective actors in the order "stop followed by open" (**Order** sub-clause). The **Pre** clause states that the cabin, cab, is currently moving.

The first line of the **Post** clause states that the cabin is now found at floor f with the isFoundAt association updated accordingly. The next (compound) expression states that if the lift has a request for this floor, then the cabin's motor was told to stop, the cabin's door was told to open, the state attributes of the cabin were updated, and the requests that were serviced by this stop were removed from the system state.

The expression, self.request->excludesAll (reqsToStopFor), not only removes the serviced request objects from the system (discussed in section 6.2), but deletes also all the asso-ciation links connected to the deleted objects. This sort of implicit removal ensures consistency of associations and is explained in section 5.1.

Also, the & operator used throughout the schema is a shorthand for logical "and" it is discussed in section 5.4. In the **Post** clause, we assert that an actor is sent an event using the "sent" shorthand, which indicates that the supplied event instance was placed in the event queue of the appropriate actor instance; this is detailed in section 5.7. Looking further at the OCL notation, an expression, such as cab.doorState = DoorState::open, means that the attribute, doorState, of the object cab has the enumeration value open (of the type DoorState) after the execution of the operation.

5 Proposals

In this section, we make a number of proposals to OCL. It has a number of subsec-tions, but there is a continuous thread of proposals for enhancements and interpreta-tions to OCL throughout. We cover such areas as the association consistency assumption, the frame problem, incremental descriptions, structuring schemas, and events and exceptions.

5.1 Consistency of Associations

An association link can only link existing objects; it is therefore a well known consis-tency constraint for class models that when an object is removed from the system state all association links connected to it have to be removed too. Although it would be pos-sible to explicitly state all association links that must be destroyed, this is quite cum-bersome in the presence of numerous associations. Therefore we propose the association consistency assumption.

Assumption 1: Removal of an object from the system implies implicitly that all association links in the system that included the destroyed object are destroyed, in addition.

5.2 Frame Assumption

The frame of the specification is the list of all variables that can be changed by the operation [18], which in our model is always a subset of all objects and all associations links that are part of the system state. The postcondition of a specification describes all the changes to the frame variables, and since the specification is declarative, the postcondition must also state all the frame variables that stay unchanged. The reason is simple: if the unchanged frame variables are left unmentioned, they are free to be given any value and the result will still conform to the specification.

Formal approaches such as Z, VDM, Larch, etc. explicitly state what happens to each one of these frame variables—even for those variables that stay unchanged. This approach soon becomes cumbersome to write and error-prone, particularly for specifications that have complex case distinctions (where the complete frame is the combination of all the variables read/changed in each different case). One approach that avoids this extra work is to imply a "... and nothing else changes" rule when dealing with these types of declarative specifications [3]. This means that the specification implies that the frame variables are changed according to the postcondition with the unmentioned frame variables being left unchanged. This approach reduces the size of the specification, thus increases its readability, and makes the activity of writing specifications less error prone. We therefore adhere to this convention.

However, there is a slight problem with this assumption in the case of implicit removal—a consequence of the association consistency assumption. For an example, let us reconsider the seventh line of the postcondition in figure 5.

    self.request->excludesAll (reqsToStopFor)

If we strictly apply the frame assumption "... and nothing else changes", as a result the associations HasIntRequest, HasExtRequest, HasCurrentRequest, and HasTargetFloor would stay unchanged which would lead to an inconsistent system state. At least three of the associations have to be changed, and will be changed following our implicit consistency of associations convention stated in section 5.1.

Also, we need to cover two more cases: what happens to attributes of frame objects that are not mentioned by the postcondition, and what happens to attributes of newly "created" objects that are not mentioned in the postcondition.

We propose the following amended frame assumption.

Assumption 2: No frame variables (including, if a variable denotes an object, the object attributes) are changed with the execution of the operation other than those that are explicitly mentioned to be changed by the postcondition, the associations that are implicitly modified as defined by the association consistency assumption, and the objects, and their attributes, that are new to the system state as a consequence of the operation.

This assumption forces all attributes of objects that are not mentioned to keep the same value with the exception of new objects added to the system state; in this case, we provide three possible interpretations: 1) attributes of new objects that are not mentioned in the postcondition can take any value, 2) the unmentioned attributes get predefined default values, or 3) the specification is incorrect if a value is not given to the respective attributes. The last interpretation gives more of a prescriptive flavor and one could probably expand this to also prohibit specifications where attribute values are constrained to a range rather than a precise value, e.g., acc.num > 0 would not be allowed in the description of an effect.

5.3 Incremental Descriptions

It is common practice in software development to tackle a problem in a piece-meal fashion—describing the problem incrementally. In a similar way, it is useful to describe postconditions incrementally, i.e., a particular effect of an operation may be defined by a combination of constraints that are defined at different places throughout the postcondition. However, declarative specifications do not in general support incremental descriptions. For example, it is *not* possible to state the effect on a given set in the following way (an extract of an *inconsistent* postcondition),

```
req.targetFloor = req.targetFloor@pre->including (flr1)
...
req.targetFloor = req.targetFloor@pre->excluding (flr2)
```

because both conditions define a different final set, but nevertheless refer to the same one: clearly a contradiction.

Set manipulations, like the two from above, are commonplace in OCL, and there are many reasons, detailed later, why an incremental description of sets is advantageous. For this purpose, we introduce the principle of minimal set into OCL to facilitate incremental description of effects on sets in postconditions.

5.3.1 Minimal Set Principle

Proposal 1: The minimal set principle is applied to the interpretation of post-conditions.

We propose to define the semantics of OCL postconditions by applying the idea of the minimal sets. For each class and each association within the system, we will consider their sets of instances and links, and claim that these are all minimal sets after execution of the operation.

Unless otherwise stated, if C is a class of the system, if SetOfAllObjects(C)@pre is the set of its instances before the execution of the operation, and SetOfAllObjects(C) is the set of its instances after the execution of the operation, then SetOfAllObjects(C) is the minimal set containing SetOfAllObjects(C)@pre and fulfilling the postcondition. Intuitively, SetOfAllObjects(C) can be constructed by adding to SetOfAllObjects(C)@pre all instances of C created by the operation. Similarly, we can come to a similar result for an association A of the system, where SetOfAllLinks(A) is the minimal set containing SetOfAllLinks(A)@pre and fulfilling the postcondition. The rule must hold for all classes and associations. Also, the minimal set principle is quite complementary to our frame assumption that states, more or less, that nothing changes other than what is explicit in the postcondition.

There is a slight problem, however, when we allow for the destruction of objects or removal of association links. For defining the semantics, the idea is then to gather the deleted entities into a temporary set, and rephrase the rule in the following way: let A be an association of the system, let us denote by SetOfLinksToRemove(A) the set of links of A destroyed by the operation, then SetOfAllLinks(A) ∩ SetOfLinksToRemove(A) is empty, and SetOfAllLinks(A) ∪ SetOfLinksToRemove(A) is equal to SetOfAllLinks(A)@pre, where SetOfAllLinks(A) is the minimal set. Minimal sets have a similar effect to re-dashing of schemas when composing them in Z [21].

Applying the minimal set principle to a postcondition, for example, we could rewrite the condition,

```
req.targetFloor = req.targetFloor@pre->including (flr)
```

as:

```
req.targetFloor->includes (flr)
```

which would be equivalent as long as no other effects have been expressed about the state of req.targetFloor.

One consequence of the minimal set principle that is not so intuitive is the case where the minimal set condition is negated. For example, the following condition:

```
not req.targetFloor->includes (flr)
```

is *not* equivalent to the condition:

```
req.targetFloor->excludes (flr)
```

because the first condition states that flr is not one of the elements added to the set req.targetFloor, where the second condition states that flr was one of the elements to be removed from the set req.targetFloor@pre.

The minimum set principle can also be applied to collections in general.

However, when it is applied to a bag, duplicates are not accounted for, e.g.,

```
Pre:    bagX = Bag {};
Post:   bagX->includes (x1) and
        bagX->includes (x1);
```

is equivalent to:

```
Post:   bagX->includes (x1);
```

An additional constraint it therefore required for the bag to contain two x1 elements, e.g., bagX->count(x1) = 2.

We take the opportunity, even though this has nothing to do with the minimum set principle, to insist that ordering of conditions does not suffice to order elements in a sequence, e.g.,

```
Pre:    seqX = Sequence {};
Post:   seqX->includes (x1) and
        seqX->includes (x2);
```

does not mean that x1 precedes x2 in seqX. The correct postcondition would be

```
seqX = seqX@pre->union (Seq{x1, x2})
```

which, using the minimum set principle, can be simplified to:

```
seqX->union (Seq{x1, x2})
```

The minimal set principle allows one to write the postconditions incrementally. For example, we could define a fragment of the postcondition for an imagined operation called swapCabins, which exchanges two cabins, cab1 and cab2, from floors f1 to f2 and from f2 to f1, respectively:

```
f1.cabinsPresent->excludes (cab1) and
f2.cabinsPresent->includes (cab1) and
f2.cabinsPresent->excludes (cab2) and
f1.cabinsPresent->includes (cab2)
```

Taking this example further we could be later asked, in a maintenance phase for example, to modify the operation by putting the cabin specialCab at the floor f1, as part of the swapCabins operation. This would simply require the following additional line in the postcondition.

```
... and
f1.cabinsPresent->includes (specialCab)
```

Such an incremental description, possible because of the minimal set principle, is easier to maintain because conditions are not definitive can be extended constructively.

```
if inPriorityMode then
            self.extRequest->includes (r1)
else
            self.extRequest->excludes (r5)
endif and
if liftAtSameFloor then
            self.extRequest->excludes (r2)
else
            self.extRequest->includes (r4)
endif and
if liftIsBusy then
            self.extRequest->includes (r6)
else
            self.extRequest->excludes (r3)
endif
```

Fig. 6. Incremental Approach

Incremental descriptions also offer one the possibility to break large case distinctions into more manageable and concise *if-then-else* conditions. Normally with a non-incremental description, one would specify each individual case completely with possibly many repetitions. Figure 6 shows an example of an incremental description using three *if-then-else* conditions. Figure 7 shows an equivalent description that is not incremental, it uses eight implication conditions.

Note that the relationship between the two approaches is exponential: there are 2^n separate cases for n if-then-else conditions. Note that we used implications in figure 7, but it is common practice to use separate pre/post pairs (see section 5.6 for more details), which would make the text even longer. Clearly, the usefulness of our incremental descriptions becomes even clearer as n gets larger.

```
inPriorityMode and liftAtSameFloor and liftIsBusy implies
            self.extRequest = self.extRequest@pre->union (Set {r1,r6})->excluding (r2) and
inPriorityMode and not liftAtSameFloor and not liftIsBusy implies
            self.extRequest = self.extRequest@pre->union (Set {r1, r4})->excluding (r3) and
inPriorityMode and not liftAtSameFloor and liftIsBusy implies
            self.extRequest = self.extRequest@pre->union (Set {r1, r4, r6}) and
inPriorityMode and liftAtSameFloor and not liftIsBusy implies
            self.extRequest = self.extRequest@pre->including (r1) - Set {r2, r3} and
not inPriorityMode and liftAtSameFloor and liftIsBusy implies
            self.extRequest = self.extRequest@pre->including (r6) - Set {r5, r2} and
not inPriorityMode and not liftAtSameFloor and not liftIsBusy implies
            self.extRequest = self.extRequest@pre->including (r4) - Set {r5, r3} and
not inPriorityMode and not liftAtSameFloor and liftIsBusy implies
            self.extRequest = self.extRequest@pre->union (Set {r4, r6})->excluding (r5) and
not inPriorityMode and liftAtSameFloor and not liftIsBusy implies
            self.extRequest = self.extRequest@pre - Set {r5, r2, r3}
```

Fig. 7. Non-Incremental Approach

5.3.2 Incremental Plus and Minus

Continuing with incremental descriptions, we can use an idea similar to minimal sets for numeric types. We propose to use the operators, "+=" and "-=" with the following meaning: the value of the numeric type in the post-state is equivalent to the value in the pre-state plus all the right-hand sides of all += operators used in the postcondition that refer to the numeric type, and minus all the right-hand sides of all -= operators that refer to the numeric type. For example:

```
obj.x += 5 and
obj.x -= 4
```

is equivalent to (and can be rewritten as):

```
obj.x = obj.x@pre + 1
```

However, care needs to be taken when the incremental style is mixed with the other styles.

```
Post: ...
obj.x += 5 and              -- line one
obj.x -= 4 and              -- line two
obj.x = obj.x@pre + 2 and   -- line three
obj.x = 2                   -- line four
```

The above example is an erroneous specification: line three is in contradiction with the result defined by the incremental plus and minus, and line four would require that obj.x@pre be either 0 or 1 depending on whether line three was brought into agreement with line one and two or vice versa.

Unfortunately, the incremental plus and minus facility cannot be extended to more complex expressions (e.g. multiplication) because it relies on the commutativity of additions and subtractions.

5.4 Shorthand Proposals for OCL

In this subsection, we propose some shorthand notations that could be used in OCL to make the job of the specifier less laborious and therefore probably less error-prone.

Proposal 2: The *else* part in the *if-then-else* construct is optional if the resulting type of the *if-then-else* expression is boolean.

We use *if-then-else* conditions for case distinction. Without our frame assumption, we would write:

```
if makeStop then
    cab.movement = Movement::stopped
else
    cab.movement = cab.movement@pre
endif
```

Taking the frame assumption into account, we are not required to state which variables stay unchanged; consequently, the *else* part, in this case, is simply true:

```
if makeStop then
    cab.movement = Movement::stopped
else
    true
endif
```

Applying proposal 2, the *else* part of the *if-then-else* condition can be made implicit:

```
if makeStop then
    cab.movement = Movement::stopped
endif
```

An implicit else true promotes a smaller, more readable postcondition. Thus, every time that a postcondition includes an *if-then* statement (without the *else* part), the expression is of type boolean and an else true is implied. To support this feature in OCL, only a syntax change would be required.

Proposal 3: *elsif* parts can be used in if-then-else constructs.

When dealing with a large number of branches by using the *if-then-else* construct, it is common to nest *if-then-else* constructs within other *if-then-else* constructs. This practice, however, can become problematic as the depth of nesting increases, having a negative impact on clarity for the reader and even the writer. Using an *elsif* part for the *if-then-else* construct can help make such situations cleaner and clearer to write and understand. The *elsif* addition is directly derivable from nested *if-then-else* constructs. For example, the following two conditions are equivalent:

if condA **then**
    effectA
elsif condB **then**
    effectB
else
    effectC
endif
	if condA **then**
	    effectA
	else
	    if condB **then**
	      effectB
	    else
	      effectC
	    endif
	endif

The required change to OCL to realize this proposal would be purely a syntactic one, i.e., the *elsif* keyword is simply added as a new part of the *if-then-else* construct. Furthermore, one could treat the new construct as a syntactic rewrite of the *if-then-else* construct.

Proposal 4: The commercial-and "&" can be used for separating conjunctive effects. It is an alternative to repeating the "pre" and "post" keywords.

OCL uses the keywords "pre" and "post" to separate system effects in a pre- and post-condition respectively [32]. However, we believe this becomes quite heavy and disruptive for the reader of large specifications. Therefore, we propose to use the commercial-and "&" as an effect description separator, because it is more discrete for use in large specifications and it has a clear usage with *if-then-else* conditions.

The commercial-and "&" and the logical-and "**and**" operators are logically equivalent. The difference between them lies in their interpretation that helps the human reader. Commercial-and, &, is used to separate conjunctive system effects, whereas logical-and, **and**, is used to separate boolean expressions that form conditions for branches leading to different effects.

For example, the following two postconditions are equivalent, but the one on the left-hand-side is written using the multiple post keywords style, and the one on the right-hand-side is written using our proposed style.

Post: effectA
Post: **if** condA **and** condB **then**
    effectB
    and effectC
  endif
Post: effectD
Post: effectE
	Post: effectA &
	  if condA **and** condB **then**
	    effectB &
	    effectC
	  endif &
	  effectD &
	  effectE

Again the change required to OCL to accommodate this proposal would be simply a syntactic one.

5.5 Interpreting Composite Values in OCL

Composite values for objects and events (section 5.7) are very useful in comparing and matching values between entities.

Proposal 5: The aggregate notation can be used for denoting composite values.

We propose the optional use of an Ada-style aggregate notation for denoting composite values. The value attributes of an object, and the parameters of an event correspond to composite values.

Fig. 8. Company Class in UML class notation

An aggregate is written by associating with each attribute a value, denoted by its name. The following aggregate conforms to figure 8:

(name => "Microsoft", headquarters => "Richmond", budget => 50.0E9)

Positional notation is also possible, but then the ordering of the values must be agreed upon by some convention, e.g. alphabetical order of the attribute names for objects:

(50.0E9, "Richmond", "Microsoft")

For clarity, it is sometimes useful to be able to qualify an aggregate by its type, e.g. the class name or the event type, yielding a so-called qualified aggregate. We propose to use the Ada-like "tick" notation, i.e. the type name precedes the aggregate, separated by an apostrophe, e.g.

Company'(50.0E9, "Richmond", "Microsoft")

Due to the "by-reference" semantics of objects and events, we propose to denote their composite value by introducing the property "all". Thus we can write expressions like the following:

company.**all** = (name => "Microsoft", headquarters => "Richmond", budget => 50.0E9)

which evaluates to true if the object referenced to by company has the corresponding attribute values. The above condition is equivalent to:

company.name ="Microsoft" **and**

company.headquarters = "Richmond" **and**

company.budget = 50.0E9

The advantage of aggregates is that related values are kept together in one place.

Proposal 6: The class or event name together with an aggregate can be used to denotate a representative object or event.

We introduce a special shorthand that makes it possible to match objects and events directly to composite values. The shorthand is defined for each object/event type. It uses the same name as the type, and it takes a composite value as parameter, resulting in a reference to the corresponding object/event in the system that has the matching composite value. For example, the expression:

    Company ((50.0E9, "Richmond", "Microsoft"))

results in all the company objects that have the corresponding composite value and chooses one, if there are more than one.

The above expression is a shorthand for the following expression:

    Company.allInstances->select (c | c.all = (50.0E9, "Richmond", "Microsoft"))->any (true)

The precondition of the any collection operator states that the supplied collection, i.e., the expression on the left-hand-side, must have at least one element satisfying the expression. This means that if there are no objects matched, then the shorthand is undefined. Thus, the specifier should ensure that the corresponding object exists for all valid system states.

Such a shorthand allows one to write concise and, we believe, intuitive expressions in postconditions, e.g.:

    region.localCompanies->includes (Company ((50.0E9, "Richmond", "Microsoft")))

which results in true if Microsoft is a member of the local companies in the region, region. This shorthand notation is particularly useful for denoting event sending, as we will see in section 5.7.

Proposal 7: The oclIsNew property can be optionally parameterized by a composite value, which states all the (initial) attribute values of the object.

We propose to allow the oclIsNew property to be parameterized with a composite value, defining the attribute values of the new object. For example, asserting that a new object has the same value as another one can be described simply by:

    myCompany.oclIsNew (john.company.all)

It is also possible to use an aggregate, which denotes the actual attribute values. For example, a postcondition could state:

    cabinX.oclIsNew ((doorState => DoorState::closed, mode => Mode::express,
                      movement => Movement::stopped))

which means that the object, cabinX, became a new element of the system state with the execution of the operation, and all its value attributes, i.e., doorState, mode, and movement, were given the enumeration values, closed, express, and stopped, respectively.

The above expression is directly equivalent to the following one:

    cabinX.oclIsNew **and**
    cabinX.doorState = DoorState::closed **and**
    cabinX.mode = Mode::express **and**
    cabinX.movement = Movement::stopped

The proposed notation ensures that all attributes of a newly created object were constrained to the given values, and none of them were forgotten.

Proposal 8: The oclIsNew property can be applied to a collection; it then takes a single parameter which signifies the number of new objects that were cre-

ated with the execution of the operation and are the only members of the collection.

We propose to allow the creation of a collection of objects by introducing the oclIsNew property for collections, where the oclIsNew property takes as parameter the number of elements to be created. Assuming colX: Collection (X), then:

    colX.oclIsNew (n)

is equivalent to,

    colX->forall (x: X | x.oclIsNew) **and**
    colX->size () = n

Both conditions state that the collection contains exactly n new objects. For example, a postcondition defining the result of initializing the ElevatorControl system could include the following extract:

    self.cabin.oclIsNew (5)

which is equivalent to the following condition:

    self.cabin->forall (c: Cabin| c.oclIsNew) **and**
    self.cabin->size () = 5

5.6 Structuring Schemas by Parameterized Predicates and Functions

For the sake of readability and usability, it is necessary to be able to structure Operation Schemas as the size of a schema increases. One common approach is to use multiple pre- and postcondition pairs for structuring operations (called case analysis in the Larch community) [30][8], where each schema describes the effect by the operation in a distinct case. We avoid this style of structuring because it leads to the case explosion problem that was demonstrated by figure 7.

Even though incremental descriptions help reduce the size of a specification, specifications can nevertheless get large and we have made the observation that they become cumbersome to write and use. This observation is backed by the results of a controlled experiment by Finney et al.; the result of the experiment gives evidence that structuring a specification into schemas of about 20 lines significantly improves comprehensibility over a monolithic specification [10].

We introduce two new concepts that help structure Operation Schemas and provide a means for reuse. We call them parameterized predicates and functions.

A *parameterized predicate* can be used in **Pre** and **Post** clauses to better support readability of schemas and to allow one to reuse commonly recurring predicates. They are inspired from those proposed in Catalysis [8]. They are used to encapsulate a 'piece' of the pre- or postcondition and therefore they can use the suffix '@pre' (in the case that it is destined for postconditions); they evaluate to true or false. They implicitly refer to self, the system object of the schema where they are instantiated. At definition, their scope is the schema (i.e. the names declared in the **Scope, Declares** and **Sends** clauses) where it is supposed to be used; it can then be used in all schemas having this scope or a wider one. When a predicate is referred to in a postcondition, it must be possible to resolve all references within the current context. For example, we could define a parameterized predicate that encapsulates the condition that the state of a cabin was changed to stopped and open, and two events were sent to the motor and the door to stop and open, respectively:

Predicate: madeStop (targetCabin: Cabin, stopTheLift: Stop, openTheDoor: OpenDoor);
Body: (targetCabin.movedBy).events->includes (stopTheLift) **and** -- stop sent to cab motor
                 targetCabin.movement = Movement::stopped **and**
                 (targetCabin.myDoor).events->includes (openTheDoor) **and** -- open sent to door
                 targetCabin.doorState = DoorState::open;

The parameterized predicate can then be used in the postcondition of the atFloor Operation Schema of figure 5, for example, in the following way:

Post: ...
  if makeStop **then**
        madeStop (cab, stop, open) **and** -- use of parameterized predicate
        self.request->excludesAll (reqsToStopFor) **and**
        ...

A *function* may be used to encapsulate a computation. They do not have any side effects, i.e. they are pure mathematical functions, and to the contrary of a system operation they do not change the system state. Functions may be used as a reuse mechanism for commonly recurring calculations.

We propose to separate the function declaration (its signature) from the function definition. In that way, they can be used as a placeholder when the need for the function is known, but its realization is deferred to a later stage of development, i.e. design or implementation. For example, we might know that we have to determine the best suited lift to service a particular request, which can be expressed by a function, e.g.

Function: bestSuitedCabin (options: Set (Cabin), requestedFlr: Floor): Cabin;

-- A function that hides the algorithm for choosing the best suited cabin to service a request

but the choice of the algorithm is deferred until design.

Functions can also be used when OCL is not suitable for expressing the algorithm, e.g. in the case of numeric computations. Functions are therefore a way to escape the limited expressive power of OCL when necessary. However, we admit that such a facility can be abused.

Functions can be referred to anywhere, in contrast to parameterized predicates, whose use is limited to pre- and postconditions. They can refer to the model elements of the Analysis Class Model. If a function does not refer to any model elements, then it is a universal function, e.g. the sine function, and it is possible to refer to it "anywhere". Functions can include an **Aliases** clause, which is local to the function, and is equivalent to the **Declares** clause of Operation Schemas, except only aliases are allowed. When referring to a function, it must be possible to resolve all references within the current context.

For example, the first line after the **Declares** of figure 5 (atFloor Operation Schema) used a function calcAllowedRequests, which returns a possibly empty set of requests to service. A possible definition of the function could be:

Function: calcAllowedRequests (c: Cabin, currentFlr: Floor, intReqs: Set (IntRequest)
　　　　　　　　　　　　　extReqs: Set (ExtRequest)): Set (Request);
Function Body: calcAllowedRequests (c: Cabin, currentFlr: Floor, intReqs: Set (IntRequest)
　　　　　　　　　　　　　extReqs: Set (ExtRequest)): Set (Request);
Aliases:
　atFloorExtremities: Boolean **is** currentFlr.num = MIN_FLOOR_NUM **or**
　　　　　　　　　　　　　currentFlr.num = MAX_FLOOR_NUM;
Post:
　if intReqs->notEmpty () **and**
　　　　(intReqs->any (true) = c.currentRequest **or** allowedToDropOff (c.mode)) **then**
　　result->includes (intReqs->any (true))
　endif &
　if extReqs->notEmpty () **and**
　　　　(extReqs->exists (r | r = c.currentRequest) **or** allowedToPickUp(c.mode)) **then**
　　if extReqs->exists (r | r = c.currentRequest) **then**
　　　result->includes (c.currentRequest)
　　else -- allowed to make a pick-up
　　　if atFloorExtremities **then**
　　　　result->includes (extReqs->any (true))
　　　else
　　　　result->includes (extReqs->select(r | r.direction = cab.movement)->any (true))
　　　endif
　　endif
　endif;

This function calculates the internal and external requests that are allowed to be serviced according to the mode of the lift, and the context, e.g., direction the lift is going, etc.

5.7 Events, Calls, and Exceptions

Operation schemas specify not only the changes to the system state, but also the *system events* that are output by the operation. Communications between the system and actors are through event occurrence delivery. In our approach, we distinguish input from output events. Input events are incoming to the system and trigger system operations. Usually, their names are the same. The parameters of the input event are the parameters of the system operation. Output event occurrences are outgoing from the system and are delivered to a destination actor.

We propose to interpret a system event occurrence as:

- having by-reference semantics;
- having unique identity;
- having an implicit reference to its sender, referred to by the keyword **sender**;
- being reliably and instantaneously delivered (no latency).

There are several kinds of system events, which can be thought of as either a specialization of SignalEvent or CallEvent in UML, depending on whether the event is asynchronous or synchronous. We will distinguish three kinds of system event types that we call Event, Exception, CallWithReturn, respectively stereotyped <<event>>, <<exception>>, and <<callwithreturn>>. They all have a single compartment containing parameters.

An Event occurrence instigates an asynchronous communication; it usually triggers the execution of an operation. An Exception occurrence signals an unusual outcome to the receiver, e.g., an overdraft of an account (section 5.7.2). A CallWithReturn occurrence triggers the synchronous execution of an operation that returns a result to the sender (section 5.7.1). The result is modelled by an Event occurrence.

Often we use the term event with the meaning of any of the above kinds or even occurrences.

We use a naming convention to differentiate the different kinds of events: suffix "_e" for an Exception, and suffix "_r" for CallWithReturn. The reason for this naming convention is to help specifiers visually differentiate between different kinds of events.

Care must be taken that all parameters of an event sent by an operation have defined values.

The System Interface Protocol defines the temporal ordering of the input events (as shown in figure 4 for the elevator control system), but the events that are output by the system during the execution of an operation are specified in the respective schema. This is achieved by stating:

- the type of the event and the destination actor type;
- the condition(s) under which the event occurrence is sent;
- the actual parameters of the event occurrence;
- the destination actor instance(s);
- and optionally any ordering constraints that the event occurrence may have relative to other events output by the same operation.

The declaration of output events is written in the **Sends** clause of the Operation Schema. The **Sends** clause is broken up into three (optional) sub-clauses called **Type**, **Occurrence**, and **Order**. The **Type** sub-clause declares the actor types together with the event types that may be sent. The **Occurrence** sub-clause declares the named event occurrences. The **Order** clause defines the constraints on the order that the events are output.

As an example, let us consider a **Sends** clause of an Operation Schema for a subsystem of the elevator control system called cabin controller, which communicates with the scheduler subsystem, the administration subsystem, the motor, and the door (figure 9).

Sends:
> **Type**:   Motor::{Stop;}; Door::{OpenDoor;}; Administration::{LogMessage;};
>   Scheduler::{GetNextRequest_r **throws** NoRequests_e;};
> **Occurrence**: stopLift: Stop; openLiftDoor: OpenDoor; gnr: GetNextRequest_r;
>   seqMessages: Sequence (LogMessage);
> **Order**: <seqMessages, stoplift, openLiftDoor>;

Fig. 9. Sends clause of an Operation Schema

It states by the **Type** sub-clause that actor instances of type Motor, Door, Administration, and Scheduler may be sent occurrences of the events Stop, Open, Message, and GetNextRequest_r respectively. It also uses the **throws** keyword to indicate that an occurrence of the exception NoRequest_e may be received by the operation instead of a reply from the call triggered by an occurrence of GetNextRequest_r.

The **Occurrence** sub-clause declares an event occurrence of type Stop, Open, GetNextRequest_r, and a sequence of event occurrences of type Message. The **Order** sub-clause states that the sequence of message occurrences are sent before the stoplift occurrence, and the stoplift occurrence is sent before the openLiftDoor occurrence.

We propose that declaring a group of events as a sequence means that they are received in the order that they are in the sequence, and events in a set or bag are not ordered. Moreover, if a collection is specified, ordering is not dealt with, but deferred to later design activities.

All event occurrences have to be created within the execution of the operation. Therefore we propose to avoid explicitly stating that they were created in the postcondition (to the contrary of new objects in the system).

Each actor has an event queue—just as the system has an event queue. If the actor is able to deal with occurrences of a given event (type), then it is possible to state that an event was placed in the actor's (input) event queue as a result of an operation.

Hence, an event is specified as delivered by asserting that it is present in the event queue of the destination actor. For example, the output of a request to the door actor of the cabin controller system can be asserted in the postcondition of the Operation Schema, corresponding to figure 9, in the following way, given that there is an association from the cabin controller to its door that has the role name myDoor.

Post:

...

(self.myDoor).events->includes (openLiftDoor)

...

In addition to explicitly writing that an event is placed on the target actor's event queue, we propose a shorthand that we have found in practice to be more intuitive to users and writers. It has the following form, where actorX denotes any identifiable actor and eventOccurrenceX denotes any appropriate event occurrence:

actorX.**sent** (eventOccurrenceX)

and is equivalent to or syntactic sugar for:

actorX.events->includes (eventOccurrenceX)

We emphasize that **sent** is just a shorthand and should not be confused with a property of the actor.

Proposal 9: The delivery of an event in an OCL postcondition is asserted by placing the event occurrence in an actor's event queue.

Note that because events have by-reference semantics, an event can be placed in several event queues (multicast).

For example, we could imagine a situation where a fire alarm triggers a system operation that stops all moving lifts. An extract of the postcondition that asserts the output of a stop event to all moving cabins could be the following, given emergencyStop: Stop and movingCabins = self.cabin->select(c | c.movement <> Movement::stopped):

movingCabins.movedBy -> forall (m | m.**sent** (emergencyStop))

5.7.1 Modeling Results Returned by Operations

In this subsection, we discuss our ideas on how to use Operation Schemas for modeling results returned by operations to other actors or subsystems.

Figure 10 shows two approaches for servicing a particular request from an actor. The two approaches produce the same result. The first approach (top) shows a blocking call from requestingActor to subsystemA. During the execution of this operation, subsystemA executes a blocking call to subsystemB. Once the call returns, subsystemA returns the result of the request to requestingActor. For modeling this situation, we will use Call-WithReturn occurrences and operations returning results.

The second approach (bottom) achieves the same result by exchanging asynchronous events. Consequently, two asynchronous calls are made to subsystemA, as opposed to a single synchronous call in the first approach. This second case is handled with sending event occurrences as we have already seen in this paper. It is our preferred approach and we recommend it for systems specified from scratch.

However, both approaches are needed when we are modeling already existing components.

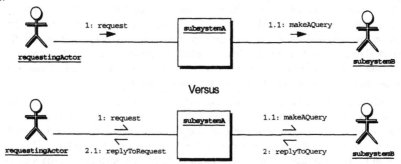

Versus

Fig. 10. Alternatives for Returning Results from "Calls"

A CallWithReturn occurrence has an associated reply event (figure 11). It is possible to navigate to this returned result.

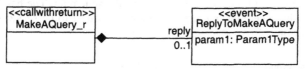

Fig. 11. Relationship between a CallWithReturn and its Reply

With the event declarations shown in figure 11, here is a postcondition fragment that asserts that a CallWithReturn occurrence was delivered to subsystemB and shows how the returned result can be accessed via reply.

subsystemB.**sent** (makeAQuery) & -- like for a non-blocking call

objX.addr = makeAQuery.reply.param1 -- note the reply event has possibly many return parameters

The first line asserts that the event makeAQuery has been delivered to the actor instance subsystemB. The second line asserts that the value attribute objX.addr was given the same value as the first parameter of the result of the call. The assumption is that the results are always available when the postcondition is evaluated.

Finally, we have to show how an operation returning a result can be specified by an operation schema. In the postcondition that describes such an operation, the reply event is referred to by the keyword **reply**, and from **reply** one can navigate to the return parameters.

For example,

Operation: SubsystemB::makeAQuery (): Param1Type;
Post:
    reply = ReplyToMakeAQuery ((param1 => Color::blue));

We could have equally replaced the last line with:

reply.param1 = Color::blue;

The reply event is implicitly sent back to the sender (who made the call), e.g., the following is redundant and may be omitted:

sender.sent (reply);

5.7.2 Exceptions

Despite our assumption for reliable communications, there are often situations where the called actor cannot provide what was requested for. We will use exceptions for handling these situations. For instance, in the example of figure 9, if the scheduler can not return a request to be serviced it might throw an exception, rather than return some "dummy" value. We require that any actor requesting a service that can throw an exception must provide an exception handler. It may choose to pass it on, but this is to be asserted explicitly in a handler. We therefore propose to add an additional clause in the schema format called **Exceptions**. This clause is used to handle all exceptions stated in the **Sends** clause (associated with the **throws** keyword).

The **Post** clause of the schema should be written in such a way that the functionality associated with exception handling is asserted within the **Exceptions** clause and not in the **Post** clause. In the case that the called operation throws an exception, instead of getting a result via the reply rolename of the output event, the caller will receive an exception in its event queue, and the semantics of the Operation Schema's postcondition will be the conjunction of the **Post** clause and the **Exceptions** clause. It is possible to write a specification that conforms to this rule because in the **Post** clause, the expression, event.reply->isEmpty (), is true if an exception occurred.

We demonstrate exception handling on a call to the scheduler. The handler deals with the case when the scheduler is unable to return a request to be serviced, and instead raises an exception called noRequests_e:

Post:
scheduler.**sent** (gnr) &
if gnr.reply->notEmpty () **then**
    self.currentRequest = gnr.reply.nextRequest
endif;
Exceptions:
noRequests_e () **handledBy**
    self.mode = Mode::express;

The **Post** clause asserts that the scheduler actor, scheduler, is delivered gnr, an event of type GetNextRequest_r, and if there is a reply, then the system's current request is equivalent to the nextRequest parameter of the reply. The **Exception** clause states that if the exception occurrence of type NoRequests_e is thrown as a consequence of a call made by the operation, then the condition after the **handledBy** keyword is fulfilled.

6 Miscellaneous Issues

In this section, we discuss how packages of OCL constraints can be used in a similar way to libraries in programming languages and how we describe "creating" and "destroying" objects in Operation Schemas. And, we describe some issues related to the navigational style of OCL over n-ary associations.

6.1 Libraries and Packages

According to UML, packages can be used to store any kind of UML model elements. OCL constraints are a subtype of model element in the meta-model. It is therefore possible to define a package that contains only constraints. Furthermore, one could well imagine that a package could be used as a library or even just a common place to store related constraints. Clearly, packages could be useful to the OCL modeler for storing invariants, extensions to OCL types, parameterized predicates, functions, etc. For example, we could imagine "importing" a certain package of functions into a schema, like one would in Java, for example. Of course, the level of reuse would depend on how generic the constraints supplied by the package are.

6.2 Creation and Destruction of Objects

Instead of explicitly asserting that an object is created or destroyed with the execution of an operation, we rather define creation and destruction in terms of what is part of system state and what ceases to be part of system state. We judge an object as part of system state if and only if it has a composition link either directly or transitively with the system. For instance, an object that is a component of a component of the system is also part of the system state by transitivity. Thus, "creating" an object requires only that one asserts that a link was added to a composition association with the system (direct or transitive), and "destroying" an object requires that one asserts that a link was removed from a composition association with the system.

We have found that this approach simplifies the description of destruction in particular, because it abstracts away from a particular implementation interpretation, i.e., we could interpret removing the link between the object and the system as either instant destruction (a call to a destructor), or as flagging the garbage collector, or even as a prompt for the system to place the object back into the program's object pool.

6.3 Navigation

OCL was created with the main purpose of providing navigation of UML models and consequently it is asymmetric with respect to associations. OCL's style of navigation has quite some advantages, e.g. there are not too many operators and they are easy to understand, but there are also some drawbacks.

First of all, the addition of a new link between two objects can be easily misinterpreted. For example, in a postcondition an expression like the following:

```
cab.intRequests->includes (req)
```

means that there is a new link between cab and req in the HasIntRequest association. It can be easily misinterpreted as being a unidirectional link from cab to req, whereas the condition is strictly equivalent to:

```
req.requestingCabin->includes (cab)
```

More seriously, it is impossible to use the navigational notation for higher-order associations, and at least awkward to use it for handling attributes belonging to association classes.

7 Related Work

The idea of Operation Schema descriptions comes from the work on the Fusion method by Coleman et al. [6]. They took many ideas for Operation Schemas from formal notations, in particular, Z and VDM. The Operation Schema notation that we present here has a similar goal to the original proposal, but we have made notable changes to the style and format of the schema. Several proposals for formalizing Fusion models with Z and variants of Z have been proposed [2] [4]. One advantage of these approaches is that they can draw upon already existing analysis tools for Z.

Z [26] and VDM [15] are both rich formal notations but they suffer from the problem that they are very costly to introduce into software development environments, as is the case with most formal methods, because of their high requirements for mathematical maturity on the user.

The Z notation is based on set theory and classical first-order predicate logic. An interesting feature of the Z specification language is the schema notation. A schema can be viewed as an encapsulated structure, associated with some properties. Using the schema notation, it is possible to specify parts of a system separately, and then compose the specifications for the parts to obtain the specification of the whole system. Schemas are commonly used in Z to represent types, state spaces and operations.

In contrast to Z, which is strictly a specification notation, VDM offers notations that provide a wider treatment of the software lifecycle. VDM supports the modeling and analysis of software systems at different levels of abstraction. Both data and algorithmic abstractions expressed at one level can be refined to a lower level to derive a concrete model that is closer to the final implementation of the system. A VDM specification written in assertional style can be refined into another VDM specification written using statements, i.e., VDM has imperative programming constructs as part of its notation. An even more complete treatment of the software development lifecycle is offered by the B-method [1], which uses a formalism that has similarities to both Z and VDM. It uses a unified notation for specification, design and implementation and is supported by the B-toolkit which provides tool support for specification, animation, design, proof obligation generation, automatic and interactive proof, and code generation.

The Catalysis approach [8], developed by D'Souza and Wills, provides action specifications. Catalysis defines two types of actions: localized and joint actions. Localized actions are what we would term operations in our approach and joint actions are related to use cases. In the endeavor to support controlled refinement by decomposition through a single mechanism, Catalysis defines actions, which can be decomposed into subordinate actions, at a lower-level of abstraction, or composed to form a superordinate action, at a higher-level of abstraction. Furthermore, Catalysis defines joint actions to describe multi-party collaborations, and localized actions to describe strictly the services provided by a type. However, joint actions lack the ability of goal-based use cases to describe stakeholder concerns due to the focus of pre- and postconditions on state changes and not the goals of the participants/stakeholders. The activity of assuring stakeholder concerns when writing use cases is often a source for discovering new requirements and business rules. It is for these reasons that we did not merge use case descriptions and pre- and postcondition descriptions of operations, but instead chose to keep them separate.

Meyer [19] proposes design-by-contract; it is an assertion language that is integrated into the Eiffel object-oriented programming language. Pre- and postconditions are placed in class methods: *require* assertions (preconditions) are checked before their respective method is executed and *ensure* assertions (postconditions) are checked after the execution of the method; if either assertion fails then an exception is raised. All assertions are made on the program state and for each class. Therefore assertions are numerous and limited to the abstraction level of the implemented program. Design-by-contract is also complemented by the BON method [28]. The BON assertion language has similarities to OCL [20].

8 Conclusion

The goal of this paper was to motivate and justify a number of enhancements and interpretations that we made to UML's Object Constraint Language while developing an approach for pre- and postcondition assertions. We proposed a number of modifications for making OCL more effective when used by developers for writing and reading pre- and postconditions: incremental descriptions, aggregates, structuring techniques, etc. Also, the paper discussed our proposal for specifying events and exceptions and delivering them to actors.

We defined a list of criteria, detailed in section 1, to measure our approach and guide its design. Currently, we believe our approach fulfils, more or less, the first five criteria and goes someway in fulfilling the last three ones—part of our future work. Our approach conforms to UML (criterion 1) and we propose a model that is sufficiently precise and consistent that the transition to design can be performed in a systematic manner (criterion 2). Also, we believe that we were able to show that with our approach usability does not necessarily have to be traded-in against rigor. For example, we believe that the application of the minimal set principle and our frame assumption makes it easier to formulate correct postconditions (criterion 3). We proposed parameterized predicates and functions to manage reuse and to support modularity (criterion 4). Our model offers both operational and representational abstraction (criterion 5): the pre- and postconditions avoid design details thanks to their declarative description and because the state of the system is defined in terms of domain concepts and not software components. Currently, we have a prototype tool that supports our approach by checking both syntax and type correctness (criterion 6). Our ideas for modeling performance constraints on the SIP (criterion 7) and concurrent operations (criterion 8) are published elsewhere [25].

Our approach has been successfully taught to students and practitioners and used in a number of small-to-medium sized projects. This leads us to believe that Operation Schemas based on OCL are not only a powerful, but indeed a usable mechanism for precisely describing operations.

For examples of our approach applied to several case studies see [35].

References

[1] J. Abrial. *The B-Book: Assigning Programs to Meanings*. Cambridge University Press, 1996.

[2] K. Achatz and W. Schulte. *A Formal OO Method Inspired by Fusion and Object-Z*. In J. P. Bowen, M. G. Hinchey, and D. Till (eds.): ZUM'97: The Z Formal Specification Notation, LNCS 1212 Springer, 1997.

[3] A. Borigda, J. Mylopoulos and R. Reiter. *On the Frame Problem in Procedure Specifications*. IEEE Transactions on Software Engineering, Vol. 21, No. 10: October 1995, pp. 785-798.

[4] J-M. Bruel and R. France. *Transforming UML models to formal specifications*. Proceedings of the OOPSLA'98 Workshop on Formalizing UML: Why? How?, Vancouver, Canada, 1998.

[5] P. Chen; *The Entity-Relationship Model—Toward A Unified View of Data*. ACM Transactions on Database Systems, 1(1), 1976, pp. 9-36.

[6] D. Coleman et al. *Object-Oriented Development: The Fusion Method*. Prentice Hall, 1994.

[7] S. Cook, A. Kleppe, R. Mitchell, J. Warmer, and A. Wills. *Defining the Context of OCL Expressions*. Second International Conference on the Unified Modeling Language: UML'99, Fort Collins, USA, 1999.

[8] D. D'Souza and A.Wills. *Objects, Components and Frameworks With UML: The Catalysis Approach*. Addison-Wesley 1998.

[9] J. Daniels et al. *Panel: Cracking the Software Paradox*. OOPSLA 2000 Companion from the Conference on Object-Oriented Programming, Systems, Languages, and Application, USA, 2000.

[10] K. Finney, N. Fenton, and A. Fedorec. *Effects of Structure on the Comprehensibility of Formal Specifications*. IEEE Proc.-Softw. Vol. 146, No. 4, August 1999.

[11] D. Firesmith. *Use Case Modeling Guidelines*. Proc. 30th Conference on Technology for Object-Oriented Programming Languages and Systems (TOOLS-30), pp. 184-193, IEEE Computer Society, 1999.

[12] M. Fowler; *Use and Abuse Cases*. Distributed Computing Magazine, 1999 (electronically available at http://www.martinfowler.com/articles.html).

[13] M. Glinz; *Problems and Deficiencies of UML as a Requirements Specification Language*. Proceedings of the Tenth International Workshop on Software Specification and Design, San Diego, 2000, pp. 11-22.

[14] J. Guttag et al. *The Larch Family of Specification Languages*. IEEE Trans Soft Eng 2(5), September 1985.

[15] C. Jones. *Systematic Software Development Using VDM*. Prentice Hall, 1986.

[16] M. Kandé and A. Strohmeier. *Towards a UML Profile for Software Architecture Descriptions*. UML 2000 - The Unified Modeling Language: Advancing the Standard, Third International Conference, York, UK, October 2-6, 2000, S. Kent, A. Evans and B. Selic (Eds.), LNCS (Lecture Notes in Computer Science), no. 1939, 2000, pp. 513-527.

[17] B. Kovitz; *Practical Software Requirements: A Manual of Content and Style*. Manning 1999.

[18] C. Morgan. *Programming from Specifications*. Second Edition, Prentice Hall 1994.

[19] B. Meyer. *Object-Oriented Software Construction*. Second Edition, Prentice Hall, 1997.

[20] R. Paige and J. Ostroff. *A Comparison of the Business Object Notation and the Unified Modeling Language*. UML '99 - The Unified Modeling Language: Beyond the Standard, Second International Conference, Fort Collins, CO, USA, October 28-30, 1999, Robert France and Bernard Rumpe (Eds.), LNCS (Lecture Notes in Computer Science), no. 1723, 1999, pp. 67-82.

[21] B. Potter, J. Sinclair and D. Till. *An Introduction to Formal Specification and Z*. Prentice Hall, 1991.

[22] M. Richters and M. Gogolla. *On Formalizing the UML Object Constraint Language OCL*. In Tok Wang Ling, Sudha Ram, and Mong Li Lee, editors, Proc. 17th Int. Conf. Conceptual Modeling (ER'98), pages 449-464. Springer, Berlin, LNCS Vol. 1507, 1998.

[23] S. Sendall and A. Strohmeier. *UML-based Fusion Analysis*. UML '99 - The Unified Modeling Language: Beyond the Standard, Second International Conference, Fort Collins, CO, USA, October 28-30, 1999, Robert France and Bernard Rumpe (Ed.), LNCS (Lecture Notes in Computer Science), no. 1723, 1999, pp. 278-291, extended version also available as Technical Report (EPFL-DI No 99/319).

[24] S. Sendall and A. Strohmeier. *From Use Cases to System Operation Specifications*. UML 2000 — The Unified Modeling Language: Advancing the Standard, Third International Conference, S. Kent and A. Evans (Ed.), LNCS (Lecture Notes in Computer Science), no. 1939, pp. 1-15; Also available as Technical Report (EPFL-DI No 00/333).

[25] S. Sendall and A. Strohmeier. *Specifying Concurrent System Behavior and Timing Constraints Using OCL and UML*. <<UML>> 2001 - The Unified Modeling Language: Modeling Languages, Concepts and Tools, Fourth International Conference, Toronto, Canada, October 1-5, Martin Gogolla (Ed.), Lecture Notes in Computer Science, Springer-Verlag, to be published in 2001. Also available as Technical Report EPFL-DI No 01/367.

[26] J.M. Spivey. *The Z Notation: A Reference Manual*. Prentice Hall, 1989.
[27] A. Strohmeier and S. Sendall. *Operation Schemas and OCL*. Technical Report (EPFL-DI No 01/358), Swiss Federal Institute of Technology in Lausanne, Software Engineering Lab., 2001.
[28] K. Walden and J.-M. Nerson. *Seamless Object-Oriented Software Architecture: Analysis and Design of Reliable Systems*. Prentice-Hall, 1995.
[29] J. Warmer and A. Kleppe. *The Object Constraint Language: Precise Modeling With UML*. Addison-Wesley 1998.
[30] J. Wing. *A Two-tiered Approach to Specifying Programs*. Technical Report TR-299, Massachusetts Institute of Technology, Laboratory for Computer Science, 1983.

Electronic Resources

[31] Klasse Objecten. *OCL Center: OCL Tools*. http://www.klasse.nl/ocl/index.htm
[32] OMG Unified Modeling Language Revision Task Force. *OMG Unified Modeling Language Specification*. Version 1.3, June 1999. http://www.celigent.com/omg/umlrtf/
[33] Software Engineering Lab., Swiss Federal Institute of Technology in Lausanne. *The Fondue Method*. http://lglwww.epfl.ch/research/fondue/
[34] Software Engineering Lab., Swiss Federal Institute of Technology in Lausanne. *Operation Schemas*. http://lglwww.epfl.ch/research/operation-schemas/
[35] S. Sendall. *Specification Case Studies*. http://lglwww.epfl.ch/~sendall/case-studies/

Author Index

Lecture Notes in Computer Science

For information about Vols. 1–2194
please contact your bookseller or Springer-Verlag